# Justice and Human Rights in Islamic Law

# Justice and Human Rights in Islamic Law

Dr. Wasiyoddin R. Mujawar

MANGLAM

MANGLAM PUBLICATIONS

DELHI-110053 (INDIA)

*Published by :*
**MANGLAM PUBLICATIONS**
L-21/1, Street No. 5, Shivaji Marg, Near Kali Mandir,
J.P. Nagar, Kartar Nagar, West Ghonda, Delhi-110053
Phone : 011-22945677, (M.) 9968367559, 9868572512
E-mail: manglam.books2007@rediffmail.com
manglam.publications2007@rediffmail.com

*Justice and Human Rights in Islamic Law*



First Edition 2009

ISBN 978-93-80013-15-2



**PRINTED IN INDIA**

Published by Ravindra Kumar Yadav for Manglam Publications, Delhi-110053 Laser Typesetting at M.K. Computers, Delhi- 53, Printed at Sachin Printers, Moujpur Delhi- 53

# PREFACE

Islam is a misunderstood religion. It is widely criticised by those, who have little or no knowledge about Islam, the faith, its teachings and its philosophy. People may wonder to hear that Islam is a progressive religion, which was first to confer fundamental rights on all the human beings and which advocated for the equality of men, women, on all basis. It opposed all discrimination, be that of caste, creed or faith. The concept of human rights is relatively newer and a modern one. Several hundred years ago, nobody in the west knew about this. But, Islam, had bestowed all rights—based on humanity—fifteen centuries ago, on Muslims and non-Muslims alike, at the time of its advent. Ironically, people in today's world and even the scholars are not aware of the hard facts in this regard. This study is an effort in the direction of providing the academic world with an authentic, exhaustive and comprehensive work on the subject, in order to remove all related misgivings and make people aware of the actual state of affairs.

Justice and Human Rights in Islamic Laws lays emphasis on the revival of true Islamic form of social justice and human rights form the beginning to present day. Rights and justice are the most important constitutional principles which have been confirmed both in the Qur'an and the Hadith. Both these concepts as formulated in Islam, are comprehensive and encompass all aspects of human life which governs all kinds of relations in life. It is insufficient to say that Islam should have been a living force in the past and it has produced a well constructed and balanced society in the time of the Prophet and in the age of the Caliphate. Since that time, there have been immense changes in human life. There have been material changes on the Earth and in its power relative to man. All these points have been carefully discussed in this book.

*— Author*

# CONTENTS

# 1

# INTRODUCTION

Equality and freedom are the most important principles upon which human rights are based. The modern democracies claim that the world is indebted to them for establishing the right to freedom, to equality and to the other rights that ensued. These countries took the credit for introducing human rights; and England known for its inherited traditions, took the credit, whereas France claimed that human rights were the outcome of the French Revolution. Other nations denied England and France any credit in this respect and claimed the credit for themselves. It has been authentically verified that the Faith of Islam introduced and established human rights in its most perfect form and on the widest scale. During the life of the Prophet Muhammad, blessings and peace be upon him, and during the reign of the Rightly Guided Caliphs, the Islamic states were the first states to adopt the principles of human rights. The modern democracies of today have not yet attained what the Faith of Islam ordained fourteen centuries ago. In the following pages we will present Islam's role in introducing and establishing the most important principles of human rights, namely equality and freedom.

## EQUALITY IN ISLAM

The three main manifestations of equality are: social equality, equality before the law political rights, and establishing justice in financial dealings. In the following study, we aim to present Islam's rulings concerning each of the aforementioned forms of equality. We will also throw light upon the rulings of Islam concerning equality between men and women.

## SOCIAL EQUALITY IN HUMAN VALUES

Islam declares that all people are as equal as the teeth of a comb, and that no person is superior to any other except by piety and righteous deeds in addition to what one strives to offer to God the Almighty, to one's homeland and to oneself. Islam accordingly abolished all forms of sectarianism and discrimination between all classes of society. It also abolished the privileges granted to people on account of their nationality, ancestry or lineage. This is demonstrated in the following Quranic verse "O mankind We created you from a single (pair) of a male and a female and made you into nations and tribes, that ye may know each other. Verily the most honoured of you in the sight of God is (he who is) the most righteous And God has full knowledge and is well acquainted (with all things)"

The Prophet Muhammad, and peace be up on him, announced in his farewell speech the constitution of Islam that was to be observed after his death. He embodied the principles of Islam in this speech saying: "O people Your God is One God and your father is one father, for you are all descendants of Adam, and Adam was created from clay.

The most honoured of you in the sight of God is the most righteous of you. No Arab is superior to a non-Arab and no non-Arab is superior to an Arab. No dark-skinned man is superior to a fair-skinned man and no fair-skinned man is superior to a dark-skinned man, except by his piety. I have declared this to you as God is my witness, and may those who are present inform those who are absent".

On one occasion Abu Dharr Al Ghiaffary and a negro slave were arguing about a certain matter in the presence of the Prophet Muhammad, blessings and peace be upon him. Abu Dhar, spoke harshly to the slave saying: "You son of a negress " The Prophet Muhammad, and peace be upon him, became very angry and said "This matter has exceeded all limits!

This matter has exceeded all limits! The son of a white man is not superior to the son of a negro except by his piety and righteous deeds". Abu Dharr was so ashamed that he lay down and placed his cheek upon the ground and said to his negro slave "Stamp upon my cheek."

## EQUALITY BEFORE THE LAW

Islam's rulings concerning civil rights do not differ from its rulings concerning the aforementioned rights. Islam treats all people equally before the law and grants them equal civil rights without any discrimination between a beggar and a prince, or a nobleman and a man of modest birth.

The Second Rightly Guided Caliph, `Umar ben Al Khattab, who was responsible for organizing the administration of justice in the muslim state upon the firm foundation of the Holy Qur'an and the Traditions of the Prophet, said in his first speech after becoming Caliph: "O people I swear by God that there is no man among you as powerful as he who is helpless until I restore his rights to him, and there is no man amongst you as helpless as he who is powerful until I restore what he had usurped to its rightful owner".

`Umar ben Al Khattab's message to Abu Mousa Al Ash'ary concerning the administration of justice embodied the greater part of the rulings of the Faith of Islam on justice. He wrote "From the servant of God, `Umar ben Al Khattab, Commander of the Faithful, to the servant of God, Ibn Qays, Peace be upon you.

The administration of justice is a religious duty and a tradition from the Prophet to be observed, so understand thoroughly the cases presented before you and enforce the sentence that you know to be just, for declaring the truth without executing justice is not just. Treat all people who stand before you equally in the way you greet them, address them and judge them. By so doing no nobleman would expect or hope for an unjust sentence in his favour and no poor man would despair of your just ruling".

Umar ben Al Khattab's last testament to his successor as Caliph was : "Treat all people equally and do not be influenced by any person who deserves punishment, and take no notice of any person's censure provided you have pronounced a just sentence. Never allow your preference or partiality for any person to influence your judgement in the affairs of the people whom God has entrusted to our authority."

The matter of equality in Islam was not limited to merely declaring principles and establishing laws, but history records that these principles and laws were executed solemnly and conscientiously during the lifetime of the Prophet Muhammad, blessings and peace be upon him, and during the reign of the Four Rightly Guided Caliphs who succeeded him, during the Golden Age of Islam which represents the principles and spirit of Islam in every respect Usama ibn Zayd, one of the most beloved companions of the Prophet Muhammad, prayer and peace be upon him, once attempted to intercede with him on behalf of Fatima daughter of Al Aswad Al Makhzoumiya who had been sentenced to the punish- ment of theft for stealing velvet material and golden ornaments.

The Prophet, blessings and peace be upon him, refused Osama's intercession, in spite of his affection for him, and reprimanded him severely saying "How can you intercede with me concerning a penalty ordained by God Almighty Allah." Then he said to the people who had witnessed the matter: "Before the advent of Islam, people of noble descent were not punished if they were guilty of theft and poor indigent people were punished for the same crime. I swear by God Almighty, that if my daughter Fatima were guilty of the crime of theft, I would sentence her to the punishment ordained by God Almighty."

A Jew once lodged a complaint to the Caliph `Omar ben Al Khattab against `Ali Abu Talib. When they both stood before the Caliph `Omar, he addessed the Jew by his name and addressed `Ali Abu Talib by his appellation of Abu Al Hasan (the Father of Hasan) as he was accustomed to addressing him. `Ali showed signs of displeasure and the Çaliph `Umar asked him if he had resented his adversary being a Jew with whom he had been obliged to stand on equal footing before the Caliph. `Ali Abu Talib replied that that had not been the cause of his displeasure, the reason being that the Caliph had addressed the Jew by his name whereas he had addressed him by his appellation of Abu Al Hasan, which is a sign of respect and veneration. `All ben Abu Talib had thus expressed his displeasure because `Umar ben Al Khattab had inadvertantly treated him with more respect than his adversary.

A son of `Amr ben Al `Aas, the governor of Egypt, once struck a man of the lower class. The man swore that he would lodge a complaint to the Caliph `Umar ben Al Khattab. `Amr ben Al Aas's son told the man to do so, boasting that the Caliph would never punish him, since he was the son of the noble ruler of Egypt. Later, during the pilgrimage season when the Caliph `Omar, his retinue, `Amr ben `Al `Aas and his son were assembled together, the man whom `Amr's son had struck went to the Caliph, and pointed to the son of `Amr ben Al `Aas and said : "This man struck me unjustly and when I threatened to complain to you, he told me that he was the son of a nobleman and that you would never punish him".

The Caliph `Umar ben Al Khattab looked at `Amr ben Al `Aas and uttered his famous words "What right have you to enslave people, whose mothers gave birth to them as free people?" He then gave the man who had lodged his complaint a whip and told him to strike the son of the nobleman - namely the son of `Amr ben Al `Aas - as he had struck him. On a certain occasion, the Caliph `Umar witnessed a man and a woman committing adultery, so he assembled the people around him and said : "How should the Caliph of the Muslims act when he witnesses the sin of adultery being committed ?"

Ali ben Abu Talib replied : "There must be four witnesses to the sin of adultery and if he cannot present these witnesses and he accuses the man and woman of adultery, he must be punished for the sin of slander without sufficient evidence, as any other person would be punished in a similar situation".`Ali ben Abu Talib then recited the following Quranic verse: "And those who launch a charge against chaste women and produce not four witnesses (to support their allegations), flog them with eighty stripes; and reject their evidence ever after ; for such men are wicked transgressors". The Caliph `Umar did not reply nor did he reveal the identity of the man and woman whom he had witnessed committing the sin of adultery.

Islam applies the principle of equality in its treatment of Muslims and non- Muslims. Islam ordains that non-Muslims living in a Muslim state or in a state under Muslim rule have the same rights and obligations as their fellow Muslims. They are subject to the Muslim laws of justice except in matters concerning their religion. Accordingly their faith and beliefs are respected by the state and the community in which they live. There is a great difference between these sublime principles of Islām and the laws of the United States of America which claims to be the most democratic country in the world. Until very recently, the laws of the United States of America discriminated between the white and black citizens.

This discrimination was manifested in all situations, dealings and even in matters of justice, such as the harshness of the verdict and the manner of its execution.

These laws even gave a white man the right to tie a black man to a tree and burn him alive or to cut him to pieces, without him having been tried in court, if the black măn had had any kind of relationship with a white woman even if she had consented to this relationship. A similar fate awaited any black person who overstepped the limits of these unjust laws. We have all read in the press about two cases which prove, beyond a shadow of doubt, the extent of the injustice of this racial discrimination in certain states of the United States of America.

The first case concerns Uthrene Lucy, a black American girl, living in the State of Alabama, who had applied to be registered as a student in the University of Alabama. The University refused her application on account of the colour of her skin, but she filed a suit against the University in the Federal Court in Birmingham, the capital of the State of Alabam. The court ruled that she be admitted to the University and accordingly notified the University officially on the first of July . However, as soon as the students heard about the court's verdict, they organized a violent demonstration of approximately seven thousand students representing the various faculties and colleges. They demanded that this black girl be killed by being hanged from a tree, in the same way that black men who had had any relationship with white women were hanged. The students made an effigy of Uthrene Lucy and burnt it in the city squares. They did not limit their violence to these demonstrations but some students actually attacked the girl, threw rotten eggs at her and even tried to lynch her. They also swore that they would never allow her to sit side by side with them in the lecture hall. These demonstrations were applauded by the authorities of the University and on February the sixth , they issued a decree suspending her from continuing her studies at the University, in spite of the verdict previously issued by the Federal Court which had granted her that right.

Uthrene Lucy was consequently forced to remain in her home to escape from the violence of hostile crowds. Nevertheless, she filed another suit against the University in the Federal Court in Birmingham where she and her sisters lived, and demanded the annulment of the University's decree of suspension. Uthrene Lucy received threatening calls on her telephone which continued to ring every two minutes for seven whole hours one night. The poor girl was accordingly forced to leave her home in Birmingha and live in another town where she would not be recognized, in order to escape from the persecution to which she had been subjected. Although the Federal Court of Birmingha had issued a verdict that Uthrene Lucy resume her studies at the University, on the twenty ninth of February , the Board of Directors of the University assembled a few hours after the verdict had been pronounced, and unanimously voted that Uthrene Lucy be expelled from the University. They had, by their decision, defied the verdict of the Federal Court of Birmingha in addition to false alleging that the girl had declared that the demonstrations directed against her had been instigated by the University authorities.

John Cadeel, a member of the Board of Directors of the University, declared in his testimony in Court that he feared that the students would kill Uthrene Lucy and that the verdict of the Federal Court had placed the girl's life in danger. The Governor of Alabama suggested that a committee consisting of both white and black citizens should be formed in order to solve racial problems in the state in a peaceful manner. Nevertheless, he himself admitted that "Every sane person knows that white and black children will never go to school together in Alabama".

The second example of racial discrimination also occurred in the city of Birmingham in the state of Alabama. It concerned a black woman who sat in a seat reserved for white passengers on a bus. In the state of Mabama black people were not allowed to sit in the seats reserved for white people. This woman refused to leave her seat and sit in the seats allotted to black passengers and was consequently arrested by the police and taken to the police station. The woman appeared in court and was sentenced to a fine, upon which all the black people in the state of Alabama boycotted the buses as a sign of their protestation. The jury in the court declared that the procedure of boycotting the buses was an illegal procedure and arrested more than a hundred negroes who had led the boycotting and tried them before a court of justice in March.

There can accordingly be no comparison between the aforementioned treatment of negroes in the United States of America and the just principles and tolerant rulings ordained by Islam, in its treatment of non-Muslims. Non-Muslims were accorded equality with Muslims in all matters in addition to being guaranteed respect for their faith, religious beliefs, rites and ceremonies.

The tolerant rulings of Islam and its just principles cannot, in any way, be compared to the brutal treatment to which the natives of the colonies were recently subjected. These people led a life humiliation and were subjected to unjust laws which are inconsistent with the basic principles of human rights. Nevertheless, those in power applied just laws to their own subjects and to the subjects of other Western communities. In many cases the colonialists did their utmost to eradicate the nation of the country they had occupied, so that their own countrymen could dominate the land completely. Examples of this Policy are manifested in the European colonists' treatment of the Red Indians the original inhabitants of North America and their treatment of the Aboriginees and Maoris the original inhabitants of Australia and New Zealand. This policy resulted in the genocide of the natives, and the minority that survived now lives in the remote districts of their country after being hunted like wild beasts by the colonists, while others live in reservations. As a result of this brutal inhumane policy, the United Nations issued a clause in its Charter which prohibits the genocide of nations.

## ESTABLISHING JUSTICE IN FINANCIAL DEALINGS AND IN THE DISTRIBUTION OF WEALTH

Islam ordains rulings which establish justice in all financial dealings and in the distribution of wealth. It also affords equal opportunities for everyone to work and improve his status in addition to narrowing the gap between the classes of society, thereby achieving justice in its most perfect form. The sublime status attained by Islam in this respect has never been equalled by any faith, code or law in ancient or modern times. In order to achieve this aim, Islam ordains the following nine rulings.

The most important ruling concerns the means of acquiring wealth or any kind of profit. Islam prohibits acquiring wealth through blackmail, fraud, or by monopolizing the necessities of life. It also prohibits exploiting the needs of the people or profiting from one's status of authority or Power, which usually result in an illegal increase of wealth. This leads to a great difference in the wealth of the various classes of the community, and by prohibiting such measures an economic balance can be achieved. Islam also prohibits usury in very definite terms and describes it as a great sin, threatening the usurers with a severe punishment from God Almighty. Islam accordingly prohibits all wealth that is the consequence of usury.

The following Quranic verses demonstrate this ruling "Those who devour usury will not stand except as stands one whom the Evil One by his touch hath driven to madness. That is because they say "Trade is like usury", but God hath permitted trade and forbidden usury. Those who after receiving direction from their Lord, desist shall be pardoned for the past their case is for God (to judge) ; but those who repeat (the offence) are Companions of the Fire they will abide therein (for ever). God will deprive usury of all blessing, but will give increase for deeds of charity for He loveth not creatures ungrateful and wicked. Those who believe and do deeds of righteousnes, and establish regular prayers and regular charity, will have their reward with their Lord on them shall be no fear, nor shall they grieve. O ye who believe ! Fear God and give up what remains of your demand for usury, if ye are indeed believers. If ye do it not, take notice of war from God and His Apostle : but if ye turn back, ye shall have your capital sums: deal not injustly, and ye shall not be dealt with unjustly. If the debtor is in a difficulty, grant him time till it is easy for him to repay. But if ye remit it, by way of charity, that is best for you if ye only knew".

Islam prohibits all forms of usury, the most predominant of which was making loans of money to those in dire need for a certain period of time at a profit previously agreed upon. If the person in debt was unable to pay back the loan with its profit at the appointed date, the period of the loan would be extended with an increase in the profit to be paid. Islam also prohibits all transactions based upon fraud, bribery or unjustly consuming people's wealth. This is expressed in the following Quranic verse:

> "And do not eat up your property among yourselves for vanities, nor use it as bait for the judges, with intent that ye may eat up wrongfully and knowingly a little of (other) people's property.
>
> The Prophet Muhammad, blessings and peace be upon him, is related to have said : "Whoever cheats my nation is not one of us" .

He also said that any transaction agreed upon by both parties concerned is blessed by God, but if they withold the truth or cheat in the transaction, all blessing shall be erased. The Prophet Muhammad, blessings and peace be upon him, said : "Nothing that has originated from ill-gotten gain will ever flourish and the Fire of Hell will be its home". He also said that if a person donated ill-gotten wealth in charity, it would not be accepted by God and if he spent ill-gotten wealth, it would never be blessed and if he left it after he died, it would be fuel to burn him in the Fire of Hell. The Faith of Islam prohibits monopolizing any goods necessary for people's livelihood, with the intention of controlling the price. This is expressed in the following Saying of the Prophet Muhammad, blessings and peace be upon him :

> "Whoever monopolizes people's food provisions for forty days will have angered God and disobeyed Him".

This prohibition applies to the monopoly of any commodity or goods in industry or trade, with the intention of controlling the market and taking advantage of the consumers' needs. This is in keeping with the Islamic principle that governs all forms of transactions and is expressed in the following Saying of the Prophet, blessings and peace be upon him, which states that no one should subject others to harm.

The Faith of Islam absolutely prohibits the exploitation of authority and power to acquire wealth, and rules that wealth acquired in this manner be confiscated and deposited in the treasury of the state for the welfare of the needy and indigent Muslims. The Prophet Muhammad, blessings and peace be upon him, himself introduced this ruling. One day Ibn Al Latbiya of the Azd tribe, gave the Prophet, blessings and peace be upon him, a share of what had been presented to him in the form of gifts and retained a share for himself. The Prophet Muhammad, blessings and peace be upon him, became furious and called upon the people to listen to what he had to say and said : "Thanks be to God and praise be to God. I have appointed men as governors to represent me in matters for which God has made me responsible and now one of you comes to me and offers me gifts and retains gifts saying that these gifts had been presented to him. If he had remained in his father's or his mother's home, would anyone have offered him a gift ? By God Almighty, if anyone takes any such gift or offering it will be wrapped around his neck on the Day of Judgement, be it a camel that growls or a cow that bellows or a sheep that bleats". Ibn Al Latbiya accordingly returned all the gifts that had been presented to him.

This principle was applied on a wider scale after the death of the Prophet Muhammad, blessings and peace be upon him. During the reign of the Caliph `Omar ben Al Khattab, he confiscated the wealth of the governors of the Islamic states, which they had gained from trade and other transactions which were prohibited. He also confiscated the gifts and wealth presented to them as a result of their status and authority.

`Omar ben Al Khattab applied this ruling to the governors of Basra and to one of the governors of Bahrein. The Caliph `Omar learnt that this governor's wealth had increased greatly during the period of his reign, so he calculated his wealth and confiscated what he believed to have been acquired as a result of his status and deposited it in the treasury of the state. This procedure demonstrates `Omar ben Al Khattab's concern for the fulfilment of justice, and this episode concerning the governor of Bahrein is evidence of the strict measures he took to prevent any form of; illicit gain. `Omar ben Al Khattab also reminded the governor of

Bahrein that he had appointed him as governor when the governor had not owned a pair of sandals and that he had been informed that the governor had recently bought horses for the sum of one thousand and six hundred dinars. The governor replied that he had possessed horses which had multiplied by breeding and that many valuable gifts had been presented to him.

The Caliph `Omar ben Al Khattab then told the governor of Bahrejn that he had calculated the money to which the governor was entitled for his livelihood and the sum that remained must be returned to the treasury of the state. When the governor objected the Caliph said : "By God I will punish you", and he flogged him till his back bled. The governor then said that he wouldd the confiscated sum of money as charity and `Omar ben Al Khattab replied that such a sum would only have been accepted by God Almighty if it had been his own wealth and he had donated it of his own free will. He finally reprimanded him saying "Have you come from the farthest regions of Bahrein to collect people's wealth for yourself and not in the Cause of God or for the welfare of the Muslims ?"

`Omar ben Al Khattab behaved in a similar manner with one of the governors of Al- Kufa when he confiscated half his wealth which he estimated had been acquired as a result of his status as governor. The Caliph `Omar ben Al Khattab also sent a message to a governor of Egypt in which he wrote that he had been informed that the governor's possessions which included a great number of slaves, livestock and valuable crockery had increased greatly: The governor replied that the land was fertile and productive and that it produced more than was needed for the expenses of their livelihood. `Omar ben Al Khattab sent him another message in which he declared that he was well informed concerning the errors of the governors and that the governor's message had proven his guilt and that he the Caliph considered him guilty. He informed him that he had dispatched Muhammad ben Muslima to confiscate half his wealth and he ordered him to obey Ibn Muslima and to submit to his commands since the whole matter was clear and decisive. The governor obeyed the Caliph's command and submitted half his wealth to Muhammad ben Muslima to be confiscated.

The Faith of Islam has established a just system of inheritance which distributes wealth between people fairly and in a just manner. It also prevents the accumulation of wealth in the hands of a minority of people by dividing the estate of the deceased person into lesser portions for a large number of his relatives, thus widening the circle of people who benefit from the estate. This just system ensures the distribution of the wealth after a few generations to a large number of people in the form of small ownerships, thereby narrowing thè gap between the classes of society and fulfilling the principle of socialism in its most sublime form. In order to ensure the establishment of these sublime principles, the Faith of Islam prohibits any procedure that violates the laws of inheritance.

This is manifested in the following Quranic verses : "Those are the limits set by God: those who obey God and His Apostle will be admitted to Gardens with rivers flowing beneath, to abide therein (for ever) and that will be the supreme achievement. But those who disobey God and His Apostle and transgress His limits will be admitted to a Fire, to abide therein :nd they shall have a humiliating punishment" Accordingly most Muslim jurists prohibit family endowments, by which the owner of property or wealth entails the profit of his property, after his death, upon a certain group of his relatives or any other person he names, according to the terms and amounts that he desires. This procedure prevents the wealth from being circulated in the normal manner and violates the laws of inheritance.

In, the law in Egypt annulled all forms of family endowments and decreed that any such endowments in the future would be considered illegal. The Faith of Islam also prohibits a person from bequeathing in his will anything to any of his heirs which would grant him more than his legitimate due, according to the laws of Islamic inheritance. The Prophet Muhammad,- blessings and peace be upon him - declared that an heir should not be included in the will. The laws of inheritance in Islam also prohibit a person from bequeathing more than a third of his estate to people who are not his heirs. This law was ordained to protect the legitimate heirs from the whims of their legators. There can be no comparison between Islam's just and fair system of inheritance and the current system of inheritance in the countries of the Western world by which a person bequeathes all or most of his estate to his eldest son, or even bequeathes all his estate to whomever he wills. These laws resulted in the accumulation of wealth in the hands of a minority of people which generated hatred and envy in the hearts of the deprived members of society and led them to feel a grudge against the society that permitted these laws. Consequently extremist subversive ideologies appeared and led to an upheaval in the economy of the society. This paved the way for the rebellions and revolutions that arose in many countries.

. The Faith of Islam imposes various forms of taxes and alms upon people's wealth and economic activities in order to achieve justice for all classes of the community. Such laws also meet the needs of the indigent and destitute, in addition to preventing the accumulation of wealth in the hands of a minority of the community. Taxes were imposed upon certain commercial activities the most important of which are:

### LAND TAXES:

This tax is either pecuniary or both pecuniary and in specie and was imposed annually upon the land, the owners of which were at peace with the Muslims before war was waged, or upon the land left to them by the Muslims after they had defeated them in warfare. The land tax that the Caliph `Omar ben A' Khattab imposed on the greater part of Iraq was five dirhams annually for every square cubits of clover or vegetables, and ten dirhams annually for every square cubits of vinegroves and palm trees. He also imposed one dirham and one measure of wheat or barley for every square cubits of land that was irrigated and produced wheat, barley or similar grain.

The land tax continued to be imposed upon the aforementioned land even after the land owners embraced Islam and this land is termed Taxed Land. The taxes were paid to the treasury of the state for the general welfare of the Muslim community. This included improving the living conditions of the Muslims, paying the salaries of government officials, the governors, the judges the jurists and the soldiers who protected the state, in addition to building mosques, bridges and paving the paths in the land.

### The Extraction of Metal Ores from the Land:

If the land was the property of a person, he would be entitled to whatever was dug out of the land be it solid or liquid, even if someone else had extracted it, since it was buried in his property, to which he had a legal right.

If the land did not belong to any person, whatever was extracted or dug out of the land belonged to the person who had extracted it, if it was a liquid like crude oil, or a solid that could not be melted like rubies, emeralds, crystal, amber, topaz or arsenic. If it was a solid that could be melted like gold or silver or a combination of a solid and a liquid like mercury, the person who extracted it was entitled to four fifths of it and was obliged to submit one fifth of it to the treasury of the state which spent it upon poor people, orphans and wayfarers. These laws were established at a time when these metals were not of paramount importance in the lives of the people. The Faith of Islam gave the ruler of the state the right to confiscate any source of wealth for the welfare of the Muslim community, in addition to having the right to estimate the tax upon it, according to the importance of the source, and according to the economical circumstances of the state.

### Hunting and Fishing:

The hunter who hunted on the land was entitled to the animals and birds that he killed. Those who fished in seas and rivers were also entitled to the fish, pearls, sponges, mother of pearl and everything else they caught in their nets. Islam did not impose any tax upon what was hunted on the land or what was caught from the seas or rivers.

However, if the ruler of the state considered that the welfare of the state necessitated imposing taxes on hunting and fishing in order to replenish the treasury of the state, he was legitimately entitled to do so. If such a situation arose, most jurists declared that the hunter and the fisherman were entitled to four fifths of what they had hunted or caught while the remaining fifth should be paid to the treasury of the state to be spent according to the needs of the indigent and needy. This principle was applied when one of the governors of the Islamic states informed the Caliph

`Omar ben Al Khattab that a pearl had been extracted from the sea of the state and `Omar ben Al Khattab commanded that a fifth of its value be deposited in the treasury of the state. He also ordered that one fifth of the value of any ambergris be deposited in the treasury of the state.

### Custom Taxes and Taxes on Merchants:

These were imposed upon merchants passing certain surveillance posts on their journeys and merchant ships passing by certain Islamic ports. These taxes were estimated at one tenth of the value of the goods. The official responsible for collecting these taxes was accordingly called Al `Ashaar, meaning he who takes one tenth. These taxes were paid to the treasury of the state for the welfare of the Muslim community in common with the other taxes.

### Other Taxes:

These taxes were imposed on the mints where coins were minted and on shops. The taxes were paid to the treasury to be spent on the welfare of the citizens of the Islamic states.

### The Faith of Islam Grants:

The Faith of Islam grants the ruler of the state the right to impose permanent taxes in certain fields if the welfare of the Muslims necessitates it, in addition to the afore- mentioned taxes. If the coffers of the treasury are empty or the state is unable to meet with the necessary requirements of the state such as paying the salaries of the soldiers in the army or the salaries of the government officials, Islam grants the ruler of the state the right to impose temporary taxes upon the wealthy citizens and upon certain economic activities and dealings, for the welfare of the state. These taxes are cancelled when the need for them no longer exists.

In addition to the various forms of taxes, Islam imposes the system of almsgiving upon four sources of wealth. The first source includes crops and fruit whereas the second source is cattle. The third source includes gold and silver and the fourth source is trade and commerce. The alms due on crops and fruit are one tenth of the produce of the land if it is irrigated by water flowing from a river or a spring or by rain. If the land is irrigated by buckets, water wheels or irrigation ditches, the alms due are half a tenth of the produce of the land, and this form of alms is imposed only on land owned by Muslims.

Some jurists decree that both land tax and alms on crop and fruit are due on the Muslims who own the above mentioned land, whereas other jurists exempt the lands taxed with land tax from fruit and crop alms. In this case, in their opinion, the owner of the land only pays the land tax.

The lands upon which alms on crops and fruit are due are called "Ushriya Lands", namely lands that submit one tenth or half a tenth of their produce as alms. Alms are due on cattle if the owner of the cattle is a Muslim and if his cattle are a specified number and graze upon common pasture most of the year. The owner must also possess the cattle for a whole lunar year. The alms due on the cattle depend upon the number and species of the cattle.

If a person owns less than five camels, alms are not imposed on him. If he owns five to nine camels that graze upon common pasture for a lunar year, the alms due are one ewe. If he owns ten to fourteen camels, the alms due are two ewes, and if he owns fifteen to nineteen camels, the alms due are three ewes. However, if he owns twenty to twenty four camels, the alms due are four ewes. If he owns twenty five camels, the alms due are a she-camel that is more than a year old in addition to five ewes. The alms accordingly increase with the increase of the number of camels owned, and alms due on cows, sheep and horses are similar to the alms due on camels and this is explained in detail in the references of Islamic jurisprudence.

The alms due on gold and silver are a quarter of a tenth of their value if they remain in a person's possession for a whole lunar year. The weight of the silver must be at least two hundred drachmas and the weight of the gold must not be less than twenty weights of what is explained in detail in the references of Islamic jurisprudence. The alms on trade and commence are a quarter of a tenth of what a person possesses for a lunar year. The value of the goods or the property must be equal to the value of the gold and silver upon which alms are due. The four classes of alms are all donated for the welfare of the members of the Muslim community as is mentioned in the following Quranic verse : "Alms are for the poor and the needy, and those employed to administer the (funds) ; for those whose hearts have been (recently) reconciled (to Truth) ; for those in bondage and in debt ; in the cause of God ; and for the wayfarer (thus is it) ordained by God, and God is full of knowledge and wisdom"

A poor person is he who does not own the sum of money, gold, silver, goods or property that obliges him to pay alms. A needy person is he who does not own anything.Those employed to administer the funds are those people responsible for collecting the alms, and they are granted a share of the alms for fulfilling their duty as collectors of alms regardless of their wealth or poverty.

There were three classes of people whose hearts had been reconciled to Islam as a result of certain circumstances. One class included people whom the Prophet Muhammad, blessings and peace be upon him, had reconciled to Islam and their people had followed their example and embraced Islam. The second class of people were those who had embraced Islam but whose faith was weak and the alms helped to strengthen their faith. The third class of people were given alms in order to ward off their evil. These three classes were granted alms during the first few years after the advent O (Islam, but after the Faith of Islam was firmly established, alms for these classes of people were cancelled. Those in bondage refers to the slaves, and a certain sum of money from the alms was used to liberate them by buying them from their owners and then granting them their liberty. Those in debt who are entitled to alms are those who do not possess the sum of money or property that imposes upon them the duty of paying alms, and cannot pay their debts.

"Those in the Cause of God", refers to those who fight in the Cause of God and are separated from their regiments and those pilgrims who are separated from their families and have no money to enable them to travel. Scholars who strive to seek knowledge are also entitled to alms. Alms are also granted to the soldiers who are separated from their regiments in times of war to aid them in joining their regiments or to assist them in joining their families if there is no war.

The wayfarer is a person who possesses wealth in his own land, but on leaving his homeland has no means of earning his living, so he is granted alms to meet with his necessary demands and to enable him to return to his homeland.

Originally all forms of alms were paid to the treasury of the state which distributed the alms to the aforementioned categories of deserving people. Nevertheless, the land owner or the merchant or the wealthy man who owns property is permitted to donate his alms himself to the deserving cases in his community. It is preferable to donate the alms collected in a district to those entitled to alms who live in the same district unless there are no deserving cases in the district. The ruler of the state, however, is entitled to use his discretion for the welfare of his subjects in distributing the alms as he sees fit, provided that the sums of money that he distributes do not exceed the sum of the alms. Almsgiving is one of the five pillars of Islam, the other four pillars being : the belief in God and that Muhammad is the Prophet of God, performing prayers, fasting and making the pilgrimage. Almsgiving plays an important role in preserving the economic equilibrium of the nation by narrowing the gap between the classes of the nation and creating a spirit of cooperation and joint responsibility in the Muslim community.

The extent of the importance of almsgiving is manifested by the fact that Abu Bakr Al Siddiq, the First Rightly Guided Caliph, fought the tribes that refused to pay alms after the death of the Prophet Muhammad, blessings and peace be upon him, although many of them had not renounced the Faith of Islam. Abu Bakr Al Siddiq considered them all apostates and declared his famous statement : "By God if they refuse to give me a camel's shackle which they were accustomed to giving to the Prophet, I will fight them until they submit it". Abu Bakr Al Siddiq carried out his resolution in spite of the opposition of many of the Companions of the Prophet Muhammad, blessings and peace be upon him. He was finally able to convince them and was accordingly able to overcome the greatest crisis that had threatened the Faith of Islam after the death of the Prophet Muhammad, blessings and peace be upon him. There is a difference between taxes and alms, since alms are not only imposed upon the profit of the capital or its products but are also due on property. If the property does not make any profit, its value will be consumed by the alms after forty years, since the alms due on property are one fortieth of its value. The same applies to gold, silver and chattels.

The Faith of Islam commands wealthy people to donate charity to the poor and needy on certain days and on specific occasions, the most important of which are:

(a) Alms on the first day of the Feast of the Lesser Bairam. Every Muslim able to do so is obliged to donate these alms to the poor and needy on the first day of the Feast of the Lesser Bairam on behalf of himself and all the members of his family. The alms were originally four pounds (lbs) of wheat or eight pounds of barley, dates, or raisins or their value. This form of alms is obligatory and not merely a commendable or righteous deed. In Egypt, if every head of a family fulfilled this obligatory religious duty on the first day of the Feast of the Lesser Bairam, all poor and indigent people would be supplied with their needs.

(b) The animals that are slaughtered and sacrificed on the first day of the Feast of the Greater Bairam and the animals slaughtered and sacrified by the pilgrims during their pilgrimage are another example of charity. In both cases, the families of the person who performs this religious duty are permitted to partake of the meat of the sacrificed animal, but most of it is distributed as charity to the poor and needy. This is referred to in the following Quranic verses : "....and when you are in peaceful conditions (again), if any one wishes to continue the`Umra on to the hajj, he must make an offering, such as he can afford,.. " Also: "And proclaim the pilgrimage among men : they will come to thee on foot and (mounted) on every kind of camel, lean on account of journeys through deep and distant highways ; that they may witness the benefits (provided) for them, and celebrate the name of God, through the Days appointed, over the cattle which He has provided for them (for sacrifice) : then eat ye thereof and feed the distressed ones in want."

The Faith of Islam has ordained charity to the poor and needy as expiation and atonement for many sins, such as breaking one's oath as is clear from the following Quranic verse : "God will not call you to account for what is futile in your oaths, but He will call you to account for your deliberate oaths : for expiation, feed ten indigent persons, on a scale of the average for the food of your families ; or clothe them ; or givea slave his freedom." This form of expiation applies to most cases of breaking the fast of Ramadan; and he who breaks the fast of Ramadan without any legitimate reason must fast the days that he had not fasted in addition, to the ordained expiation. Old people and people who have chronic ailments whose physical condition prevents them from being able to fast are only obliged to feed an indigent person two meals for every day they cannot fast. Both the expiation and the sacrifice are given to the poor

and needy and are estimated in terms of grain or the value of grain. Expiation is also ordained for a man's oath that his wife be to him as if she were his mother namely that there was to be no marital intercourse between them. This was a Pre- Islamic custom which Islam strove to eliminate, and imposed upon the husband who wanted to resume marital relations with his wife as one of the forms of expiation that are mentioned in the following Quranic verses : "But those who divorce their wives by Zihar, then wish to go back on the words they uttered, (it is ordained that such a one) should free a slave before they touch each other this are ye admonished to perform and God is well acquainted with (all) that ye do. And if any has not (the wherewithal), he should fast for two months consecutively before they touch each other. But if any is unable to do so, he should feed sixty indigent ones.

"The Faith of Islam also imposes expiation for certain circumstances during the pilgrimage as is expressed in the following Quranic verse "And complete the Hajj or `Umra in the service of God. But if ye are prevented (from completing it), send an offering for a sacrifice, such as ye may find, and do not shave your heads until the offering reaches the place of sacrifice. And if any of you is ill or has an ailment in his scalp, (necessitating shaving), (he should) in compensation either fast, or feed the poor, or offer sacrifice ; and when you are in peaceful conditions (again), if any one wishes to continue the `Umra on to the Hajj, he must make an offering, such as he can afford, "

The Faith of Islam ordains that wealthy people support their poor and needy relations and those relatives who are unable to earn their living. This system is explained in detail in the books of Islamic jurisprudence. Islam also commands the people in every district to cooperate with each other and to assist one another. It is therefore the solemn duty of wealthy people to aid and assist the poor and to feed those people who are unable to earn their daily bread. Some jurists declared that, the state was responsible for the death of any citizen who had died of starvation. In such a circum, the man's relatives are all obliged to pay blood money to his immediate family, since the Faith of Islam considers that his wealthy relatives who did not assist him in his ordeal were responsible for his death.

There are many verses in the Qur'an which ordain kindness and generosity to one's neighbours, whether they be living near to one's home or at a distance. The following Quranic verse is an example of this principle "Serve God and join not any partners with Him ; and do good - to parents, kinsfolk, orphans, those in need, neighbours who are near, neighbours who are strangers,..." The Prophet Muhammad - blessings and peace be upon him - enjoined kind and generous treatment to one's neighbours in more than one of his Sayings. He said : "He is not one of us who goes to sleep at the end of the day, after having had enough to eat, while his neighbour is hungry". It has been related that a man visited Abdullah ben Abbas while a sheep was being slaughtered, and Ibn Abbas said to his servant who had slaughtered the sheep : "Do not forget to give our Jewish neighbour a share of the meat". He uttered this sentence `three times and the man who had witnessed this incident asked him why he had repeated his request so many times and Ibn Abbas told him that the Prophet Muhammad, blessings and peace be upon him, always recommended them to treat their neighbours generously so often that he believed that he would give them the right to inheritance.

The Faith of Islam ordains that the treasury of the state support any person who cannot earn his living. This includes old men and women who have no relatives to support them. In this respect Islam does not differentiate between Muslim and non-Muslim subjects. The Caliph `Omar ben Al Khattab once saw an old non-Muslim man begging in the streets, so he granted him immediate financial support from the treasury of the state and uttered his famous statement : "We will not have treated you justly if you pay your taxes to the state during your youth and the state leaves you to beg in your old age".

The Faith of Islam grants the ruler of the state the right to distribute the state's wealth in a manner that achieves an economic balance between the classes of the community, even if this necessitates granting wealth to a certain class or group of people. The Prophet Muhammad, blessings and peace be upon him, introduced and established this just tradition after divine inspiration had been revealed to him. The Prophet Muhammad, blessings and peace be upon him, granted all the wealth of the spoils of the battle against the tribe of Al Nadeer to the Muhajirin namely those who had emigrated from Mecca to Al Medina, in addition to two poor men of the Ansaar who were the original inhabitants of Al Medina, in order to narrow the gap between the wealth of the Ansaar and that of the Muhajirin.

By so doing, there existed a balance between the wealth of both the Ansaar and the Muhajirin who made up the Islamic community. This incident is referred to in the following Quranic verses : "What God has bestowed on His Apostle (and taken away) from the people of the townships, - belongs to God - to His Apostle and to kindred and orphans, the needy and the wayfarer ; in order that it may not (merely) make a circuit between the wealthy among you. So take what the Apostle assigns to you, and deny yourselves that which he withholds from you. And fear God ; for God is strict in Punishment. (Some part is due) to the indigent Muhajirs, those who were expelled from their homes and Their property, while seeking Grace from God and (His) Good Pleasure, and aiding God and His Apostle : Such are indeed the sincere ones." Al Ansaar are " the wealthy among you", referred to in the Quranic verse.

In addition to the aforementioned rulings, Islam takes every opportunity to urge wealthy people to donate charity to the poor and needy, in order to earn the Grace of God and His Reward.

The Faith of Islam also prohibits the hoarding of wealth and avoiding donating it in the Cause of God. Such miserly conduct is considered a great sin and these misers are threatened with a severe punishment on the Day of Judgement. Countless Quranic verses declare this ruling in almost every chapter of the Holy Quran. The following Quranic verses are examples of the aforementioned ruling : "It is not righteousness that ye turn your faces towards East or West; but it is righteousness - to believe in God and the Last Day, and the Angels, and the Book, and the Messengers ; to spend of your substance, out of love for Him, for your kin, for orphans, for the needy, for the wayfarer, for those who ask, and for the ransom of slaves ; " Also : "They ask thee what they should spend (in charity). Say Whatever ye spend that is good, is for parents and kindred and orphans and those in want and for wayfarers. And whatever ye do that is good, - God knoweth it well."

Also "O ye who believe Spend out of (the bounties) We have provided for you, before the Day comes when no bargaining (will avail), nor friendship nor intercession. Those who reject Faith - they are the wrong doers". "The parable of those who spend their substance in the way of God is that of a grain of corn it groweth seven ears, and each ear hath a hundred grains. God giveth manifold increase to whom He pleaseth and God careth for all and He knoweth all things. Those who spend their substance in the Cause of God, and follow not up their gifts with reminders of their generosity or with injury,- for them their reward is with their Lord on them shall be no fear, nor shall they grieve"

"And the likeness of those who spend their substance, seeking to please God and to strengthen their souls, is a garden high and fertile heavy rain falls on it but makes it yield a double increase of harvest, and if it receives not heavy rain, light moisture sufficeth it. God seeth well whatever ye do."

"O ye who believe ! Give of the good things which ye have (honourably) earned, and of the fruits of the earth which We have produced for you, and do not even aim at getting anything which is bad, in order that out of it ye may give away something, when ye yourself would not receive it except with closed eyes. And know that God is Free of all wants, and Worthy of all praise

"And whatever ye spend in charity or devotion, be sure God knows it all. But the wrong-doers have no helpers. If ye disclose (facts of) charity, even so it is well, but if ye conceal them, and make them reach those (really) in need, that is best for you. It will remove from you some of your (stains of) evil. And God is well acquainted with what ye do".

"Those who (in charity) spend of their goods by night and by day, in secret and in public, have their reward with their Lord on them shall be no fear, nor shall they grieve

"By no means shall ye attain righteousness unless ye give (freely) of that which ye love ; and whatever ye give, of a truth God knoweth it well".

"Serve God and join not any partners with Him And do good - to parents, kinsfolk, orphans, those in need, neighbours who are near, neighbours who are strangers, the Companion by your side, the wayfarer (ye meet), and what your right hands possess for God loveth not the arrogant, the vainglorious; - (nor) those who are niggardly or enjoin niggardliness on others, or hide the bounties which God hath bestowed on them for We have prepared, far those who resist Faith, a Punishment that steeps them in contempt"

"And there are those who bury gold and silver and spend it not in the Way of God :nnounce unto them a most grievous penalty - on the Day whenheat will be produced out of that (wealth) in the fire of Hell, and with it will be branded their foreheads, their flanks, and their backs. - "This is the (treasure) which ye buried for yourselves : taste ye, then, the (treasures) ye buried "

God Almighty ordains that this form of charity is the religious legitimate right of the poor and needy as is expressed in the following Quranic verses:

"And those in whose wealth is a recognized right for the (needy) who asks and him who is prevented (for some reason from asking) "

"So give what is due to kindred, the needy, and the wayfarer. That is best for those who seek the Countenance, of God, and it is they who shall prosper"

There are numerous Quranic verses which demonstrate that Islam considers that it is the religious duty of the person who possesses wealth, bestowed upon him by God Almighty, to spend it in His Cause. This is expressed in the following Quranic verse : "Believe in God and His Apostle, and spend (in charity) out of the substance whereof He hath made you heirs. For, those of you who believe and spend (in charity), - for them is a great Reward".

The Faith of Islam urges wealthy people to donate the wealth tht exceeds their needs in the Cause of God Almighty. It has been related that Abu Dhar Al Ghaffary said that on one occasion, the Prophet Muhammad, blessings and peace be upon him, walked with him in the direction of Mount Uhud and told him that he would not wish to possess as much gold as the size of Mount Uhud and spend it in the Cause of God then die leaving two carats of gold that had not been spent in the Cause of God, Abu Dhar asked him if he had meant two tons of gold and the Prophet, blessings and peace be upon him, replied that he had meant two carats of gold, which had not been spent in the Cause of God.

This incident urged Abu Dhar to encourage wealthy people during the reign of the Caliph `Othman ben `Affan to donate the wealth that exceeded their needs in the Cause of Islam and for the welfare of the poor and indigent members of the community. He also advised them not to squander their wealth or to spend it extravagantly on luxuries and warned them againt hoarding it and never lost an opportunity of reminding them of the needs of the poor and indigent.

Abu Dhar's appeal to the wealthy to donate their wealth in charity exceeded the rulings ordained by Islam, namely paying one's taxes and alms. However, the form of charity advocated by Abu Dhar raises the donor to a sublime status in the Grace of God.

Certain scholars misunderstood Abu Dhar's approach to donating charity as being an inclination towards communism. However, Islam and communism are the exact opposites of each other, since Islam ordains that wealthy people pay alms and encourages them to donate charity for the welfare of the poor and needy. These rulings establish and confirm individual ownership of property and wealth, in addition to preventing any conflict between the wealthy and the poor indigent members of the community. Communism, on the other hand, prohibits all forms of individual ownership and calls for the common ownership of all property, which paves the way for conflict between the classes. Thus Abu Dhar's advocation for charity cannot in any way be compared to communism.

The aforementioned examples are proof that the Faith of Islam has administered justice between people in matters of finance, trade and commerce in a manner unprecedented by any other faith in the past or in the present era. The Islamic community that adheres to the teachings of Islam and applies its rulings and laws on the economic level is an ideal community that encourages people to work and grants every person the reward his efforts deserve. It also encourages ambition and distinction in every branch of work and affords equal opportunities to everyone to make a profit in the various branches of trade and commerce. One of the most important aims of this community is to stabilize the economic balance by striving to narrow the gap between the classes.

The economic relationship between the members of such a community is thus established upon a system of cooperation, sympathy and justice, thereby affording every individual a dignified and honourable life, which is the aim of

## EQUALITY BETWEEN MEN AND WOMEN IN ISLAM

The Faith of Islam abolished the principle of discrimination between men and women as human beings. It also abolished any discrimination between them before the law and in civil rights, and Islam ordained tht men and women be equal in that respect. Islam declared that men and women are equal as human beings in this world and in the Hereafter. This is expressed in the following Quranic verses : "And their Lord hath accepted of them, and answered them "Never will I suffer to be lost the work of any of you, be he male or female ye are members one of another . "... to men is alloted what they earn, and to women what they earn " "We have honoured the sons of Adam..."By the "sons of Adam", is meant the offspring of Adam, namely the human race with its men and women. The Faith of Islam not only permitted the Muslim woman to acquire knowledge, but also commanded her to do so in so far as it would assist her in her life in this world and in the Hereafter. The Prophet Muhammad - blessings and peace be upon him - said that the quest for knowledge is the obligation of every Muslim man and woman.

Before the advent of Islam, Hafsa, the daughter of `Omar ben Al Khattab had beentaught the fundamentals of writing by a woman called Al Shifaa' Al `Adawiya and after the Prophet, blessings and peace upon him, married Hafsa, he asked Al Shifaa' Al Adawiya to continue teaching her how to improve her handwriting. The Faith of Islam permits the Muslim woman to hold any post outside her home, provided that she assumes it in a respectable dignified manner that does not in any way subject her to any embarrassing situation that does not observe the teachings of Islam. Her employment must not harm her reputation in any way, nor must it prevent her from carrying out her duties as a wife and a mother.

Islam permits the working woman to associate with the male sex in public according to the rulings and teachings of the Qur'an and the Traditions of the Prophet, blessings and peace be upon him.

Islam grants the Muslim woman equal civil rights and grants her the right to manage her own business affairs such as participating in legal contracts that deal with the sale or the purchase of any property or goods, in addition to her legal right to grant gifts and to contract a will. Islam also grants her the right to personally manage her wealth and supervise all her financial affairs. These rights naturally necessitate associating with the male sex and it is a well-known historical fact that `Aisha daughter of Talha - the granddaughter of Abu Bakr Al Siddiq fought side by side with men in the battles against the infidels and that she fought bravely with spears and arrows. The Prophet Muhammad, blessings and peace be upon him, led men and women together into battle and granted Sa'eeda, daughter of Ka'b, the same share of the spoils as the men in the Battle of Khaybar. He also seated Umaya, daughter of Qays Al Ghafiriya, behind him on his camel on their way to the Battle of Khaybar after the battle was won, awarded her a medal for her outstanding courage in battle, in the same way that heroes are awarded medals today. Umaya wore this medal all her life and according to her desire, the medal was buried with her when she died.

Another example of courageous womanhood is Um Hakim, daughter of Al Harith who Participated in the battle against the Romans while she was still a newly-wed bride. Her husband had been martyred before her eyes, but instead of wailing over his dead body, she seized the pole of the tent in which her marriage had been consumated and killed Seven of the enemy at the archway which is still known as the Archway of Um Hakim. From the above mentioned incidents, it is clear that Islam Permits the association of the two sexes, provided that no immorality ensues. In order to Preserve a moral and chaste community, Islam ordains certain rulings and terms and prohibits certain matters. Islam prohibits a man and a woman from being alone together unless, according to Islamic laws, they are religiously prohibited from marrying one another, such as a brother and sister or a maternal aunt or uncle or a paternal aunt or uncle or a father and mother or a grandfather or a grandmother or a grandchild.

A Muslim woman's apparel must clothe her completely except for her face and hands. Islam also ordains that she must not ostentatiously display her beauty, and her conduct and speech should be dignified, So as not to arouse any temptation in those with whom she is conducting her business. This is expressed in the following Quranic verses "Say to the believing men that they should lower their gaze and guard their modesty ; that will make for greater purity for them and God is well acquainted with all that they do. And say to the believing women that they should lower their gaze and guard their modesty; that they should not display their beauty and ornaments except what (must ordinarily) appear thereof ; that they should draw their veils over their bosoms and not display their beauty except to their husbands, their fathers, their husbands' fathers, their sons, their husbands' sons, their brothers or their brothers' sons, or their sisters' sons, or their women, or the slaves whom their right hands possess, or male servants free of physical needs, or small children who have no sense of the shame of sex ; and that they Should not Strike their feet in order to draw attention to their hidden ornaments. And O ye Believers I turn ye all together towards God that ye may attain Bliss." Also "O Prophet ! Tell thy wives and daughters and the believing women, that they should cast their outer garments over their persons (when abroad)." The following Quranic verses are addressed to the wives of the Prophet Muhammad, blessings and peace be upon him "O Consorts of the Prophet ! Ye are not like any of the (other) women if ye do fear (God), be not too complaisant of speech, lest one in whose heart is a disease should be moved with desire but speak ye a speech (that is) just. And stay quietly in your houses and make not a dazzling display, like that of the former Times of Ignorance ""be not too complaisant of speech..." means not to speak to men in a soft voice which might arouse temptation.

"And stay quietly in your houses..." means that they should not go out unless there be a specific reason for doing so "Make not a dazzling display, like that of the former Times of Ignorance" means that they should not make an ostentations display of their ornaments as did the women of the Pre-Islamic era. Although these verses are addressed to the wives of the Prophet, blessings and peace be upon him, Muslim women are encouraged to follow in their footsteps since they are the ideal of Muslim womanhood.

The Faith of Islam ordains equlity between men and women before the law and in all civil rights. This applies to unmarried girls and to married women. The laws of marriage in Islam differ from the laws of Christianity in the Western World by preserving the Muslim woman's right to retain her surname after marriage. Her marriage does not cancel her civil rights or her capacity to participate in legal contracts or her right to possess property or wealth. Thus a Muslim woman retains her family's name after marriage in addition to being entitled to all the civil rights due to men. She owns property in her own name and her wealth belongs to her alone and cannot be appropriated by her husband. The following Quranic verses refer to the dowry which is a woman's legitimate right in the event of divorce "But if ye decide to take one wife in place of another, even if ye had given the latter a whole treasure for dower, take not the least bit. of it back : would ye take it by slander and a manifest wrong ? And how could ye take it when ye have gone in unto each other, and they have taken from you a solemn covenant?"

Also : "It is not lawful for you (men), to take back any of your gifts (from your wives),.."If a man is forbidden to claim what he had given to his wife as a gift, it is only logical that he cannot appropriate any of her own personal wealth or property or any possession of any kind. If a wife in the event of a divorce or during marriage, of her own free will, relinquishes her claim to her dowry which is her due, her husband is allowed to regain it. This is clear from the following Quranic verse "And give the women (on marriage) their dower as a free gift ; but if they, of their own good pleasure, remit any part of it to you, take it and enjoy it with right good cheer." A husband has no right to dispose of his wife's wealth or property without her consent or without being granted power of attorney to act on her behalf. It is also a wife's right to cancel the power of attorney granted to her husband and to grant it to whomever she wills.

Most civilized modern democracies have not yet attained this elevated status of equality. In France, until recently, a French woman had no civil rights, since the French law denied her these rights. This is stated in the th clause of the French Civil Law "A married woman, even if her marriage is based upon the separation of her property from her husband's property, does not have the legal right to endow or dispose of her property or mortgage or exchange her property without her husband's written consent and participation in the contract."

Although certain amendments were made later concerning this law, its negative bearing upon the legal status of the French woman exists upto this very day. When a woman marries in the Western World, she officially takes her husband's surname to be her surname and by so doing yields her individuality and is integrated into her husband's personality.

The Faith of Islam does not discriminate between men and women except in matters when this discrimination is due to the nature of their sex, for their welfare and for the welfare of the community, the family and in particular for the welfare of women.

There are five issues where discrimination between men and women is ordained by Islam, namely : financial responsibilities, inheritance, the custodianship of the family, testimony and divorce. During the next stage of a woman's life, namely during her marriage, the Faith of Islam charges the husband with the responsibility of supporting his wife and family and does not charge the wife with any financial responsibilities. Nevertheless, Islam preserves all the Muslim woman's civil rights which include her right to possess and dispose of her wealth and property without any intervention from her husband. A wife is not obliged to participate in the financial support of her family even if she is wealthy enough to do so, for supporting the family is the sole responsibility of her husband, this being his religious and legal duty.

In the event of divorce, the husband is also charged by Islam with all the expenses that ensue. He is charged with paying the dowry agreed upon in the event of divorce, in addition to his divorced wife's financial support which includes her housing, food expenses and, apparel in addition to the children's expenses which include the wages of their wet nurses who breast feed them, their clothes and their education. The Muslim woman, on the other hand, is not charged with spending a single penny on herself or on her children.

It is obvious from the aforementioned, Islamic rulings that Islam has raised the status of the Muslim woman and has preserved her dignity in her father's home before marriage, in her own home during her marriage, and even in the event of her divorce. This status has not been attained by any other religion in the past or in the modern world of to day.

## THE DISCRIMINATION BETWEEN MEN AND WOMEN IN ISLAM

### Financial Responsibilities

The Faith of Islam is a faith of mercy and compassion and it protects the Muslim woman from having to work for her sustenance and guarantees her subsistence so that she would not be subject to the evils that are frequently related to drudgery and toil. She is accordingly not required to earn her living and this is the responsibility with which men are charged.

If a Muslim girl or woman is not married, her expenditure is the religious and legal obligation of her male relations, according to the laws of jurisprudence. If there is no male relative financially capable of supporting her, her livelihood is the solemn obligation of the treasury of the state. This ruling is applied in all stages of a girl's or woman's marriage which include the period during which the girl or woman prepares for marriage, the duration of her marriage, and in the event of divorce the period during its procedures. Men are thus charged with the financial support of women in all the stages of women's lives.

During the period preceding marriage, the Faith of Islam imposes upon the prospective husband a number of financial obligations concerning his forthcoming marriage without incurring any expense upon the bride's family. The husband's responsibilities include the dowry and the preparation of the marital home.

### The Laws of Inheritance

The Faith of Islam ordains that the males' share of inheritance be greater than the females' share, in most cases. The male inherits double the share of the female when the inheritance is shared between sons and daughters or between brothers and sisters. A widow's share of her husband's estate is half a widower's share of his wife's estate. Occasionally the father's share of his deceased son's estate is more than the mother's share. Nevertheless the mother's and father's share of the inheritance is sometimes equal if they have a son or more than two daughters.

The difference in the shares of the inheritance between males and females is based upon the financial responsibilities with which men alone are religiously charged. Men's financial obligations according to the laws of Islam are infinitely greater than women's financial responsibilities. A man is the head of his family and its custodian who is financially responsible for the maintenance of all its members if he is married and will be responsible for his family in the future if he is a bachelor. Islam also charges men with the financial support of their relatives whereas a Muslim woman, however wealthy she may be, is not even financially responsible for herself.

The laws of inheritance in Islam are accordingly fair in so far as they grant males a greater share of the inheritance, in order to enable them to fulfil their financial responsibilities with which

Islam has charged them. On the other hand Islam does not burden Muslim women with any financial obligations.

The Islamic laws of inheritance for women are fair and generous for she is granted half the share of her male counterpart's inheritance although she is not obliged to spend any of it supporting herself or her family, since that is the religious duty with which her husband, father, brother, paternal uncle or her nearest male relative is charged.

There are certain cases when males and females are granted equal shares of the inheritance as is the case when the family consists of a father, a mother, a son and two or more daughters. If one of the children dies, the father and the mother each inherit one sixth of the inheritance as is stated in the following Quranic verse : "For parents, a sixth share of the inheritance to each, if the deceased left children ;..." [Surah IV verse ]. Another case is when the deceased leaves no direct heir and maternal brothers and sisters all together inherit one third of the estate to be divided equally between them regardless of their sex. This is stated in the following Quranic verse "If a man or woman whose inheritance is in question, has left neither ascendants or descendants, but has left a (maternal) brother or a sister, each one of the two gets a sixth ; but if more than two, they share in a third ; ..." [Surah IV, verse ]. In this case the male does not take double the female's share. "In what your wives leave, your share is a half, if they leave no child but if they leave a child, ye get a fourth ; after payment of legacies and debts. In what ye leave, their share is a fourth, if ye leave no child but if ye leave a child, they get an eighth ; after payment of legacies and debts". [Surah IV, verse ].

### The Custodianship of the Family.

There are two reasons why the right to the custodianship of the family is granted to men by the Faith of Islam. The first reason is that men are charged with the financial support of their families and it is only fair that the person charged with the financial support and maintenance of any group of people should have the right of being that group's custodian who supervises their affairs.

The constitutions of the democracies of the modern world are likewise based upon this principle. The citizens of the state who pay taxes, which are spent on the public utilities of the state, have the right to have a say in their affairs and supervise the executive power of the land, in addition to participating in the legislation of the state. Referendums, general elections and representation in parliament are also based upon the same principle.

A referendum grants the citizens of a state direct supervision over the affairs of their country, whereas their indirect supervision is realised in the system of parliamentary representation by which they elect the members of parliament in a free election. Constitutional legislators sum up this principle in the following statement: "He who pays has the right of supervision". The second reason for granting a man authority and custodianship over his family is due to the indisputable fact that women are more emotional than men and that their disposition affects their judgement. God Almighty created women in this manner to enable them to pursue the principal role in their life namely that of motherhood and all that such a role entails, which includes nursing their babies and caring for them day and night. Such a vital role requires a sensitive compassionate nature more than its need for contemplation and meditation. On the other hand, men do not usually follow their emotions as is the case with women, and in most cases men are influenced by their reason and their perception. Accordingly a man's nature and disposition qualify him to be the head of the family and to supervise its affairs. These two reasons are stated in the following Quranic verse : "Men are the protectors and maintainers of women, because God has given the one more (strength) than the other, and because they support them from their means"

This custodianship which Islam grants man over his family is merciful, guiding and loving. It also includes principles that preserve a woman's dignity and protect her rights and welfare in every respect. The aim of this custodianship is one of protection and affection and not of absolute power or domination. Islam thus ensures the welfare of the family and of women themselves by taking into account all the circumstances and situations that exist in a woman's life.

If a Muslim girl or woman is unmarried, her father or her guardian is her custodian and he is therefore charged with supporting and providing for her financially so that she would not be forced to earn her living in a manner that might lead to her disgrace or the disgrace of her family. The custodianship in this case preserves the woman's dignity and protects her from any possible embarrassment.

A Muslim girl who is eligible for marriage, being of sound mind and body, has the right to choose the man she is going to marry, after the consent of her guardian be he her father or otherwise. Her guardian however cannot force her to marry any person against her will.

It has been related that a girl went to `A'isha, wife of the Prophet, blessings and peace be upon him, and complained to her that her father had married her to his brother's son in order to elevate her status. `A'isha told her to wait until the Prophet, blessings and peace be upon him, returned home so that he could advise her what to do. When he returned and heard the girl's complaint he said : "A girl has more right to her choice than her guardian". The girl said: "O Prophet of God, I will obey my father, but I came to you so that women will understand that men do not have the right to force women in this matter".

She meant that men did not have the right to force women into marriage against their will. If a girl or woman chooses a husband and her guardian refuses him, without having a legitimate reason for his refusal, she can take the matter to court and the Judge can marry her to the man of her choice. The following Quranic verse refers to not preventing divorced women from remarrying their former husbands if they desire to do so "When ye divorce women, and they fulfil the term of their (`Iddat), do not prevent them from marrying their (former) husbands, if they mutually agree on equitable terms".

Islam is greatly concerned with the issue of compatability between husband and wife. The wisdom of this ruling is that marriage is not only a relationship between two people but is a relationship between two families. An incompatible marriage usually brings more embarrassment upon the wife's family than the husband's family. Accordingly the Faith of Islam grants the girl's or the woman's guardian the right to prevent her from marrying a person who would bring disgrace upon her and upon her family. This is the guardian's right, yet he cannot force her to marry against her will but is permitted to advise her and convince her. The Faith of Islam also grants the judge of the State the right to intervene in matters of marriage in which guardians are unfair or exceed the limits of their authority.

Abu Hanifa, one of the four founders of the schools of Muslim Law, declared that a Muslim woman has the right to marry herself whenever she wishes provided that her husband is compatible by religious standards and that her guardian has no right to prevent her marriage except on the grounds of incompatibility.

The current laws in Egypt are based upon Abu Hanifa's ruling. Abu Hanifa's School of Muslim law and the other schools of Muslim law agree that the custodianship and supervision granted to men by Islam in this stage of a girl's or a woman's life, in common with the other stages of her life are for her welfare and protection.

After a woman is married, this custodianship and supervision is transferred from her father or guardian to her husband. This does not in any way belittle the woman nor does it affect any of her civil rights of purchasing, selling, entering into contracts or disposing of her wealth and property independently without requiring her husband's consent. In fact her husband does not have any right to intervene in her affairs without her consent or her granting him power of attorny, which she can cancel any time if she so wishes.

The man's custodianship and supervision over his wife as head of the family is manifested in his right to supervise the policy of the household with the cooperation of the wife, who must obey him within the recognized ordained limits. These rights granted to men impose upon them certain obligations such as financially supporting their wives and families in addition to protecting their rights. Husbands are also commanded to treat their wives fairly, kindly and generously. A husband must be tolerant and lenient when dealing with the problems that exist in every marriage. He is also religiously charged with correcting his wife's errors in a gentle and understanding manner. The Prophet, blessings and peace be upon him, stated that the best people are those who are kind to their families. The passage from the following Quranic verse summarizes the aforementioned relationship between husband and wife "And women shall have rights similar to the rights against them, according to what is equitable ; but men have a degree of advantage over them". In Islam women's rights are equal to their obligations and men's obligations are equal to their rights, and even the degree that God grants man is not without obligations since it charges him with the support, maintainance and protection of his wife and family.

## The Testimony of Men and Women in Islam

Islam does not rely upon a woman's testimony in serious crimes such as adultery, and relies upon the testimony of women in matters concerning women that are understood only by women. In other matters the testimony of two women is equal to the testimony of a man and since Islam demands the testimony of two men in most matters, a man must corroborate the testimony of the two women. The reason for this discrimination is that God Almighty created women with extremely emotional and sensitive natures in order to enable them to fulfil their vital duties in life, the most important of which is the role of motherhood and all the love and affection it demands. Motherhood requires a sensitive, tender and compassionate nature and a woman's emotions are usually stronger than her reasoning and this in itself is not a shortcoming in a woman's character. Occasionally a woman's emotions overwhelm her to the extent that she may not be able to estimate an event clearly and may interpret it in a manner that may not be precise, without her realising it. Islam accordingly takes this into consideration and in order to ensure that justice is executed, ordains the above mentioned laws of testimony regarding women.

The reason why the testimony of two women is equal to the testimony of one man is built upon the basis that there is hardly any possibility that two women would be emotionally affected in the same way by the same event. They can also correct each other's testimony if one of them forgets a fact or misunderstands a matter. This is mentioned in the following Quranic verse "And get two witnesses, out of your own men, and if there are not two men, then a man and two women, such as ye choose, for witnesses, so that if one of them errs, the other can remind her".

## THE RIGHT OF DIVORCE IN ISLAM.

Many orientalists criticize the Faith of Islam because it grants the right of divorce to men only. It accordingly behooves us to explain the laws of divorce in Islam clearly and in detail. Many people have either misinterpreted or misunderstood the facts that govern the issue of divorce in Islam and have consequently presented a distorted picture of the matter.

The system of divorce in Islam is the most ideal system of divorce ordained by any religion. If we consider the system of divorce, in the countries of the Western world that adhere to Christianity we must understand the following facts. Christians follow one of three Churches, namely the Catholic, Orthodox or the Protestant Church.

The Catholic Church prohibits divorce and does not permit the annulment of marriage for any reason, however serious the reason may be. Adultery itself is not a justifiable cause for divorce and the only procedure permitted in the event of adultery is a separation between the husband and wife. The state of marriage nevertheless, exists legally between them and accordingly neither of them can marry again, since they would be committing the crime of bigamy. The Catholic Church ordained this law according to Mathew's Gospel which states: "What therefore God hath joined together, let no man put asunder." Certain groups that seceded from the Catholic Church permit divorce only in the event of adultery being committed by the husband or wife, but they also prohibit them from marrying again.

The Christian Churches that permit divorce in the event of adultery base their ruling on Mathew's Gospel as uttered by Christ : "Whosoever shall put away his wife, saving for the cause of fornication, causeth her to commit adultery".The prohibition of a divorced man and a divorced woman from entering into a second marriage is based upon the following ruling from Mathew's Gospel : "Whosoever shall marry her that is divorced committeth adultery" According to the original laws of Christianity, if discord between a husband and wife reaches a point when reconciliation is an impossibility and marital life becomes intolerable and the life of the whole family, adults and children alike, is threatened with disasterous consequences, they are commanded to remain in their miserable marriage whatever the consequences may be since : "What therefore God hath joined together let no man put assunder".

Even if a husband and wife hate each other and all human attempts fail to reconcile them to each other, since one has no control over one's emotions which are controlled by God alone, they are commanded by the Church to spend the rest of their lives together, however miserable their lives may be. If either a husband or a wife does not abide by the sacred contract of marriage and deviates from morality and all attempts fail to reform him or her, Christianity prohibits divorce and the injured husband or wife is commanded to remain married to the person who has sinned against the Law of God, for the rest of his or her life. Occasionally separation between a husband and wife is permitted, but neither of them is permitted to marry again, according to the aforementioned verses of Mathew's Gospel.

If either a husband or a wife becomes mentally deranged and is a threat and a danger to the family, Christianity does not permit a divorce. If a husband contracts a serious infectious disease for which there is no remedy, or if he is impotent or sterile and cannot father a child, the Christian faith prohibits divorce although the marital relationship between husband and wife and the birth of offspring are the foundation of marriage. A husband may abandon his wife and family for many years without his family knowing whether he was alive or had died or had been sentenced to life imprisonment, but the Christian faith will not grant the abandoned wife divorce. The same prohibition applies in the event of a husband who cannot or will not support his wife and family that has no other means of maintainance and may accordingly force the wife to lead a life of sin.

An Egyptian Christian woman, Mrs Zahiya`Aziz Murqos, filed a suit of divorce against her husband who had abandoned her without any financial support and had been unable to pay her the money for her maintainance which the court had decreed, as a result of his straitened means. The court refused her suit on the grounds that the laws of Christianity ordain that the bond of marriage is a sacred bond as is stated in the Gospel and is one of the seven secrets of the Church, emphasizing that what God has joined, no human being should set asunder. The court stated that some church officials and members of the general religious board had responded to the demands of people of weak faith and had granted them divorce for reasons which had not been ordained in the Gospel, and that the only reason for divorce permitted by the Gospel was adultery. These were the reasons stated by the Court for refusing a divorce to Mrs. Zahiya `Aziz Murqos. The Christian faith also prohibits the divorce of a husband and wife whose treatment of each other may lead to their serious harm or injury, after all attempts to reconcile them fail. Even if a husband and wife both feel that their married life has become intolerable and they both desire and agree to terminate their marriage, so that each one of them may begin a new life, they are prohibited from doing so by the Church.

When the Christians in the countries of the Western world realized that they could not adhere to the rigid laws of divorce as ordained by the Gospel, they introduced civil laws which permitted them to annul the marriage contract in certain cases. The great English philosopher, Bentham, expressed his opinion on the matter of divorce in his book "The Principles of Legislation", in which he wrote that a permanent marriage is undoubtably the ideal state for people and the most suitable for their needs, in addition to being the most favourable for the welfare of the family. He then stated that if a woman should stipulate that her husband should never be separated from her even if hatred should replace love, that would be an intolerable situation.

He continued to state that this stipulation exists without women demanding it, since the laws of the Church declare to the bride and bridegroom that they marry in order to be happy, but that they must understand that they have entered a prison the door of which is locked and that they will never be allowed to leave the prison, even if they fight each other with the weapons of enmity and hatred. The English philosopher also declared that if death alone could terminate a marriage the number of murders would have increased greatly. Christians have introduced civil laws which permit divorce and thus deliver them from having to resort to murder or suicide in order to liberate themselves from this prison. Abiding by civil law in matters of marriage and divorce and abandoning the laws of their faith is a unique manifestation of the Christians of the Western world. People of other religions including the Brahmas, Budhists and even the Magians and Pagans adhere or adhered to the laws of their faith in matters of marriage and divorce even if they introduced laws in other matters. They were accordingly able to live their lives without the problems that arise from the prohibition of divorce.

Some Christians however disregarded the laws of theifaith marriage and divorce after realizing that these laws do not take human nature, with all its inherent weakness, into consideration. The Christian priests and clergymen could not stem the opposition to the laws of the Christian faith concerning divorce, nor could they deny the logic of man's natural needs, so they let matters drift and passed judgement on divorce only in the most serious and critical circumstances concerning royal families or other symbols of authority. They also chose the most opportune time from the political perspective in order to demonstrate their power and status. When King Edward the Eighth of England declared his intention to marry a divorced woman and the policy of the government was opposed to this marriage, the Church refused to grant him permission to marry Mrs Simpson and remain on the throne of Great Britain. He was consequently obliged to choose between his throne and the woman he loved, and he chose the woman he loved and relinquished the throne.

It beloves us to mention that neither the Church nor the nation objected to their king having an illicit relationship with Mrs Simpson but that they only objected to his intention of marrying her. When Princess Margaret Rose, sister of Queen Elizabeth the Second of Great

Britain, declared that she intended to marry Captain Townsend whom she loved, the Church refused to permit her to marry him as he had divorced his wife. The fact that Captain Townsend's divorce had been granted him by civil and religious law, since his wife had been found guilty of adultery for which sin, the Protestant Church of England permits divorce, had no influence upon the Church's refusal.

In Europe and in North America, the courts grant divorce to husbands and wives according to man-made civil laws, thereby violating the laws of their faith. The people who advocate that we abandon our Islamic laws of divorce and abide by these civil laws do not realize that such a procedure would result in chaos and corruption. Although thousands of cases of divorce were filed and granted in Europe and in the United States of America, the Church did not object and did nothing to prevent such a phenomenum. An example of the Church's policy, which takes into consideration the political circumstances of the land, is that when the British Prime Minister, Sir Anthony Eden, divorced his wife, who had eloped with her lover to the United States of America, and married another wife, the Church did not object to his second marriage since it was not an opportune time to oppose the marriage.

The laws of Christianity concerning divorce and man-made civil laws concerning divorce are deficient with the result that the welfare of the family has invariably been sacrificed. There are two trends in the civil laws concerning divorce, the first of which is extremely lax in its attitude towards the sacred bond of marriage, and permits divorce on the slightest pretext. This is the case in certain states in the United States of America. It was therefore quite an ordinary occurrence in these states for a woman to be married in the morning and to be granted a divorce in the evening. Such laws of divorce are undoubtably responsible for the breaking up of family life.

The second trend in the laws of divorce bases its rulings upon the spirit of the Chritian faith although it is not as rigid in its rulings. It only permits divorce in certain cases with extremely complicated procedures. Accordingly such divorces are only valid after a lengthy period as is the case in France and most Catholic countries. The French civil law only permits divorce in three cases, the first of which is in the event of the adultery of either the husband or wife. The second case is in the event of either the husband or the wife being subjected to brutal treatment. The third instance is if either the husband or wife is sentenced to imprisonment for a criminal offence. A person's chronic malady, physical disability and insanity itself even if it results in harmful and cruel treatment to the spouse, are not, according to French law, legitimate reasons for divorce. Absence from one's husband or wife for a lengthy period of time and extreme discord between a husband and wife are also not considered legitimate reasons for divorce according to the French law, even if both the husband and wife desire the divorce. In order that divorce be granted if one's husband or wife is sentenced to prison, the crime committed must be a major crime. Proof of brutal and cruel treatment of wives and husbands is also a very difficult matter to prove to the court. Accordingly, most people who file for divorce do so on the grounds of adultery.

The concerned party presents the evidence of the adultery of his or her spouse to convince the court that adultery has been committed. On the other hand a husband and wife often present false evidence of adultery and perjure themselves in court in order to be granted a divorce. Divorce which is granted on the grounds of adultery brings disgrace upon the husband, wife and their children. In addition to this, divorce invariably incurs exorbitant expenses which can only be afforded by the wealthy. The final decree of divorce also takes years before it becomes valid during which time the husband and wife are separated from one another. As a result of these complications and the lengthy period that the divorce takes to become legalized, many men take mistresses and women lovers thereby completely destroying any family life that had previously existed. Such relationships have become so common in the United States of America and in Europe, that they are regarded as ordinary occurrences. In addition to the fact that the family has lost its value in society, the fatherhood of many children is unascertained and a source of doubt.

Thus the civil laws of divorce either destroy the sacredness of the bond of marriage by permitting divorce on the slightest pretext, or are so rigid that divorce is only granted after disgracing the family concerned and subjecting its members to a most complicated and expensive procedure. In both cases the family is sacrificed. After presenting the laws of Christianity concerning divorce and the civil laws introduced in the matter of divorce and the complications of both the religious and the civil laws, it behoves us to present the laws of divorce as ordained by the Faith of Islam. These laws have been severely criticized by non-Muslims who claim that these laws are not based upon equality between men and women. The Faith of Islam permits divorce because it ordains laws that take human nature into consideration and divorce is sometimes the only solution to serious problems of marital discord. However, Islam does not permit divorce without enforcing definite terms which ensure safeguarding the rights of both the husband and wife and guarantee the execution of their obligations and duties in a just and fair manner. The bond of marriage in Islam is a sacred bond which is venerated and solemnly respected. The following Quranic verse refers to the marriage bond "And how could ye take it when ye have gone in unto each other, and they have taken from you a solemn covenant ?"Such a bond is thus regarded with the utmost veneration. Islam does its utmost to make people detest divorce and urges Muslims not to resort to it as far as is humanly possible. The Prophet Muhammad, blessings and peace be upon him, said "Divorce is the most detested permissible legitimate act in the eyes of God". He also said "Marry and do not resort to divorce, for the Throne of God Almighty shakes with every divorce In addition to discouraging divorce on principle, Islam ordained certain rulings that guaranteed avoiding divorce except when it was the only solution to marital discord.

Islam states that one should not resort to divorce as a result of any matter that can be remedied or that might improve in the future. Even if a husband dislikes some qualities in his wife's nature, Islam does not consider this a justification for divorce. He should not contemplate divorce if his feelings for his wife have undergone a change or if he has begun to dislike her. Any minor matters that aggravate a husband in his wife's conduct-providing that this does not include immorality or disobedience of the Faith - are not justifiable reasons for divorce, since one's emotions are fickle and inconstant.

One should consequently never allow oneself to be controlled by one's whims when making decisions concerning important matters upon which the future of one's family depends, for a person whom one dislikes today may be beloved on the morrow. A husband who dislikes a certain trait in his wife might discover that she possesses other qualities that appeal to him. This is mentioned in the following Quranic verse : "...live with them on a footing of kindness and equity. If ye take a dislike to them, it may be that ye dislike a thing, and God brings about through it, a great deal of good".

The Prophet Muhammad, blessings and peace be upon him, said that a believer should not hate his believing wife for if he dislikes a certain quality in her, she may possess another quality that pleases him.

A man went to `Omar ben Al Khattab, the Second Rightly Guided Caliph, to ask for his advice about divorcing his wife. `Omar told him not to divorce her and when the man replied that he did not love her, `Omar said "Woe betide you ! Are homes built only upon love? Where then is the role of care, affection and avoiding censure ?" He meant that if a marriage were not built upon love, it could be built upon two other important factors, one of which includes the care, affection and consideration which binds the members of the family to one another and teaches them their rights and their obligations. The other important factor is avoiding being the object of censure or blame for one's actions such as breaking up a home and family and being the cause of their misery.

The system ordained by Islam aims at avoiding divorce and the husband and wife who are at discord with each other are commanded to do their utmost to overcome their differences by dealing with each other compassionately and considerately as is mentioned in the following Quranic verse "If a wife fears cruelty or desertion on her husband's part, there is no blame on them if they arrange an amicable settlement between themselves ; and such settlement is best".

When a husband and wife fail to reconcile their differences with each other, Islam ordains that the matter of their discord be discussed at a family meeting in which the husband and the wife are each represented by a member of their families. These representatives act as mediators, and it is their duty to discuss and consider the problems that had caused the discord and to do their utmost to reconcile the points of view of the husband and wife until a reconciliation between them is effected. The Faith of Islam, in its concern for the happiness of the family, does not wait until discord actually takes place, in order to resort to this method of reconciliation, but it commands the husband and wife to do so if they fear that discord may occur and they feel that they are unable to deal with the matter.

This is stated in the following Quranic verse : "If ye fear a breach between them twain, appoint (two) arbiters, one from his family, and the other from hers ; if they wish for peace, God will cause their reconciliation : for God hath full knowledge, and is acquainted with all things". The Faith of Islam has also ordained certain financial and social obligations in the event of divorce, so as to discourage people from resorting to it. Islam ordains that when a man divorces his wife, he must pay her the delayed dowry agreed upon in the marriage contract, in addition to the expense of her maintainance of food, drink and living quarters for a certain period of time, known as the " iddat ". The custody of the children is granted to the mother until they grow up. In the event of her death or inability to look after her children, the custody of her children is granted to her relations. The husband is legally and religiously charged with his children's financial maintainance, and for wet nurses to breast feed them even if their mother breast feeds them herself, as is stated in the following Quranic verse "And if they suckle your (offspring) give them their recompense"

If all attempts at reconciliation made by the mediators of both families fail, and the husband insists upon divorce, that in itself signifies that the stability of the family is in danger and that the chief elements upon which a marriage is founded no longer exist. In such circumstances Islam permits divorce and at the same time guarantees the welfare and the future of the family. Even if a divorce takes place, Islam grants the husband an opportunity to reconsider the divorce if there is the slightest possibility that married life be resumed.

The Faith of Islam ordains that after a husband divorces his wife once, he is given two options, one of which is to restore his wife during her " iddat " or period of waiting which is approximately three months for a wife who is not pregnant. The wife's return to her husband in this case needs no legal procedure and is valid as soon as the husband utters the words "I have restored my wife", or words to that effect. In order to encourage a husband to restore his divorced wife, Islam ordains that she live in her marital home during her period of waiting. This is stated in the following Quranic verse "O Prophet When ye do divorce women,divorce them at their prescribed periods,.nd count (accurately) their prescribed periods and fear God your Lord and turn them not out of their houses, nor shall they (themselves) leave, except in case they are guilty of some open lewdness" .

Islam also favours restoring one's divorced wife as is stated in the following Quranic verse : "And their husbands have the better right to take them back in that period, if they wish for reconciliation "The Quranic verse describes the restoration of the divorced wife to her marital life as redressing the divorce. If a husband does not restore his wife during her period of waiting, she will have been divorced for the second time. Islam, which always guards the welfare of the family, permits the husband after the second divorce to restore his wife, but charges him with paying her a new dowry and contracting a new marriage contract. In the event of the husband restoring his wife during her period of waiting or marrying her for the secondtime with a new marriage contract and a new dowry, and then deciding to divorce her, he is permitted the same opportunities of restoring his wife that he had previously been granted.

After a husband divorces his wife twice he is left with the right to divorce her only one more time. A third divorce signifies that married life has become intolerable and that the husband and wife have failed to make a success of their marriage. It is at this stage that the Faith of Islam ordains permanent divorce between them. The only chance of their remarrying is if the wife marries another man after her final divorce from her first husband and is divorced by her second husband. If she and her first ex-husband believe that after their long separation from one another, and after the change in their circumstances, they can succeed in living a happily married life, Islam permits them to do as, as is expressed in the following Quranic verses "So if a husband divorces his wife (irrevocably), he cannot after that, re-marry her until she has another husband and he has divorced her. In that case there is no blame on either of them if they re-unite, provided they feel that they can keep the limits ordained by God. Such are the limits ordained by God, which He makes plain to those who understand".

The Imam Malik related that during the lifetime of the Prophet Muhammad, blessings and peace be upon him, Abdullah, the son of `Omar ben Al Khattab divorced his wife during her menstrual period, and Omar asked the Prophet, blessings and peace be upon him, his opinion on the matter. He told `Omar that his son must restore his wife until her menstrual course be terminated and she purifies herself from it then to wait till she purifies herself from the following menstrual course, after which he can divorce her or restore her.

Such is the system of divorce in Islam and these are the laws ordained according to the Quran and the Traditions of the Prophet, Divorce that does not adhere to the laws of Islam is not valid. This is clear from the ruling given by the Prophet - blessings and peace be upon him - concerning `Omar ben Al Khattab's son who had divorced his wife during her menstrual course, which is not considered a period during which divorce can be pronounced. Ibn Jurayh related through Abu Al Zubayr that he had heard `Abdel Rahman ben Ayman ask Abdullah ben `Omar about this matter and that `Abdullah had replied that the Prophet, blessings and peace be upon him, had told him that his utterance of divorce had not been legitimate.

`Omar ben Al Khattab, the Second Rightly Guided Caliph legalized a certain system of divorce which was not founded upon the aforementioned laws of divorce. This included considering a divorce irrevocable if a man uttered the vow of divorce three consecutive times in one sitting. The reason for enforcing this ruling was that `Omar ben Al Khattab noticed that many men had made light of the sanctity of marriage and had underestimated the gravity of divorce. These men had often uttered the oath of divorce in order to intimidate their wives or to force them to obey them, so `Omar ben Al Khattab punished them by introducing this new system of divorce to make them realize the sanctity of marriage so that they would not utter false threats of divorce. He told them that God had granted them an opportunity for tolerance and deliberation in the Islamic laws of divorce, but that they had not heeded them, so they deserved a penalty in keeping with their sin. `Omar's ruling was only temporary as a remedy for the ill use of divorce that had spread and was thus a disciplinary measure. The Egyptian law of the year decreed that any oath of divorce that specifies more than one divorce is considered only one divorce. In fact there is no valid law of divorce that is not mentioned in the Qur'an or the Traditions of the Prophet. The laws of divorce in Islam guarantee every person his or her rights and it is sinful for any man to believe that he can divorce his wife whenever he pleases, since the laws of divorce in Islam are based upon a precise and just system which God ordained for mankind, men and women alike, in order to remedy the discord and misery to which some families are subjected.

The laws ordained by Islam concerning divorce are divine laws and the following Quranic verses dealing with divorce invariably state that the laws are ordained by God who prohibits breaking these laws and warns against the harm that ensues "These are the limits ordained by God ; so do not transgress them. If any do transgress the limits ordained by God, such persons wrong (themselves as well as others)."

Also "Such are the limits ordained by God, which He makes plain to those who understand". "Those are limits set by God and any who transgresses the limits of God, does verily wrong his own soul.. " "But do not take them back to injure them, (or) to take undue advantage ; if any one does that, he wrongs his own soul. Do not treat God's Signs as a jest,..." "And know that God knoweth what is in your hearts, and take heed of Him ..."

The Faith of Islam ordains certain provisions and stipulations concerning divorce so that it would not be the result of a whim. Islam grants the husband the opportunity of reconsidering his decision and grants the relations of the husband and wife an opportunity to intercede and reconcile them. Even after the failure of all the aforementioned attempts at reconciliation, the Qur'an states that two witnesses must witness the divorce : "Thus when they fulfil their term appointed, either take them back on equitable terms or part with them on equitable terms ; and take for witness two persons from among you, endued with justice, and establish the evidence (as) before God. Such is the admonition given to him who believes in God and the Last Day. And for those who fear God, He (ever) prepares a way out ....". "A way out" can be interpreted to mean a way out of divorce. The Shiites decree that there must be witnesses to a divorce, and that this is an essential factor without which the divorce is not valid and has no consequences. This opinion adheres to the Quranic verses and grants the husband a final opportunity to reconsider his intention and not finalize the divorce. It is also an opportunity for the two witnesses who are summoned to witness the divorce, and are usually close friends or relatives of the husband and wife, to make a final attempt to deter the husband from concluding the divorce.

If divorce occurs, the Faith of Islam does its utmost to ensure generous and compassionate treatment of the divorced woman in addition to guaranteeing her her rights and safeguarding her from any harm to which she might be subjected. The laws of financial support for the divorced wife and her children, the custody of the children, financial support during the period of waiting, financial maintenance for nursing the children are all in the divorced woman's favour and this is verified by the following Quranic verses : "When ye divorce women, and they fulfil the term of their (Iddat), either take them back on equitable terms or set them free on equitable terms; but do not take them back to injure them, (or) to take undue advantage ; if any one does that, he wrongs his own soul. Do not treat God's Signs as a jest, but solemnly rehearse God's favours on you, and the fact that He sent down to you The Book and Wisdom for your instruction. And fear God, and know that God is well acquainted with all things. When ye divorce women, and they fulfil the term of their (Iddat), do not prevent them from marrying their (former) husbands, if they mutually agree on equitable terms. This instruction is for all amongst you, who believe in God, and the Last Day. That is (the course making for) most virtue and purity amongst you. And God knows and ye know not."

Also : "O Prophet ! When ye do divorce women, divorce them at their prescribed periods, and count (accurately) their prescribed periods and fear God your Lord : and turn them not out of their houses, nor shall they (themselves) leave, except in case they are guilty of some open lewdness ; those are limits set by God :nd any who transgresses the limits of God, does verily wrong his (own) soul : thou knowest not if perchance God will bring about thereafter some new situation. Thus when they fulfil their term appointed, either take them back on equitable terms or part with them on equitable terms ; ..." Also : "Let the women live (In Iddat) in the same style as ye live, according to your means annoy them not, so as to restrict them. And if they carry (life in their wombs), then spend (your ) on them until they deliver their burden and if they suckle your (offspring), give them their recompense :nd take mutual counsel together, according to what is just and reasonable. And if ye find yourselves in difficulties, let another woman suckle (the child) on the (father's) behalf ".

Also : "But if ye decide to take one wife in place of another, even if you had given the latter a whole treasure for dower, take not the least bit of it back would ye take it by slander and a manifest wrong ? And how could ye take it when ye have gone in unto each other, and they have taken from you a solemn covenant ?"

In addition to divorce between a man and his wife who consumated their marriage and lived together as man and wife, Islam permits the divorce of a man and his bride who have signed the marriage contract, but have not consumated their marriage, if there is a good reason to do so, so that each one of them can begin a new life with the Grace of God.

In such a situation, Islam ordains that the man must pay the girl or woman half the dowry agreed upon, in addition to compensation for divorcing her. This procedure is ordained as compensation for the divorced bride and the compensation is estimated by the ruler of the state according to the means of the husband and the extent of the injury caused to the bride by the divorce.

The following Quranic verses mention this matter : "There is no blame on ye if ye divorce women before consumation or the fixation of their dower ; but bestow on them (a suitable gift), the wealthy according to his means, and the poor according to his means ; - a gift of a reasonable amount is due from those who wish to do the right thing.

And if ye divorce them before consumation, but after the fixation of a dower for them, then the half of the dower (is due to them), unless they remit it or (the man's half) is remitted by him in whose hands is the marriage tie ; and the remission (of the man's half) is the nearest to righteousness. And do not forget liberality between yourselves . For God sees well all that ye do."

In addition to the aforementioned cases of divorce there are four other kinds of divorce, the first of which is if a wife stipulates in her marriage contract that the right of divorce be in her hand and her husband agrees to the condition, she has the right to divorce her husband according to some schools of jurisprudence with certain provisions.

The second kind of divorce occurs and is legal if there is a breach of one of the terms stipulated by the wife in the marriage contract. If the husband is responsible for this breach, certain schools of jurisprudence consider this sufficient to legalize the divorce, provided that the term stipulated does not violate the basic elements of marital life or the laws ordained by God Almighty.

The third kind of divorce is pronounced by the judge in a court of law as the result of the husband's failure to support his family or in order to safeguard his wife and family against any harm that might threaten them. The absence of a husband from his wife and home for a lengthy duration is also another reason for this kind of divorce and the Egyptian law, number twenty five, for the year legalized divorce for the aforementioned reasons.

The fourth kind of divorce occurs by the mutual consent of a husband and wife. In this case, the wife usually renounces all or some of her rights as a divorced woman, or grants her husband a sum of money upon which they both agree.

This kind of divorce is known as divorce by compensation, and takes place when a wife feels that her marital life has become intolerable and fears that if she is not divorced she may not be able to abide by the laws ordained by God. This kind of divorce is mentioned in the following Quranic verse: "It is not lawful for you, (men), to take back any of your gifts (from your wives), except when both parties fear that they would be unable to keep the limits ordained by God, If ye (judges) do indeed fear that they would be unable to keep the limits ordained by God, there is no blame on either of them if she gives something for her freedom. These are the limits ordained by God ; so do not transgress them. If any do transgress the limits ordained by God, such persons wrong (themselves as well as others)."

The objections and criticism concerning the system of divorce in Islam is based upon the claim that it constitutes a violation of equality since the right of divorce is granted to men and not to women.

It is claimed that since a husband and wife are partners in a marriage and in their life together, granting the right of divorce to only one of them is inconsistent with the basis of the marriage contract and with the equality that should be granted to both sexes in that respect. People who criticize the Islamic system of divorce claim that the marriage contract should only be annulled by the mutual consent of both parties, namely the husband and the wife.

These people misunderstood many important facts in this matter, such as that when a Muslim girl or woman agrees to the contract of marriage with her prospective husband she does so in full knowledge of the laws ordained by God Almighty, one of which is that the man alone has the right of divorce in accordance with the laws of the Faith of Islam. By signing the marriage contract, she is quite aware of and agrees to renouncing her right of divorce of her own free will.

People who object to the laws of divorce in Islam have also overlooked the recognized fact that women are more emotional and temperamental than men and are frequently unable to control their feelings. In addition to this, by the laws of Islam, they incur no financial responsibilities on themselves in the event of their divorce. If the right of divorce were granted to women, their emotions might affect their better judgement, and trifling misunderstandings might provoke them to divorce their husbands, thereby ruining their lives and the future of their families.

As a rule, men are not as temperamental as women and are seldom motivated by their emotions. A husband who resorts to divorce also incurs grave financial responsible for the welfare and maintenance of his family. It is therefore only natural that he be granted the right of divorce with the restrictions of the aforementioned provisions and rulings which are ordained in order to safeguard the wife and the family against any harmful consequences.

Recently a suggestion has been forwarded to deny the husband and wife the right of divorce and to grant the right of divorce to the judge in a court of law. By this system a wife could only be divorced after she had filed for divorce in a court of law and had convinced the judge that she had the right to be divorced. Such a system would mean that the French civil law would replace the laws of God Almighty.

We have mentioned how the French civil laws of divorce were responsible for breaking up the families involved in divorce suits and how this led to the deterioration of the morals of the community.

Most divorce suits involve sordid details and embarrassing situations which ought not to be made public. If a husband and wife have no other option but to publicly announce embarrassing and sordid details in order to be granted a divorce, by doing so they would disgrace themselves and ruin their reputation and the reputation of their family. If on the other hand they feared for their reputation and the reputation of their family and refused to mention the sordid details which would have enabled them to win a divorce case, they would spend the rest of their lives in an intolerable mabased upon deceit and infidel.

Although the Faith of Islam establishes the system of arbitration by mediators between the husband and wife in matters of discord between them, it guarantee! the dignity and privacy of their personal life.

The arbitrators or mediators according to the rulings of Islam are persons chosen by the wife and husband. They are chosen for this specific purpose and accordingly neither the husband nor the wife are subjected to any embarrassment when they declare the reasons of the discord. The arbitrators accordingly safeguard the reputation of the husband and wife and everything that is mentioned is strictly confidential. The dignified conduct of the mediators is only natural since their relationship with the husband and wife is that of trust and confidence.

The laws of divorce as ordained by the Faith of Islam are just and fair. They have been ordained for the welfare of the husband and wife, the family and the community. These laws preserve and guarantee the rights of both the husband and wife and do not wrong either of them. These divine laws grant the husband certain rights and grant the wife certain rights to compensate her in the event of divorce. This is mentioned in the following Quranic verse "And women shall have rights similar to the rights against them, according to what is equitable ; but men have a degree (of advantage) over them."

Divorce in Islam is the solution to problems that cannot otherwise be solved just as surgery is the only remedy to certain maladies. Islam takes a medium course that does not prohibit divorce as does Catholicism, nor does it abuse the sanctity of the marriage contract as does the civil law in some countries in Europe and North America, which more often than not subjects the husband, wife and the family to humiliation and disgrace.

2

# FREEDOM IN ISLAM

The Faith of Islam has based all its laws upon the principle of freedom and has applied it to all aspects of life. This includes political freedom, freedom of thought, freedom of religion and civil rights.

## POLITICAL FREEDOM

Political freedom is the right granted to every sane adult to participate in the administration of the affairs of his country and to observe the executive power by which representatives are elected in a free election or by a general referendum.

The Faith of Islam adheres to this principle and the choice of the Caliph himself is left to the Muslim citizens of the State. The sound choice of the Caliph is thus based upon a free pledge of allegiance, and it was upon this democratic principle that the Four Rightly Guided Caliphs were chosen. Islam also prohibited the executive power from legalizing any important matter in the affairs of the state without the approval of the subjects of the state. The executive power was also obliged to answer to the people for all its procedures concerning the state

The speech made by Abu Bakr Al Siddiq after the Muslims had pledged allegiance to him as Caliph of the Muslims after the death of the Prophet Muhammad, blessings and peace be upon him, demonstrates this principle. He said : "O people I have been summoned to rule you and I am no better than you. If you see me acting justly, aid and assist me, and if you see me doing wrong, rectify me and guide me to do what is right. Obey me provided I obey God's commands in ruling you, but if I disobey the commands of God, I will not be entitled to your obedience". In another speech Abu Bakr said : "If I am in the right, follow me, but if I swerve from righteousness rectify me". `Omar ben Al Khattab, the Second Rightly Guided Caliph, said to his people "If you ever see any deviation from righteousness in my conduct, rectify me". A man stood up and said "If we see any deviation from righteousness in your conduct, we will rectify it by the sword". `Omar ben Al Khattab was very pleased to see that the Muslims were aware of their rights and their duty to safeguard justice and righteousness in their state.

When some citizens of the state criticized Othman ben Affan - in certain matters, he said "I repent and will refrain from doing anything that the Muslims criticize and when I come down from the pulpit, let those who wish to express their opinion on any matter come to me, and by God if a slave refers to any mistake I may have made, I will accept his criticism and feel as humiliated a slave".

In order to confirm this sacred principle of freedom, God Almighty commanded the Prophet Muhammad, blessings and peace be upon him, not to be autocratic in matters that concerned the Muslims, and commanded him to consult the Muslims in certain matters that concerned them. This is mentioned in the following Quranic verse "It is part of the Mercy of God that thou dost deal gently with them. Wert thou severe or harsh-hearted, they would have broken away from about thee so pass over (their faults), and ask for (God's) forgiveness for them ; and consult them ; in affairs (of moment)."

The Prophet, blessings and peace be upon him, accepted the unanimous opinion of his Companions even if he was not personally convinced by it. If his Companions' opinion was not unanimous, he agreed to the opinion of the majority as was the case in the Battle of Uhud when he was against going to battle, but he agreed to his Companions' demand to fight and his opinion proved to be correct, for the Muslims were defeated in this battle.

When a serious or urgent matter that affected the security of the state occurred and no such matter had been mentioned in the Quran or in the Traditions of the Prophet, the Muslim Caliph would hold a general referendum by assembling the people whom the matter concerned and would seek their opinion. The opinion of the majority would be adopted after the result of the referendum would be made clear. This procedure adhered to the Spirit of Islam and the principle of consultation that was ordained by the Faith of Islam. Thus Islam adopted the principle of political freedom in a manner that does not exist in many of the modern democracies of the world.

## FREEDOM OF THOUGHT

Islam's principle concerning freedom of thought does not differ from its principle concerning political freedom. Islam grants every human being the right to express his or her opinion in the manner that he or she chooses. Islam considers that one of the most important characteristics of a Muslim is his conviction that he should declare what he believes and not fear censure or opposition.

The Prophet Muhammad, blessings and peace be upon him, and the Four Rightly Guided Caliphs who succeeded him, adhered to this principle, and freedom of thought was guaranteed and sanctified. During this Golden Age of Islam in which its principles were the true representation of the Faith, there is no record of any attempt by those in authority to prohibit or restrain any expression of free thought.

The principle of the freedom of thought was also guaranteed during the Ommayad Dynasty and at the beginning of the Abbassid Dynasty. The Caliphs of these two dynasties only opposed the opinions that incurred the danger of the security of the state or spread sedition among the people of the nation.

During the reign of `Omar ben Abdel Aziz and Al Ma'moun, son of Haroun Al Rashid, people were granted the right to discuss, in the Caliph's presence, matters that concerned the Caliph's right to rule over them, without fearing any retribution from those in authority.

Freedom of thought includes the freedom of scientific and academic thought which means that every person has the right to declare what he believes concerning the phenomena of nature, astronomy, animal life, plant life and mankind, according to the theories by which he is convinced. Islam grants Muslims this freedom in common with the other branches of freedom and never attempts to dictate any particular theory or precept concening cosmic, human, animal or plant phenomena. Islam does not even indirectly suggest any theory concerning the aforementioned matters, but urges people to meditate upon the phenomena of the universe in order to understand the general laws that govern it. Freedom of thought accordingly encourages one to contemplate and to attempt to discover more about the manifestations of the universe that had not previously attracted one's attention, and to ponder upon the order, arrangement and recurrence of these phenomena. It also leads to the realization that such matters are worthy of meditation, examination and merit scientific and academic research.

Matters that we take for granted are in fact wonders that are created by God Almighty such as night and day, the sun and the moon, the sequence of the seasons of the year, the reproduction of animals and the propagation of plants, in addition to the floating of certain bodies on water and other scientific phenomena.

The following Quranic verses are evidence of the aforementioned phenomena :

"Do they not look at the camels, how they are made? And at the sky, how it is raised high? And at the mountains, how they are fixed firm ? And at the Earth, how it is spread out".

"And among His Signs are the ships, smooth-running through the ocean (tall) as mountains. If it be His Will, He can still the Wind then would they become motionless on the back of the (ocean). Verily in this are Signs for everyone Who patiently perseveres and is grateful".

"Do they see nothing in the government of the heavens and the earth and all that God hath created ?"

"A Sign for them is the earth that is dead : We do give it life, and produce grain therefrom, of which ye do eat. And We produce therein orchards with date-palms and vines, and We cause springs to gush forth therein"

"Glory be to God, Who created in pairs all things that the earth produces, as well as their own (human) kind and (other) things of which they have no knowledge. And a Sign for them is the

Night : We withdraw therefrom the Day, and behold they are plunged into darkness :nd the Sun runs his course for a period determined for him : that is the decree of (Him). The Exalted in Might, The All- Knowing, And the Moon, We have measured for her mansions (to traverse) till she returns like the old (and withered) lower part of a date-stalk. It is not permitted to the Sun to catch up the Moon, nor can the Night outstrip the Day Each (just) swims along in (its own) orbit (according to Law). And a Sign for them is that We bore their race (through the Flood) in the loaded Ark ; and We have created for them similar (vessels) on which they ride"

"See they not that it is We Who have created for them - among the things which Our hands have fashioned - cattle, which are under their dominion ?"

"Seest thou not that God sends down rain from the sky, and leads it through springs in the earth ? Then He causes to grow, therewith, produce of various colours "

"Seest thou not that God makes the clouds move gently, then joins them together, then makes them into a heap ? - then wilt thou see rain issue forth from their midst. And He sends down from the sky mountain masses (of clouds) wherein is hail : He strikes therewith whom He pleases and He turns it away from whom He pleases. The vivid flash of His lightning well-nigh blinds the sight. It is God Who alternates the Night and the Day verily in these things is an instructive example for those who have vision "

"And among His Signs is the creation of the heavens and the earth, and the variations in your languages and your colours verily in that are Signs for those who know. And among His Signs is the sleep that ye take by night and by day, and the quest that ye (make for livelihood) out of His Bounty : verily in that are Signs for those who hearken. And among His Signs, He shows you the lightning, by way both of fear and of hope, and He sends down rain from the sky and with it gives life to the earth after it is dead verily in that are Signs for those who are wise".

It is clear from the aforementioned verses that there is no suggestion of imposing any specific scientific theory or precept on the Muslims. These Quranic verses urge human minds to meditate and ponder upon the phenomena of the Universe in order to discover the laws that govern these phenomena. Every human being is then perfectly free to adhere to the theories that he believes to be true.

Freedom of opinion, freedom of speech, freedom of the press and freedom of scientific thought which the modern democracies claim to have introduced, have all been established by the Faith of Islam more than twelve centuries before these modern democracies existed.

**FREEDOM OF RELIGION**

The Faith of Islam is founded upon liberal and tolerant principles, and another manifestation of its tolerance is that it guarantees the freedom of religion and the freedom of belief.

With the establishment of the Faith of Islam, it ordained three principles concerning the freedom of religion and the freedom of belief.

The first principle was that no one was to be forced to renounce his religion and to conform to Islam. This is expressed in the following Quranic verse "Let there be no compulsion in religion : Truth stands out clear from Error"

The Muslims adhered to this principle in their wars with their enemies who followed different faiths and they granted the nations that they conquered freedom of religious belief. They paid taxes and obeyed the ruler of the Muslim state, in return for the state's defence of them against any attack. Their religion, religious rites, houses of worship - churches or synagogues - were regarded with respect and safeguarded against any harm. After Jerusalem surrendered, `Umar bn Al Khattab said to its people "Omar grants the people of this land protection and security for them, for their churches and their crosses. None of them is to be forced to renounce his religion or is to be harmed".

The second principle ordained by the Faith of Islam is the freedom of religious debate. God Almighty advises the Muslims to adhere to logic and reason in their discussions with people of other religions. Muslims are to base their discussions upon convincing those who listen to them by presenting proof and evidence to support their argument. In the following Quranic verse, God Almighty addresses the Prophet Muhammad, blessings and peace be upon him : "Invite (all) to the Way of thy Lord with wisdom and beautiful preaching; and argue with them in ways that are best and most gracious : . .."God addresses the Muslims in the following Quranic verse : "And dispute ye not with the People of the Book, except with means better (than mere disputation) " God Almighty also adresses people of other faiths in the following Quranic verses Say : "Produce your proof if ye are truthful""Have ye any (certain) knowledge ? If so, produce it before us . . .

"Say : "Do ye see what it is ye invoke besides God? Show me what it is they have created on earth, or have they a share in the heavens? Bring me a Book (revealed) before this, or any remnant of knowledge (ye may have), if ye are telling the truth!"

The Caliphs of the Abbassid Dynasty held meetings in which they discussed religious matters and many scholars who adhered to various religious sects, schools of jurisprudence and different faiths attended these religious debates. They discussed issues on belief and the various creeds, and made comparisons between religions. Each one of them declared his opinion in complete frankness without the slightest apprehension of being reprimanded. The Caliphs did not only tolerate these discussions, but they actually encouraged them and personally participated in them.

The third principle established by Islam is that true faith is the result of one's indisputable and absolute conviction concerning one's belief and not the result of blind imitation. Islam accordingly abolished the principles upon which people had previously based their adherence to their faiths before the advent of Islam. These principles had been based upon blind imitation without conviction, and the Faith of Islam encourages people to base their faith and belief on their personal conviction and to spread their faith by sound proof and logic. Islam urges people to ponder and meditate and to refuse what is not supported by proof and evidence. Many scholars of religion declared that faith which is based upon blind imitation is not true faith. God Almighty condemned the infidels for their blind imitation of their forefathers' religion and for refusing to ponder and meditate on the divine Truth. This is mentioned in the following Quranic verses : "When it is said to them : "Follow what God hath revealed" they say : "Nay, We shall follow the ways of our fathers". What even though their fathers were void of wisdom and guidance ?"

"And when it is said to them "Come to what God hath revealed ; come to the Apostle" they say `Enough for us are the ways we found our fathers following'. What even though their fathers were void of knowledge and guidance ?" Sheikh Muhammad Abdu said that he who adheres to blind imitation in his faith without conviction or reasoning is in the same category as infidels. In fact a person is not a true believer unless he understands his religion and is convinced by it. He who is accustomed to believing without convinction or reasoning and performs deeds - even if they are righteous - without comprehension, is not a true believer in the Faith.

Belief and faith in one's religion is not meant to harness man to goodness as animals are harnessed to their labour, but to promote his reasoning and his soul by knowledge, so that he would perform good deeds because he would understand that they are good and righteous and approved by God Almighty. He would also abstain from sin because he would understand its sinful consequences and the extent of its evil.

## CIVIL RIGHTS

Civil rights are granted to every sane person who is of age, by which he is charged with certain obligations and entitled to participate in marriage contracts and contracts of sale or purchase of property. He is also entitled to donate bequests, make a will, mortgage property and other legal rights.

Slaves were denied all civil rights and were therefore unable to execute a contract of any kind. They were deprived of the right of ownership and were themselves owned by their masters. They were in fact a mere commodity of their masters who could sell them whenever they wanted.

Some orientalists criticized Islam for permitting slavery which destroys the principle of the freedom of man. It behoves us to draw attention to the fact that the economic and social circumstances that existed during the era that preceded the advent of Islam, considered slavery a normal institution and that any attempt to abolish it with a stroke of the pen would have failed. Islam did not introduce slavery, nor did it approve of it, except in certain circumstances which it abolished gradually step by step. The institution of slavery was firmly established in the world before the advent of Islam and was the basis upon which all fields of economy and production were founded. Accordingly any attempt to reform or abolish such an institution would have met with certain failure, since those in authority would have crushed such an attempt. Even if the authorities had enforced a law to abolish slavery, an upheaval in the stability of the economy of the states of the world would have occurred and a number of serious consequences would have resulted. The damage that would have resulted can be compared to what we would be subjected today, if with a stroke of the pen the institutions of Banks or joint stock companies were to be abolished, or if the employment of workmen were prohibited and every person who owned land or property was forced to work on it himself. Imagine what would happen if railways were abolished and if the use of the power of steam were prohibited. Slaves in the past can be compared to the power of steam upon which the economy of the modern world depended.

Islam aimed at abolishing slavery gradually without incurring any negative consequences on the stabilily of the community. In order to achieve this noble aim, tile Faith of Islam followed a policy that led to the gradual decline of the sources of slavery, in addition to ordaining religious rulings that encouraged the liberation of slaves. Thus Islam introduced a gradual yet effective system by which slavery was finally abolished.

Slavery existed as a result of many circumstances before and after the advent of Islam. The captives of civil wars or wars against a foreign enemy were invariably either executed or taken as slaves and people who were kidnapped were also enslaved. People who had committed serious crimes such as murder, adultery and theft were sentenced to be slaves of the state or of the families against whom their crimes had been committed. People who failed to pay their debts were sentenced to be slaves of their creditors, and fathers had the right to sell their offspring as slaves. Indigent and impoverished people could sell their liberty for a certain sum of money, thereby enslaving themselves. The offspring of slaves were also slaves and the children of a female slave were slaves even if their father was a free man. All these circumstances increased the number of slaves to the degree that the number of slaves in some nations exceeded the number of free men and women. With its advent, Islam abolished all forms of slavery save inherited slavery and slavery of captives of war. However, the Faith of Islam ordained certain laws which guaranteed the gradual decline and abolishment of slavery.

One of the rulings ordained by Islam was that the offspring of a female slave, fathered by her master was to be born free after his father had confirmed that he was the father. Accordingly this situation which had previously increased the number of slaves no longer existed, and the number of slaves gradually decreased.

Captives captured during wars were enslaved except those captured in wars between Muslims regardless of their being the aggressors or otherwise. In wars waged between Muslims and non-Muslims certain rulings concerning the enslavement of the captives were enforced. The captives enslaved were those who had been captured in a war that was religiously justifiable, namely a war that had been proclaimed by the Caliph according to the rulings of Islam, which permits warfare for three reasons. The first of these reasons is self defence and this is stated in the following Quranic verse "Fight in the cause of God those who fight you, but do not transgress limits ; for God loveth not transgressors"

Warfare is also justified by Islam when the enemy break their oath of peace or a truce and intend to harm the Faith of Islam as is stated in the following Quranic verse : "But if they violate their oaths after their covenant, and taunt you for your Faith, fight ye the chiefs of Unfaith for their oaths are nothing to them that thus they may be restrained".

The third reason which justifies warfare concerns matters related to the welfare and the security of the Muslim state and the suppression of sedition, as is mentioned in the following Quranic verses : "And fight them on until there is no more tumult or oppression, and there prevail justice and faith in God ; but if they cease, let there be no hostility except to those who practice oppression"."And fight them on until there is no more tumult or oppression, and there prevail justice and faith in God altogether and everywhere ; but if they cease, verily God doth see all that they do".

The wars led by the Prophet, blessings and peace be upon him, against the Pagan Arabs, the Jews or the Romans were only waged according to these three rulings of Islam. If any wars were waged for any other than the aforementioned reasons, the captives were not enslaved. Even when captives were enslaved according to the aforementioned rulings of Islam, slavery was not always enforced, since the ruler of the state was invested with the power of granting captives freedom, unconditionally or for a ransom or for labour agreed upon. Captives could also, at the command of the ruler of the state, be exchanged for Muslim captives captured by the enemy, or for a tax to be paid for their freedom. The captives captured at the Battle of Badr earned their freedom by each teaching ten Muslims to read and write.

Islam thus ordained certain rulings concerning the slavery of captives of war in a manner that guaranteed the gradual decline of slavery. After the establishment of the Islamic State and the organization of its relations with other nations, the circumstances that had led to slavery seldom arose or existed. This signifies that Islam only permitted this form of slavery for a limited period. Islam's concern for the principle of freedom is demonstrated in the laws it ordained to encourage the emancipation of slaves. Before the advent of Islam, the only means by which a slave could be emancipated depended upon his or her master's decision to do so. Apart from this possibility, slaves and their offspring were doomed to remain slaves for the rest of their lives. Most of the laws of that era in history prohibited masters from emancipating their slaves except in special circumstances with severe terms and after complicated legal and religious proceedings. In some cases the state imposed a heavy fine upon the master who liberated a slave. The fine was paid to the state the emancipation of slaves was considered an encroachment upon the rights of the state.

Islam opened wide the gateway for the emancipation of slaves and paved the way for the abolition of slavery. The Faith of Islam ordained that any mention of emancipating a slave, uttered by the slave's master be binding, even if it had been a slip of the tongue or had been uttered in jest. In the opinion of Abu Hanifa, the master who had been forced to emancipate his slave must grant him his freedom and that even if the slave's master had not been sober, when he granted his slave his freedom, the emancipation of the slave was still binding and legitimate. It is obvious from the aforementioned rulings that Islam encouraged the emancipation of slaves on the slightest pretext.

If the master of a slave mentioned in any manner that his slave or slaves were to be emancipated after his death, this entitled the slaves to be free men or women upon his death. Islam guaranteed the rights of such slaves who had been promised freedom after the death of their masters, by prohibiting their masters to sell them, ransom them, offer them as gifts or transfer their ownership to any person during their lifetime. If a female slave was promised freedom after her master's death, her offspring would also be liberated, regardless of the consent or refusal of the heirs of their deceased master.

According to the Faith of Islam, a slave could buy his freedom from his master after agreeing upon the sum of money to be paid. In order to make such an agreement possible, Islam permitted slaves to sell and buy goods and participate in contracts in order to save the amount of money agreed upon to buy their freedom. Islam also urged all Muslims to assist such slaves by donating money as charity to help them achieve their freedom. This matter is mentioned in the following Quranic verse "And if any of your slaves ask for a deed in writing (to enable them to earn their freedom for a certain sum), give them such a deed if ye know any good in them yea, give them something yourselves out of the means which God has given to you".

Islam even specified a certain sum of wealth from the treasury of the state to help these slaves pay for their liberty. The aforementioned Quranic verse verifies the ruling to agree to allowing slaves to purchase their liberty, if they express their wish to do so. Ibn Jurayh asked `Ataa' ben Abu Rabah if he was obliged to consent to his slave's desire to purchase his liberty, and Abu Rabah replied that he considered it an obligation and he supported his opinion by reciting the aforementioned Quranic verse.

The same law applies to female slaves and to the children they bear after signing the deed with their masters, who are obliged to emancipate the female slaves' children with their mothers without any compensation from them.

The Faith of Islam ordained that a number of sins and crimes that frequently occurred be expiated by emancipating slaves. One of these crimes is manslaughter as is mentioned in the following Quranic verse "Never should a Believer kill a Believer ; but (if it so happens) by mistake, (compensation is due) : if one (so) kills a Believer, it is ordained that he should free a believing slave,... " When a Muslim breaks his oath, granting a slave his freedom is ordained as means of expiation, as is mentioned in the following Quranic verse "God will not call you to account for what is futile in your oaths, but he will call you to account for your deliberate oaths for expiation, feed ten indigent persons, on a scale of the average for the food of your families ; or clothe them ; or give a slave his freedom".

A man who says to his wife that she be to him as if she were his mother or words to that effect, meaning that there would be no marital relations between them, and then desires to retract his oath in order to have marital relations with his wife, must first grant a slave his freedom as expiation, before being able to resume marital relations with his wife. This ruling is expressed in the following Quranic verse : "But those who divorce their wives by Zihar, then wish to go back on the words they uttered, -(it is ordained that such a one) should free a slave before they touch each other .... ". If a person had committed a sin that necessitated emancipating a slave as expiation, and he did not own a slave, the Faith of Islam ordained that if he had the means, he was to buy a slave and then grant him his freedom.

In addition to all these rulings, the Faith of Islam urged people to grant slaves their freedom without expiation, since emancipating a slave was one of the most righteous commendable and sublime deeds that merited the blessings and Grace of God. The Prophet Muhammad, blessings and peace be upon him, often compared the performance of a virtuous deed that deserved the greatest reward of God, to granting a slave his freedom. Islam also ordained that a certain portion of the alms collected and placed in the treasury was to be allotted to the emancipation of slaves by buying them from their masters and then granting them their liberty, or by completing the sum of money already saved by the slaves for their liberation. This is mentioned in the following Quranic verse : "Alms are for the poor and the needy, and those employed to administer the (funds) ; for those whose hearts have been (recently) reconciled (to Truth) ; for those in bondage...". This means that alms were to be used to assist those in bondage by buying them and the granting them their freedom.

Islam commanded Muslims to treat their slaves kindly : "Serve God, and join not any partners with Him ; and do good to parents, kinsfolk, orphans, those in need, neighbours who are near, neighbours who are strangers, the Companion by your side, the way-farer (ye meet), And what your right hands possess : for God loveth not the arrogant, the vainglorious. "What your right hands possess", refers to one's slaves. God Almighty ordains the kind treatment of slaves in the same verse where He commands man to worship Him and to treat his parents, relations and neighbours generously, and this signifies the importance of this ruling.

The Prophet Muhammad, blessings and peace be upon him, said : "Fear God in your treatment of slaves". He also said that the Angel Gabriel had recommended kind treatment of slaves so often that he believed that servants and slaves should not be treated as such. The Prophet Muhammad, blessings and peace be upon him, said: "He who owns a slave must allow him to partake of the same food that he eats and clothe him with the same kind of clothes that he wears". When the Caliph `Omar ben Al Khattab travelled with his slave to Jerusalem to negotiate with the Patriarch concerning the surrender of the town, after the army of Abu `Ubayda ben Al Jarah had besieged it, he went with only one camel. `Omar the Caliph and his slave took turns in riding the camel and as they approached Jerusalem, it was the slave's turn to ride the camel. The Caliph `Umar bn Al Khattab was not embarrassed by the fact that his slave rode ahead of him on the camel and that he followed him on foot as they entered Jerusalem.

On another occasion, in Mecca, `Umar bn Al Khattab saw a group of slaves standing while their masters were eating their meal. Enraged, `Omar told their masters that they should treat their slaves as they treat themselves and he commanded the slaves to eat from the same bowl with their masters.

The Faith of Islam prohibited people from treating their slaves harshly, and some schools of jurisprudence ruled that the slave that had been treated cruelly by his master was entitled to be liberated. In such a situation, the person in authority would order that the slave be emancipated and that his master be dof his ownership.

The son of `Umar bn Al Khattab said that he had heard the Prophet Muhammad, blessings and peace be upon him, say that whoever beats his slave must liberate him as expiation for his sin.

The Faith of Islam also protected slaves from people who were not their masters, and if a slave was attacked, the penalty would usually be the same penalty as that of attacking a free man. Even in the event of a free man murdering a slave, his penalty would be the same penalty for murdering a free man. Abu Hanifa supported this opinion by the following Quranic verse "We ordained therein for them : `Life for life..."

Islam did not deprive slaves of all civil rights as was the case with other faiths. It granted them certain humane rights such as the right of a slave to have a family. A slave, according to the Faith of Islam, had the right to marry a female slave or a free woman. Similarly a female slave had the right to marry a slave or a free man. They were entitled to the same terms and marriage contract by which free people were married, apart from the fact that the master of the slave or the female slave had the right to supervise their marriage contract.

No religion prior to Islam granted slaves the right to marry and raise a family in the legal sense of the term. The relationship between male and female slaves before the advent of Islam and even after its advent according to the laws of other religions, was not a marriage relationship. The masters of the slaves chose their mates for them for the express purpose of increasing their offspring and accordingly increasing the number of their slaves, in the same way animals are reared and bred.

In other religions, intermarriage between slaves and free men and women, was prohibited. If a free woman married a slave, she would be sentenced to a severe punishment which in many cases was the death penalty.

The Faith of Islam granted the slave the right to divorce his wife whereas his master was not granted the right to divorce the slave's wife. It has been related that a slave complained to the Prophet, blessings and peace be upon him, that his master had married him to his female slave, and then had wanted to divorce her from him. The Prophet, blessings and peace be upon him, ascended the pulpit and addressed the people saying that the right of divorce is the right of the husband alone and not the right of his master.

The Faith of Islam is therefore a faith that is based upon the principle of the equality and freedom of all human beings, and aims at promoting the welfare of the human race.

3

# ISLAM AND SEX

Islam considers sex as one of the essentialhuman needs that must be properly satisfied. It is a necessity of the humanbeing that. It require favorable consideration. In fact, Islam considers it oneof the requirements of life that should be properly and lawfully satisfied.Moreover, Islam does not treat it as a distasteful, filthy, or heinous act ofman. Allah (subhanahu wa ta'ala) states in the Glorious Quran Sura Al-Imran [TheFamily of Imran] (3:14):" Fair in the eyes of men is the love of thingsthey covet: women and sons; heaped-up hoards of gold and silver; horses branded[for blood and excellence]; and [wealth of] cattle and well-tilled land. Suchare the possessions of this world's life; but in nearness to Allah is the bestof the goals [to return to]". In addition, Allah'sMessenger (peace and blessings of Allah be upon him) is reported to have said,which reads as follows:" Three items of this world were made attracted [orlikeable] to me: women, perfume [but] the [utmost] pleasure of my eyes [soul] isin prayer".

Infact, Islam forbids controlling and deprivation of the sexual behavior. This is,simply, because Islam is the natural religion commensurate to pure human innate.Islam does not, at any time, conflict with the requirements of the human'srequirements or desires. Islam rather attempts to answer and fulfill all humanneeds and requirements. Islam does so by setting certain lawful limits andrestrictions to ensure satisfying these needs in a right and lawful manner.Islam endeavors to keep the sex within the framework of human needs and elevatesit above the savage and uncivilized way. Allah's Messenger (peace and blessingsof Allah be upon him) is reported to have said, which reads as follows:"People enter Jannah, Paradise mostly based on Taqwa of Allah (subhanahu wata'ala) [full respect and obedience of the Commands of Allah (subhanahu wata'ala) and His Messenger (peace and blessings of Allah be upon him)], and basedon their good conduct. [While] most people enter the Hellfire because of the[ill use] of the mouth and private parts".

We shall attempt to present in thisbooklet, the method, which Islam instituted for Muslims to regulate the use ofthe sex. In fact, Islam sets the mode for the better advancement of man, if hefollows the Islamic rules on the subject. Islam looks at the proper use of thesex as an act of worship, Ibadah. A Muslim would be rewarded when he practicesthis act, as he is rewarded when he does any other acts of prescribed types ofworship. Allah's Messenger (peace and blessings of Allah be upon him) alluded tothis concept when he said, which reads as follows:" [A Muslim] would havean intercourse with his spouse ad would be rewarded for it. The Companions (mayAllah be pleased with him) asked: Oh Messenger of Allah! A person would berewarded while satisfying his sexual need? Allah's Messenger (peace andblessings of Allah be upon him) replied: Yes. Isn't it that he would be punishedhad he practiced sex illegally? The same applies if a Muslim practiced a lawfulintercourse with his spouse. As such, he would be rewarded".

The only acceptable wayfor sexual satisfaction in Islam is a lawful "marriage". In fact, Islam urgesMuslims to seek marriage and encourages them to practice it. Allah's Messenger(peace and blessings of Allah be upon him) is reported to have said, which readsas follows:" Whoever is financially capable of marriage but does notmarry, he does not belong to Me [i.e., Allah's Messenger (peace and blessings ofAllah be upon him)]". " Islam regards marriage as a natural necessity in order toachieve tranquility and peace of mind for the Muslim. To the society, Islamregards marriage as a place to foster love, affection, closeness, andself-denial. Further, Islam regards marriage as a requirement to maintain thehuman race. Yet, Islam regards marriage as a mean for better moral values,preservation of honor and dignity, and preservation of the moral values of thehuman society. Thus, neglecting marriage or rejecting it is regarded as a denialof all the normal human behaviors and pure code of social ethics". Hence, the objective ofmarriage in Islam is to achieve tranquility and peace of mind for both spouses.Allah (subhanahu wa ta'ala) states in Quran Sura Rum (30:21):" And amongHis Signs is this, that He created for you mates from among yourselves, that yemay dwell in tranquility with them, and He has put love and mercy between your[hearts]: verily in that are Signs for those who reflect".

In fact, one of the objectives of marriage is to protectboth spouses against indulgence in unlawful sexual practices that may lead tocorruption and immoral acts [such as prostitution, fornication and adultery orelse] in the society. Allah (subhanahu wa ta'ala) states in Quran Sura Baqarah(2:187):" They are your garments and ye are their garments". Undoubtedly, there are certain individuals who reject thecall of Islam for purity and chastity. Such individuals advocate unlicenecedsexual freedom. We believe that such people do not enjoy a normal and naturalhuman satisfaction. As for Islam, it refuses to degrade Believers to the stateof lower creatures, such as animals. Animals alone are left to practice sexualfreedom as they wish and without any restrictions. Islam regards it a great sinfor man to place his semen in a womb that is unlawful to him. Allah's Messenger(peace and blessings of Allah be upon him) states, whihc read as follows:"There is no greater sin after the sin of associating partners with Allah(subhanahu wa ta'ala), than a man placing his semen in a womb [private part of awoman] that is unlawful for him to place".

## ISLAM AND PURITY

Islam instructs Believers purity andchastity. Islam further bestows on Believers on dignity and honor. Islam guidesand directs its followers in the right direction by which they would be, Allahwilling, morally respectable and productive. Listen to the story of the youngman who came to Allah's Messenger (peace and blessings of Allah be upon him)asking him to permit him to practice adultery, as he can't live without it,after embracing Islam. The Companions (may Allah be pleased with him) loudlyrejected the young man appeal and denied it wholeheartedly. Allah's Messenger(peace and blessings of Allah be upon him), however, called the young man closerto him and said, which reads as follows:" Do you accept [to see] yourmother committing adultery?" The young man replied negatively. Thus, Allah'sMessenger (peace and blessings of Allah be upon him) said, which readsasfollows:" As such, other people refuse to see their mothers [or any other femalein their families] being indulgent in adultery. Allah's Messenger (peace andblessings of Allah be upon him) further asked the young man, which reads asfollows:" Do you accept [to see] your sister committing adultery?" The young manreplied negatively. Thus, Allah's Messenger (peace and blessings of Allah beupon him) said, which reads as follows:" As such, other people refuse to seetheir sisters committing adultery as well". Allah's Messenger (peace andblessings of Allah be upon him) further asked, which reads as follows:" Do youaccept [to see] your daughter committing adultery?" The young man repliednegatively. Thus, Allah's Messenger (peace and blessings of Allah be upon him)said, which reads as follows:" As such, other people refuse to see theirdaughters committing adultery as well". Thus, we notice that Allah's Messenger(peace and blessings of Allah be upon him) was not harsh at all on the youngman, but he rather prayed for the well-being of this young man saying:" OhAllah! Purify the heart of this young man, chastise his private parts, andenable him to lower his gaze". This young man is reported to have said:" ByAllah! I had never sought unlawful relations again ever".

This is Islam. It is areligion that doesn't condone monasticism and total negligence of the worldlyaffairs. Islam doesn't to reject all worldly goods and pleasures completely.Allah's Messenger (peace and blessings of Allah be upon him)is reported to havesaid, which reads as follows:" By Allah! I am, Allah's Messenger (peaceand blessings of Allah be upon him), the most God respectful amongst you andmost obedient to His Commands. However, I observe fast [for some days] and breakit [for other days]. I [stand up during the night] offering prayers [for sometime], and I also sleep [some times of the night]. I also marry [women]. Hence,whoever chooses any other way, other than my Sunnah, tradition, he doesn'tbelong to me".

Islam doesn't condone a blind and uncontrolled satisfaction of personal whimsand caprices. Muhammad Qutub, the renowned contemporary Muslim scholar, says:"We can find no problem for 'sex' in Islam. Islam erects barriers before allhuman desires, including sex, which do not totally block them or deny them.Nevertheless, Islam rather, elevates and controls such human desires. Islamdesigns these barriers like that of the regulating devices on a river duringflood seasons. As such, the regulating devices attempt to raise the level ofwater temporarily to a level that can't normally reach, then it let the waterrun at a higher level. Similarly, Islam controls the level of human desires byraising it to a higher plateau. Islam sets rules and regulations for the sex notto restrict or deny it completely, but rather to permit it within the scope thatAllah (subhanahu wa ta'ala)permits to practice such human desires. These are thelimits set by Allah (subhanahu wa ta'ala) as He states in the Glorious QuranSura Baqarah (2:229):" These are the limits ordained by Allah; so do nottransgress them if any do transgress the limits ordained by Allah, such personswrong [themselves as well as others]". Allah (subhanahu wa ta'ala) , inHis vast wisdom knows that these are the "safe" and "secured" limits to drainsuch energies stored in man through human desires. By releasing such energies inan organized, controlled and safe manner, man can achieve a great level ofsuccess for himself and his society. Nevertheless, even Jahiliyah, state ofignorance, acknowledges the necessity to organize, regulate, and control all thehuman desires, except for "sex". Sex, among all human desires drives, is thecrazy one. Imagine if such a crazy drive is left without control, regulation,and restrictions, what would happen to the society, its morals, honor, andindividuals? Jahiliyah doesn't permit the drive and desire of ownership withoutregulations. If such a desire left unrestricted, we could see man wanting topossess and own whatever he likes, through any mean. However, man made lawsclassify such acts as a punishable crime of theft by law. The same is practicedinsofar as the food, clothing and housing drives and desires. All these drivesand desires are controlled by laws and not left for personal or emotionalwhims".

## ISLAM AND MARRIAGE

Islam commands its followers to marry asearly as they are able. Muslims should not fear poverty nor should theyapprehend increase of family members as result of marriage, and thus, because ofthat, they stay away from marriage. Allah (subhanahu wa ta'ala) states in QuranSura Nur [The Light] (24:32):" Marry those among you who are single, orthe virtuous ones among your slaves, male or female: if they are in poverty,Allah will give them means out of His Grace: for Allah encompasseth all, and Heknoweth all things".

Moreover, Allah's Messenger(peace and blessings of Allah be upon him) is reported to have said, which readsas follows:" Allah (subhanahu wa ta'ala) takes it upon Himself to helpthree types of people. These are: A warrior, who is striving in the cause ofAllah (subhanahu wa ta'ala). A contracted slave, who wants to pay off the valueset for his freedom of slavery, and, a person, who seeks marriage to chastisehimself". Ifa male Muslim can't afford to marry because of poverty, he is commanded tochastise himself. Allah (subhanahu wa ta'ala) states in Quran Sura Nur [TheLight] (24:33):" Let those who find not the wherewithal for marriage keepthemselves chaste, until Allah gives them means out of His Grace".

Allah's Messenger (peace and blessings of Allah be upon him)gives advice that makes it easier to a certain extent for a person, who isunable to marry for dearth of marriage expenses. This advice harnesses hisdesire to marry and enables him to control his sexual desires. Allah's Messenger(peace and blessings of Allah be upon him) is reported to have said, which readsas follows:" Oh young men! Whoever is capable [financially and otherwise]to [afford the expenses] of marriage, let him do so. [Marriage] helps onecontrol his eyesight and chastise his private parts. But, he who can't affordthe marriage expenses, let him observe fast as it would [act] as a protector forhim".

TheGlorious Quran further illustrated the best example of subduing the sexual drivein the story of Prophet Yousuf (peace and blessings of Allah be upon him)[Joseph]. Prophet's Yousuf (peace and blessings of Allah be upon him) story isset as one of the best examples for the Muslim youth. Allah (subhanahu wata'ala) states in Quran Sura Yousuf (peace and blessings of Allah be upon him)(12:23-24):" But she in whose house he was, sought to seduce him from his[true] self: she fastened the doors, and said: Now come, thou [dear one]! hesaid: Allah forbid! Truly [thy husband] is my lord! He made my sojournagreeable! Truly to no good come those who do wrong! And [with passion] did shedesire him, and he would have rejected her, but that he saw the evidence of hisLord: thus [did We order] that We might turn away from him [all] evil andshameful deeds: for he was one of Our servants, sincere and purified".

Yousuf (peace and blessings ofAllah be upon him) overlookedthe adverse results stemming from his denial to the request of the prestigiouslady. The result of rejecting her request for evil acts was imprisonment. Allah(subhanahu wa ta'ala) states in Quran Sura Yousuf (peace and blessings of Allahbe upon him) (12:32-34):" She said: There before you is the man about whomye did blame me!

I did seek to seduce him from his [true] self but he did firmlysave himself guiltless! And now, if he doth not my bidding, he shall certainlybe cast into prison and [what is more] be of the company of the vilest! He said:O my Lord! The prison is more to my liking than that to which they invite me:unless Thou turn away their snare from me, I should [in my youthful folly] feelinclined towards them and join the ranks of the ignorant. So his Lord hearkenedto him [in his prayer], and turned away from him their snare: verily He hearethand knoweth [all things]".

## ISLAM AND SEXUAL STIMULANTS

Islam bans all actions that lead to arousethe sex other than the permissible. Islam, out of precautious, bans allactivities that lead to unlawful practices. It is a bare fact that when a personis sexually aroused and overwhelmed with sexual emotions he would be tempted toinvolve even in prevented courses. Such a person will not hesitate to resort toany means to gratify his sexual passions. Such a sexually charged and arousedperson may tend to discharge such drive unlawfully. The sexual prevention may beattained with mutual consent of the two parties involved, or by force, or rape.Both, adults and minors may participate in such unlawful activities. Someindividuals may tend to discharge it by another unlawful mean that ishomosexual, lesbian, or masturbation. All the above-cited forms are unlawful inIslam.

## MEANS TO RESTRICT STIMULANTS

Islam commands to apply the followingmethodology in order to restrict sexual intercourse:

. Islam commands parents to separate male and female children, who reach theage of puberty and maturity as they sleep. Allah's Messenger (peace andblessings of Allah be upon him) is reported to have said, which read asfollows:" Command your children to [begin] offering prayers [on a regularbasis] at age seven. [Then] discipline them if they don't maintain it [on aregular basis] when they become ten years of age. [Moreover] separate [malechildren from females] when they sleep at that age". Islam ordains, through Allah's Messenger's command andinstruction (peace and blessings of Allah be upon him), to avoid any contactbetween males and females while sleeping together alone in the same bed or room.Such contact may arouse the potential sexual urges. . Islam ordains that Muslim women be segregated from stranger males. This isordained, Allah (subhanahu wa ta'ala) knows best, in order to maintain the honorand preserve the dignity of both and in order to avoid any sexual intimacybetween both. Allah (subhanahu wa ta'ala) states in Quran Sura Ahzab [TheConfederates] (33:59):" Oh Prophet! Tell thy wives and daughters, and thebelieving women, that they should cast their outer garments over their persons[when abroad]: that is most convenient, that they should be known [as such] andnot molested. And Allah is Oft-Forgiving, Most Merciful". Islam, however, gave a permission to the elder,unmarriageable ladies, who are neither sexually desirous nor sexuallyattractive, to wear normal modest attire such as long garments and basic headcover [other than covering the face] and do not wear any facial makeup, toappear as such before stranger males. Allah (subhanahu wa ta'ala) states inQuran Sura Nur [The Light] (24:60):" Such elderly women as are past theprospect of marriage, there is no blame on them if they lay aside their [outer]garments, provided they make not a wanton display of their beauty: but it isbest for them to be modest: and Allah is One Who sees and knows allthings".

. Islam commands to protect and lower the eyesight against all unlawfulscenes. Eyesight may generate a sexual desire in the eyes of the beholder. Assuch, this may develop later on to a wanting, eager and meditating evil desire,and eventually executing these desires, unlawfully. Allah (subhanahu wa ta'ala)states in Quran Sura Nur [The Light] (24:30-31):" Say to the Believing menthat they should lower their gaze and guard their modesty: that will make forgreater purity for them: and Allah is well acquainted with all that they do.

Andsay to the believing women that they should lower their gaze and guard theirmodesty; that they should not display their beauty and ornaments except what[must ordinarily] appear thereof...".

Furthermore,Allah's Messenger (peace and blessings of Allah be upon him) is reported to havesaid, which read as follows:" The look [of the eyesight] is a poisonousarrow of Iblis [Satan]". Imam Ibn-ul-Qayyim is reported to havecommented on this issue as follows: "While eyesight or eye contact is thebeginning of the sexual stimulants, Allah (subhanahu wa ta'ala) began with itfirst, prior to the protection and chastising of the private parts. In fact, allsexual drives begin with an eye contact.

Similarly, the greatest fire beginswith the smallest fire spark. A person begins with an unlawful look, then thisdevelops into a thought in the mind and heart, then this develops into a step oran action of movement towards the sexual partner, and finally this would end upin a sin of an unlawful sexual intercourse. Therefore, it is wisely said:'whoever preserves the following four items, would surely preserve his faith.These are as follows:

1. Eyesight or looks and gaze.
2. [Evil] thoughts that cross the mind and heart.
3. [Sexually seductive] words that are uttered [with evil and unlawfulintention] or flirting with women or men.
4. Steps [that lead to unlawful sexual practices].

Furthermore, asit is potentially possible to unlawfully glance at something, Muslims arecommanded not to prolong such unlawful looks. Allah's Messenger (peace andblessings of Allah be upon him) is reported to have said to Ali (may Allah bepleased with him) which read as follows:" Oh Ali [Listen]! Don't continuewith looking [at unlawful items], as the first look is [permitted] for you,while the second is not".

Islam urged and encouraged itsfollowers and Believers to seek the Pleasure of Allah (subhanahu wa ta'ala) byprotecting their looks. Allah's Messenger (peace and blessings of Allah be uponhim) is reported to have said, which read as follows:" Whoever lowers hisgaze by not looking at the charms of a [stranger] woman, Allah (subhanahu wata'ala) would substitute him for this with a faith, which he would feel itssweetness in his heart".

. Islam ordains both adult and mature males and females to seek permissionprior entering any private residence. Such permission, Allah (subhanahu wata'ala) knows best, is ordained in order to avoid looks at any unlawful scene.Allah (subhanahu wa ta'ala) states in Quran Sura Nur [The Light] (24:58):"Oh ye who believe! Let those whom your right hands possess, and the [children]among you who have not come of age ask your permission [before they come to yourpresence], on three occasions, before morning prayer; the while you take offyour clothes for the noonday heat; and after the late-night prayer: these areyour three times of undress: outside these times it is not wrong foryou or forthem to move about attending to each other: thus does Allah make clear the Signsto you: for Allah is full of knowledge and wisdom".

In addition, Allah (subhanahu wa ta'ala) states in Quran Sura Nur(24:59):" But when the children among you come of age, let them [also] askfor permission, as do those senior to them [in age]: thus does Allah make clearHis Signs to you: for Allah is full of knowledge and wisdom". . Islam bans impersonation for both sexes; males and females. Allah'sMessenger (peace and blessings of Allah be upon him)is reported to have said,which read as follows:" May Allah (subhanahu wa ta'ala) curseimpersonating men [as females], and may Allah (subhanahu wa ta'ala) curseimpersonating females [as males]".

. Islam bans listening to sexually oriented songs and the like. Naturally,such acts would mentally prepare and lead normal people to commit unlawfulbanned sexual practices. In fact, Muslim scholars of early generations describedsexually motivating songs and singings: "It is the essential mean for committingadultery". . Islam bans sitting alone, for an extensive period, with young men, i.e.,minor males, especially the attractive looking ones among them. Allah'sMessenger (peace and blessings of Allah be upon him) is reported to have said,which read as follows:" The fornication of the eye is to look [at unlawfulitems or actions]. The fornication of the tongue is to speak [using unlawfulwords, phrases, terminology, descriptions and stories]. The fornication of thehand is to commit [unlawful acts or actions]. The fornication of the foot is towalk [even steps] to an unlawful place or activity. The fornication of the earis to listen [to unlawful items such as songs, stories, words, secrets and thelike]. Yet, the human soul wishes for all of that or promises to obtain.However, the private parts would either confirm [any of these actions andactivities] or falsify them". . Islam bans male Muslims to be alone with any female, other than immediaterelatives that are not permissible for marriage, or a spouse. Such privacy maylead to satanic seduction. Consequently, this may lead to adulterous acts orfornication. Allah's Messenger (peace and blessings of Allah be upon him) isreported to have said, which read as follows:" Any man, who sits in aprivacy with a female, [whom he can marry], would be accompanied by Satan as thethird companion to the two".

In fact, Allah's Messenger (peace andblessings of Allah be upon him) explained the best method to be with a femalesaying, which read as follows:" A man must not be alone with a woman,unless one of her male (Mahram) immediate relatives [i.e., a husband, a father,a son, a brother, a nephew, a grandson] is present with them".

Islam further bans any mingled activities. This is because such activitiesand meeting may lead to suspicious relationships between non-related males andfemales. In fact, Allah (subhanahu wa ta'ala)states in Quran Sura Ahzab [TheConfederates] (33:53):" And when ye ask [his one of his wives] foranything ye want ask them from behind a barrier [partition]: that makes forgreater purity for your hearts and for theirs". Professor Muhammad Qutub in his book,'Man between Materialism andIslam', comments as follows:" Innocent co-ed was a mammoth myth came fromthe West [i.e., Europe and the North Hemisphere]. The West, at the beginning ofits dissolvence, wanted to treat its' sexual pressure. The Western socialscientists and psychologists exaggerated the immense value of co-ed. Later, theydenied it all and never mentioned it after that.

They truly discovered the realpicture and results of co-ed. As such, physiatrists, psychologists, andneurologists withdrew completely from their previous opinion regarding co-ed.Those even denied slow dance [innocent] parties, co-ed tea parties, and co-edpicnics under the supervision of parents and teachers. Today, the same scholarsclaim that any co-ed meeting would stir the sex and not the opposite.

Thepersonal feelings may be suppressed, or they are forced to be suppressed becauseof social circumstances. At other times, such personal feelings would besuppressed due to shyness before other people. Consequently, suppression ofpersonal feelings would instigate psychological or mental anxiety andapprehension. Such anxiety occurs because of the social co-ed meetings. At suchpoint, one of two things may take place. A young male may seek a different placewhere he can freely practice his personal feelings and emotions without anybarriers or controls. Or else, the young male would remain under severe anxietythat may lead to certain disorders. Therefore, we can easily wonder: "What aninnocent meeting these co-ed meetings are!" . Islam bans a wife to describe the physical details of another woman. This isso to prevent the slightest attraction of that married man to the other woman.Allah's Messenger (peace and blessings of Allah be upon him)is reported to havesaid, which read as follows:" A woman must not see another woman [exposedin a private females meeting], then describes the details of that woman to herhusband".

Islam bans women to get out of their homes wearing full make up and perfume.Such a practice would attract the attention of males to them. As such, the womanmay be trapped into unlawful relationships with males who are awaiting suchopportunities. Allah (subhanahu wa ta'ala) states in QuranSura Ahzab [The Confederates] (33:33):" And stay quietly in your houses,and make not a dazzling display, like that of the former Times ofIgnorance".

In fact, Islam bans a female to speaksoftly and in an attractive tone with a male who is not related to her. Thispractice is a mean of protection for the female against males who are desirousfor adultery and fornication. A female Muslim must speak with a male only asnecessary. Allah (subhanahu wa ta'ala) states in Quran

Sura Ahzab [TheConfederates] (33:33):" Oh Consorts of the Prophet! Ye are not like any ofthe [other] women: if ye do fear [Allah], be not too complaisant of speech, lestone in whose heart is a disease should be moved with desire: but speak ye aspeech [that is] just".

Islam further bans nudity and displaying women's physical attractions. Allah(subhanahu wa ta'ala) states in Quran Sura Aaraaf [The Heights] (6:26):"Oh ye Children of Adam! We have bestowed raiment upon you to cover your shame,as well as to be an adornment to you. However, the raiment of righteousness,that is the best. Such are among the Signs of Allah, that they may receiveadmonition!". . Islam instructs women allowed to appear before lawful relatives to do sowith casual clothes and ornamentations. Allah (subhanahu wa ta'ala) states inQuran Sura Nur [The Light] (24:31):" ...and not display their beauty exceptto their husbands, their fathers, their husbands' fathers, their sons, theirhusbands' sons, their brothers or their brothers' sons, or their sisters' sons,or their women, or the slaves whom their right hands possess, or male servantsfree of physical needs, or small children who have no sense of the shame of sex;and that they should not strike their feet in order to draw attention to theirhidden ornaments. And, Oh ye Believers! Turn ye all together towards Allah, thatye may attain Bliss". . Islam bans a woman to travel alone. A woman must travel with an immediaterelative described earlier as Mahram. This escort or companion must be one ofthe following relatives: a husband, a father, a brother, or a relative whom sheis not allowed to marry on a permanent basis.

Allah's Messenger (peace andblessings of Allah be upon him) is reported to have said, which read asfollows:" A woman must not travel without a Mahram. No male must enter theprivacy of a woman without an immediate Mahram is available with that woman. Aman raised a question to Allah's Messenger (peace and blessings of Allah be uponhim) saying: Oh Messenger of Allah! My wife set out to perform pilgrimage whileI have registered for such and such Ghazwah [Fighting Troops, what should Ido?]. Allah's Messenger (peace and blessings of Allah be upon him) instructedthe man as follows: Go and join your wife for pilgrimage".

## ISLAM AND FEMALE PROTECTION

The real intent of Islam underlying all therulings, restrictions, procedures, and commands for women is their ownprotection. Islam aims at preserving their honor, and upholding their dignity.Travel usually requires a lot of efforts and other expenses. Women, by natureare weak [in comparison with men]. Women are bound to have menses, after birthconfinement, child nursing, and pregnancy. Women are, also, easily vulnerable todeception, as they usually follow their emotions, which may be, at times,misleading. Women are commonly passionate and easily influenced by theenvironment. A woman needs some kind of protection against evil people whiletraveling. Generally, a woman may not be able to defend herself physicallyagainst others due to her very nature. She also needs someone to care for herproperly and take care of her needs. Islam requires a Mahram, immediate relativeof a woman to take care of all her needs and provide her the best security andsafety he could. Islam requires this from a Mahram, in order to suffice womenany need for a stranger.

## ISLAM AND PERSONAL DESIRES

Allah's Messenger (peace and blessings of Allah be upon him) commands a man,who glances a woman, which stimulates his sexual instinct to return home to hisfamily [if he is a married man] and approach his wife. This should facilitatehim to satisfy his sexual desires in a lawful and proper manner. By the sametoken, he would be deterred from the trap of satanic way of seduction. Allah'sMessenger (peace and blessings of Allah be upon him) is reported to have said,which read as follows:" A woman approaches in a shape of Satan and walksaway in the same shape. Therefore, if a [married man] notices [physically]something of a woman that arouses him [sexually], let such a man go back to hishome and approach his wife. Doing so would cool him if".

Islam commands both spouses to satisfy their personal [sexual] desire witheach other when either spouse is interested to do so. Islam bans a woman torefuse her husband's request to satisfy his needs. If a woman denies herhusband's request, he may be led to evil thoughts searching for unlawful sourcesof satisfaction, or else, he would develop mental pressure. Both such situationsare detrimental, both physically and mentally. Islám, therefore, is insistent onthis issue. Allah's Messenger (peace and blessings of Allah be upon him) isreported to have said, which read as follows:" If a man calls his wife tosleep with him and she does not respond, causing him to be angry with her,angels will [continue] to curse her until the morning".

Islam applies the same towards the husband. A husband must satisfy hiswife's sexual desire in order to protect her against evil thoughts and actionsas well.Ibn Hazm, a renowned Muslim scholar comments as follows: "Ahusband must have an intercourse with his wife once a month, in the leastpossible ways, while he is capable of doing so. Otherwise, such a person isdisobeying Allah (subhanahu wa ta'ala). The evidence to this from Quran is fromSura Baqarah (2:222):" But when they have purified themselves, ye mayapproach them in any manner, time, or place ordained for you by Allah. For Allahloves those who turn to Him constantly and He loves those who keep themselvespure and clean".

Islam entitles a wife to seek a court judgment against her husband if heneglects to satisfy her sexual needs as well. This just and safe way maintainsthe peace, equality, and satisfaction in the family and society. · Allah (subhanahu wa ta'ala) promised individuals, who attempt to spreadchaos and evil activities in the Islamic community to pour on them the severestpenalty. Allah (subhanahu wa ta'ala) states in Quran Sura al-Nur (24:19):"Those who love [to see] scandal published broadcast among the Believers, willhave a grievous Penalty in this life and in the Hereafter: Allah knows, and yeknow not". If this is the case of the scandalousindividuals, what about the doers and supporters of such unlawful activities?Surely, it is much more disastrous.

## ISLAM AND MARRIAGE

Islam permits Muslims to satisfy theirsexual needs only through lawful marriage. Allah (subhanahu wa ta'ala) ordainedman to be different than all other irrational creatures.Sayyid Sabeq, inhis book, 'Fiqhu-Sunnah', comments as follows:" Islam controls and organizes thesexual behavior and needs. A perfect system is laid down by Allah (subhanahu wata'ala) to maintain and preserve the honor, dignity, and respect of man. Allah(subhanahu wa ta'ala) ordained that a mutual acceptance and agreement must besecured for a marriage relationship between a man and a woman. The man and thewoman who are to establish a marriage contract and relationship must perform a"Request" and an "Acceptance". Both spouses to be must have witnesses to testifythat marriage contract. Thus, a proper and safe way for this relationship isestablished. Moreover, the progeny, which is a byproduct of this relationship isalso protected, well preserved, and properly cared for. In addition, the womanin Islam is also protected by such contract against unlawful and harmfulrelationships. Islam established the basis of a nucleus family that is nourishedby the mother, and supported by the father. Thus, the products of this marriageare lawful relationship, which would grow up in a fine and suitable environment.This is the system that Islam accepts and maintains for its Believers and assuch, it ruins all other unlawful and meaningless relationships".

## Wife Selection in Islam

Islam established its own theory for aprocess of spouse. The issue of marriage in Islam is not an issue of mere sexualsatisfaction. Islam considers marriage an institution to establish a family.Therefore, Islam urges marriage seekers to select a long lasting relationship,establish a beloved, and caring family, which should serve the society. Allthese conditions would not be fulfilled unless there is a pious and righteouswife, who is mindful of the commands of Allah (subhanahu wa ta'ala) and carefulabout all duties entrusted to her. However, other issues of social life must notbe neglected. Allah (subhanahu wa ta'ala) states in Quran Sura al-Nur(24:32):" Marry those among you who are single, or the virtuous ones amongyour slaves, male or female: if they are in poverty, Allah will give them meansout of His Grace: for Allah encompasseth all, and He knoweth all things". Allah's Messenger (peace and blessings of Allah be upon him)explained the issues that urge a Muslim to marry. He also, emphasized theeverlasting factor for marriage, which is righteousness. Allah's Messenger(peace and blessings of Allah be upon him) is reported to have said, which readas follows:" A woman would be sought for marriage for the following fouritems: for her wealth, beauty, [honorable] lineage, or for her [strongcommitment to] Islam. [When you seek a woman to marry], may Allah (subhanahu wata'ala) bless your hands; seek the one with a strong commitment tofaith".

Islam seeks to prepare the best men as husbands. Islam caresa lot for the woman and urges Muslims to be the best for their families, andwives in particular. Allah's Messenger (peace and blessings of Allah be uponhim) is reported to have said, which read as follows:" The most perfectBelievers in terms of faith are those, who possess the best character andmanners. The best among you are those who are best to their women. I, as Allah'sMessenger (peace and blessings of Allah be upon him), am the best among you tomy family".

In addition, Islam idealizes a wife asthe best woman. Allah's Messenger (peace and blessings of Allah be upon him)describes such a woman as follows, which read as follows:" [She is thatwoman] who pleases [her husband] when he looks at her, obeys him when hecommands [instructs or requests], fulfills his demands and preserves hiswealth".

Allah's Messenger (peace and blessings of Allah be upon him)is also reported to have said concerning the same subject, which read asfollows:" The best gain a Muslim acquires after [commitment to] Islam is abeautiful wife who pleases him when he looks at her, obeys his commands,protects his privacy when he is absent, and protects his wealth".

### Lawful Sight of a Prospective Bride

Islam aims at long lasting maritalrelationship. If both, strong commitment to Islam and sound moral background areensured in a marriage, good looks leads to a successful marital relationship. Abridegroom, however, and his bride, both must enter into this relationship withfull conviction, mutual acceptance, and preliminary satisfaction of theessential marriage requirements. Therefore, Islam permitsboth spouses to look at each other. A man came to Allah's Messenger (peace andblessings of Allah be upon him) and informed him that he sought marriage from aspecific woman of Ansars. Allah's Messenger (peace and blessings of Allah beupon him) is reported to have said, which read as follows:" Did you lookat her? The man answered negatively. Allah's

Messenger (peace and blessings ofAllah be upon him) is reported to have said: Look at her. There is something[funny] about the eyes of Ansari women [i.e., some blemishing effect]". This is, of course, a wise advice so as the bridegroom wouldnot regret later if had seen the bride before marriage. He may think, 'I wouldhad changed my mind had I known her to be like that!'

Allah's Messenger (peace and blessings of Allah be upon him) explained thewisdom of the lawful sight of the bridegroom to the bride, prior to concluding amarriage contract. Allah's Messenger (peace and blessings of Allah be upon him)is reported to have said to a man who came and told him about his engagement ofa certain woman. Allah's Messenger (peace and blessings of Allah be upon him) isreported to have said, which read as follows:" Did you look at her? Theman replied negatively. Allah's Messenger (peace and blessings of Allah be uponhim) commanded him: 'Go and see her. It is hoped that you both would becomelovable to each other".

Love and affection, between a husbandand wife, are normal feelings according to Islam. Therefore, so long as thislove is pure, innocent, and lawful, Islam condones it and nourishes it by lawfulmeans. A man came and asked Allah's Messenger (peace and blessings of Allah beupon him) which read as follows:" Oh Messenger of Allah! I have an orphangirl in my custody. Two men sought her for marriage. One is rich and the otheris poor. We like the rich and she likes the poor. [to whom should we offer herin marriage?]. Allah's Messenger (peace and blessings of Allah be upon him)said: Nothing is known to be better for people who love one another thanmarriage". Additional aspects on marriage preference o Islam urges Muslims to intercede between two loving and righteous spouses,if their marriage is on the verge of breaking. For example, a man calledMogheith was noticed following his wife Burairah, after she obtained divorcefrom him. The ex husband cried and begged his divorcee to come back to him [as aloving wife]. Upon noticing this Allah's Messenger (peace and blessings of Allahbe upon him) is reported to have said to Ibn Abbas (may Allah be pleased withhim), which read as follows:" Isn't it amazing how much Mogheith lovesBurairah and how much she hates him? Allah's Messenger (peace and blessings ofAllah be upon him)turned to Burairah and requested her: I wish you return to him[as a wife]! urairah asked: Oh Messenger of Allah! Do you command me to returnto him? Allah's Messenger (peace and blessings of Allah be upon him)said: No, IAllah's Messenger (peace and blessings of Allah be upon him) just intercedingfor him. She said: I have no need for him".

A Muslim guardian of a woman may, based on the acceptance and approval ofthe woman, propose her for marriage to someone who is well acquainted with hischaracter and qualities. A guardian is usually keen to serve the interest of thewoman he is entrusted him for guardianship. Allah (subhanahu wa ta'ala) statesin Quran Sura al-Qasas (28:22-27):" And when he arrived at the watering(place) in Madyan, he found there a group of men watering (their flocks), andbesides them he found two women who were keeping back (their flocks). He said:What is the matter with you? They said: We cannot water (our flocks) until theshepherds take back (their flocks): and our father is a very old man. Therefore,he watered (their flocks) for them; then he turned back to the shade, and said:O my Lord! Truly am I in (desperate) need of any good that Thou dost send me!Afterwards one of the (damsels) came (back) to him, walking bashfully. She said:My father invites thee that he may reward thee for having watered (our flocks)for us. So when he came to him and narrated the story, he said: Fear thou not:(well) hast thou escaped from unjust people. He said: I intended to wed one ofthese my daughters to thee, on condition that thou serve me for eight years; butif thou complete ten years, it will be (grace) from thee. But I intend not toplace thee under a difficulty: thou wilt find me, indeed, if Allah wills, one ofthe righteous. He said: Be that (the agreement) between me and thee: whicheverof the two terms I fulfill, let there be no ill-will to me. Be Allah a witnessto what we say".

## Marriage Contract, Dowry and Wedding

Islam requires specific conditions in a marriage. The first requirement isthe acceptance and approval of both parties. Allah's Messenger (peace andblessings of Allah be upon him) is reported to have said, which read asfollows:" A widow or divorcee [woman] must not be [forced to] marriedunless she approves it. The virgin, also, must not be [forced to] marryingunless she is sought permission. The Companions asked: How could we seek herpermission? He (peace and blessings of Allah be upon him) replied: If sheobserved silence it means she gave her permission". . If a woman is forced to marry without her consent, she has the right tobreak that marriage. This is based on the action of Allah's Messenger (peace andblessings of Allah be upon him) when a woman called Khansa bint Jutham wasforced to marry, without her consent. She came to Allah's Messenger (peace andblessings of Allah be upon him) and informed him that her father offered her inmarriage without her consent. Allah's Messenger (peace and blessings of Allah beupon him) declared that marriage null and void. Of course, this is done with theintent to ensure the protection of the Muslim family. In addition, this wouldhelp eliminate the vices in the society, as it would protect against anymarriage betrayals resulting from the dislike of spouses to one another. . The role of a legal guardian is also another requirement of a validmarriage. This is based on the Hadith reported of Allah's Messenger (peace andblessings of Allah be upon him) saying, which read as follows:" A marriagewould not be valid unless a [bride] guardian and two just witness are [all]present".Again, all this is done in order to preserve the relationships among the familymembers. A [sound and matured] guardian is also keen and more careful to choosethe best for his guarded woman. Thus, he would exert every possible effort toselect the most suitable marriage partner for her.

If there is no guardian, or if the guardian forbids his guarded woman tomarry, despite the mutual agreement of male and female, the guardianship wouldautomatically transfer to the judge or authorities. This is based on the Hadithreported of Allah's Messenger (peace and blessings of Allah be upon him) whichread as follows:" The governor [judge] is the guardian for [a woman orminor] who has no [relative] guardian". . A dowry is another requirement for the validity of marriage. A dowry must bepaid to the bride. Allah (subhanahu wa ta'ala) states in Quran Sura al-Nisa [TheWomen] (4:3):" And give the women [on marriage] their dower as a freegift; but if they, of their own good pleasure, remit any part of it to you, takeit and enjoy it with right good cheer".

Muslims must not be extravagant in dowries. This is based on the Hadithreported of Allah's Messenger (peace and blessings of Allah be upon him) saying,which read as follows:" The signs of a good fortune of a woman are: theease of engagement [when marriage is sought], the ease of dowry, and the ease ofrelationship with her relatives". Omar, the second Caliph (may Allah bepleased with him) said: " Don't exaggerate when you request for a dowry for yourbrides. If there were an honor to be given in this world, or a piety in theSight of Allah (subhanahu wa ta'ala), Allah's Messenger (peace and blessings ofAllah be upon him)would have earned the best of these. I don't know of anymarriage, which Allah's Messenger (peace and blessings of Allah be upon him)performed, either for his wives, or for his daughters, that exceeded twelveUqiyah". . In addition, all other lawful conditions that both parties agree upon forthe marriage contract must be executed after marriage. This is based on theHadith reported of Allah's Messenger (peace and blessings of Allah be upon him)saying, which read as follows:" The most entitled contracts' provisions tofulfill are that of the marriage contract".

Islam ordains a wedding party to celebrate their happiness for the occasion.Such a party should invite the relatives and friends of the bride and thebridegroom in order to publicize and announce the marriage in the community.This is based on the Hadith reported of Allah's Messenger (peace and blessingsof Allah be upon him) saying when he noticed that he had married, which read asfollows:" May Allah (subhanahu wa ta'ala) bless you. Throw a [wedding]party, even if you slaughter [and prepare] one [head of] a female sheep".

Islam does not condone lavishness on the wedding party. Allah (subhanahu wata'ala) states in Quran Sura Isra [The Night Journey] (17:27):" Verilyspendthrifts are brothers of the Evil Ones; and the Evil One is to his Lord[Himself] Ungrateful". . Islam exhorts the invitees for a wedding party to attend it, unless he has avalid excuse. Allah's Messenger (peace and blessings of Allah be upon him) isreported to have said, which read as follows:" [Attempt to] liberate theprisoner, honor the call of an inviter, and visit an ill person". . Islam urges the people who attend the wedding meal party to pray for theinviters, as he (peace and blessings of Allah be upon him) instructed, whichread as follows:" Oh Allah! Forgive them, be Merciful to them, and blesswhat You have provided them". Also, to pray for them, which read as follows:" MayAllah (subhanahu wa ta'ala) bless her for you, may Allah bless you, and mayAllah gather both of you on good things". . Islam permits the use of the flat drum only at this occasion, as well asmorally encouraging songs and chanting. This is based on the Hadith reported ofAllah's Messenger (peace and blessings of Allah be upon him)saying to ourbeloved mother of Believers Aeshah (may Allah be pleased with him) who attendeda wedding of an Ansari woman:" Did you have any fun [singing and playingthe flat drum]? Ansar people liked to listen to that".

### The Etiquette at the Night of Wedding

At the first meeting after wedding night, the bridegroom is advised topresent himself in a pleasant manner, with sweet conversations, and in a verykind way to the bride. This is the first meeting of a new life style. Doing sowould bring the two spouses closer together. Allah's Messenger (peace andblessings of Allah be upon him) did the same on the night of marriage to Aeshah(may Allah be pleased with him). He sat next to her, requested a jug of milk,and drank of it, and then he passed it to her. She also drank of the same glass.Allah's Messenger (peace and blessings of Allah be upon him) told her to passthe jug to her peers, as reported by Imam Ahmad.

It is also an act of Sunnah to hold the hair bangs of the bride and offer aSunnah supplication, as reported in Hadith, which read as follows:" OhAllah! I seek of you [to grant me] the best of this woman and the best of hercharacteristics. Oh Allah! I seek refuge with you to protect me against all theevils of this woman and her evil characteristics".

### Joking and Playing between Spouses

Islam regards the fulfillment of sexualinstinct as natural, but with regulated and specific conditions. This sexualfulfillment is described in Quran Sura Rum (30:21), as follows:" And amongHis Signs is this, that He created for you mates from among yourselves, that yemay dwell in tranquility with them, and He has put love and mercy between your[hearts]: verily in that are Signs for those who reflect". Islam therefore encouraged the establishment of suchrelationship and stressed to promote it. Allah's Messenger (peace and blessingsof Allah be upon him) is reported to have said, which reads as follows:"Allah's Messenger (peace and blessings of Allah be upon him) asked his CompanionJaber (may Allah be pleased with him): Did you marry? Jaber (may Allah bepleased with him) replied affirmatively. Allah's Messenger (peace and blessingsof Allah be upon him)asked: Is she a virgin or a divorcee or widow? Jaber (mayAllah be pleased with him)stated that she was a widow. Allah's Messenger (peaceand blessings of Allah be upon him) commented: Why didn't you get a virgin, asyou would have fun with each other!". Islam, in fact,places a great value for the fun between the two spouses. Allah's Messenger(peace and blessings of Allah be upon him) is reported to have said, which readsas follows:" All the fun that man has is vain except for three items:shooting arrows, disciplining [training] a gorse and having fun with his wife.These three items are but truthful [or lawful] means of fun".

In fact, Islamencourages best grooming for both spouses. Decent grooming promotes love andincreases affection between spouses. Allah's Messenger (peace and blessings ofAllah be upon him) is reported to have said, which reads as follows:"Truly, Allah is Beautiful and He likes beauty".

Ibn Omar (may Allah be pleased withhim) also reported that Allah's Messenger (peace and blessings of Allah be uponhim) is reported to have done as Ibn Omar (may Allah be pleased with him) does,which reads as follows:" Ibn Omar (may Allah be pleased with him) used twotypes of perfume and said: this is the way that Allah's Messenger (peace andblessings of Allah be upon him) perfumed himself". Ibn Abbas (may Allah be pleased withhim) is reported to have said, which reads as follows:" I try to look bestto my wife, as I like her to look best to me. I also do not like to demand allmy rights onto her, as I, as Allah's Messenger (peace and blessings of Allah beupon him) , am afraid she would also demand her full right onto me [in such acase I wouldn't be able to fulfill it for her]. Allah (subhanahu wa ta'ala)states in Quran Sura al-Baqarah (2:228): And women shall have rights similar tothe rights against them, according to what is equitable; but men have a degree[of advantage] over them. And Allah is Exalted in Power, Wise".

## Limits of Fun between Spouses Bed Fun

Both spouses are permitted to see each other in the nude. Both are alsoentitled to enjoy one another to the utmost. Mu'awiyah (may Allah be pleasedwith him) asked Allah's Messenger (peace and blessings of Allah be upon him),which reads as follows:" Oh Messenger of Allah! To what extent should weprotect [cover] our private parts? Allah's Messenger (peace and blessings ofAllah be upon him) is reported to have replied: Protect [cover] your privateparts [fully] except from your spouse or those whom your right handpossess".

Both spouses are entitled to enjoy each other fully in terms of sexualintercourse in any position, if the husband approaches his wife in the properplace, i.e., where a baby is delivered. Tirmithi reported that Omar (may Allahbe pleased with him) came to Allah's Messenger (peace and blessings of Allah beupon him) and declared, which reads as follows:" Oh Messenger of Allah!I've destroyed myself! Allah's Messenger (peace and blessings of Allah be uponhim) asked: What cause you to say this? Omar (may Allah be pleased with him)replied: I've changed the method of my intercourse tonight. [i.e., he approachedhis wife from the back, but in the proper place]. Allah's Messenger (peace andblessings of Allah be upon him) did not comment on the issue [as he doesn't haveany jurisdiction to say]. Allah (subhanahu wa ta'ala) revealed to Allah'sMessenger (peace and blessings of Allah be upon him) , on the spot, thefollowing verse in Sura al- Baqarah (2:223): Your wives are as a tilth unto you:so approach your tilth when or how you will; but do some good act for your soulsbeforehand; and fear Allah, and know that ye are to meet Him [in the Hereafter],and give [these] good tidings to those who believe"

Allah's Messenger (peace and blessings of Allah be upon him) is reported to havesaid, at this point, which reads as follows:" You may approach her fromthe front, or from the back, provided that you avoid the anis and while the wifeis in menses". This Hadith, however, means that a husband must avoid doinganything with his wife while she is in menstruation period. Aeshah (may Allah bepleased with him) reported that:" While I was in menstruation, I woulddrink from a cup, then Allah's Messenger (peace and blessings of Allah be uponhim) would take the cup, place his lips in the same place of mine on the cup,and drink. I would also take a piece of meat on the bone; bite of it, then putit down. Then, Allah's Messenger (peace and blessings of Allah be upon him)would take the same piece and eat from it, placing his lips in the same place ofmine". Similarly, a husband and wife may enjoy each other, while in menstruation, ifthey avoid the actual intercourse. Allah's Messenger (peace and blessings ofAllah be upon him) is reported to have said, which reads as follows:" Youmay do anything [with each other as a husband and wife, while in menstruation]except of actual intercourse". Jaber (may Allah be pleased with him) is reported to havesaid, which reads as follows:" Jews used to believe that if a husbandapproaches his wife from the back, in the proper place, the born child would becross-eyed. Allah (subhanahu wa ta'ala) revealed, the following verse in Suraal-Baqarah (2:223): Your wives are as a tilth unto you: so approach your tilthwhen or how you will; but do some good act for your souls beforehand; and fearAllah, and know that ye are to meet Him [in the Hereafter], and give [these]good tidings to those who believe".

It is Sunnah to utter the name of Allah (subhanahu wa ta'ala) beforeapproaching one's wife sexually. Allah's Messenger (peace and blessings of Allahbe upon him) is reported to have said, which reads as follows:" If ahusband, before he approaches his wife sexually, supplicates as follows: OhAllah! Protect us from Satan, and make him away from us. If the two spouses geta child as a result of this sexual intercourse, Satan would not be able to harmthe child".

The husband must play with his wife, talk to her nicely, and kiss her inorder to arouse her sexually. In addition, a husband must wait for his wife tosatisfy her sexual desire. Allah's Messenger (peace and blessings of Allah beupon him) is reported to have said, which reads as follows:" If a husbandhas an intercourse with his wife he must be truthful with her. If he gotsexually satisfied before she does, then he should wait for her to get hersatisfaction". In addition, Omar bin AbdulAziz (may Allah be pleased withhim) is reported to have narrated the following Hadith of Allah's Messenger(peace and blessings of Allah be upon him), which reads as follows:" Don'tapproach your wife sexually and have intercourse with her right away. You shouldwait until she is as sexually aroused as you are. The man asked: Oh Messenger ofAllah! What should I do [in order to achieve that?] He (peace and blessings ofAllah be upon him) replied: Kiss her, touch her, and try to arouse her. If younotice that is she is as ready sexually as you are, then perform theintercourse".

In addition, it is also an act of Sunnah to perform a complete ablution bytaking a full bath, or a partial ablution, as one does to offer a prayer, if thehusband desires to have another intercourse with her. Allah's Messenger (peaceand blessings of Allah be upon him) is reported to have said, which reads asfollows:" If a husband has an intercourse with his wife once, and wantedto repeat it again, let him perform an ablution". This good practice is purer, more hygienic andenables the person to have a stronger sexual strength and desire.

## Fun while Taking a Bath

A fun with the wife is not confined to thebed only. A husband may have fun with his wife all the time, if privacy for bothis well secured and maintained. It is reported of mother Aeshah (may Allah bepleased with him) that she said, which read as follows:" Allah's Messenger(peace and blessings of Allah be upon him) and I, bathed of the same pot ofwater that we placed between both of us. He (peace and blessings of Allah beupon him) would beat me to take the water until I say to him, let me have some!Let me have some!".

## Fun at Home

Mother Aeshah (may Allah be pleased withhim) was once asked, which read as follows:" What would Allah's Messenger(peace and blessings of Allah be upon him) do first when he entered his home?She replied: He brushed his teeth with his Siwak, the wooden toothbrush. I wouldthink that he cleans his mouth and makes it smell better in order to hug hisfamily and kiss them". Mother Aeshah (may Allah be pleased with him) alsoreported that, which read as follows:" Allah's Messenger (peace andblessings of Allah be upon him) kissed one of his wives and went straight out tothe Masjid to offer his prayers. He did not perform Wudu ablution".

## Fun with Wife Outside the House

As we pointed out earlier, fun with thewife is permitted at all times and at all places if the full privacy is securedand maintained. No body must see a husband and wife having fun or playing witheach other in public. Mother Aeshah (may Allah be pleased with him) is reportedto have said, which read as follows:" While I was young, before I put muchweight on me, Allah's Messenger (peace and blessings of Allah be upon him) and Iwere on a trip. He advised his Companions (may Allah be pleased with him) to goahead of him and called me to race with him. I beat him in running.

Then,Allah's Messenger (peace and blessings of Allah be upon him) did not ask me anymore to race with him for a while. Later on, after I gained weight and forgotthat I've beaten him in the race, I was again on a trip with him. He advised hisCompanions (may Allah be pleased with him) to go ahead of him for a distance.Then, he told me: come let's have a running race! I totally forgot the previousincident when I beat him in the race. Mother Aeshah (may Allah be pleased withhim) commented: Oh Messenger of Allah! How can I race with you and I am as heavyas you can see? He (peace and blessings of Allah be upon him) said: You must doit. Thus, we raced and he beat me this time. He (peace and blessings of Allah beupon him) began laughing and said: Oh Aeshah (subhanahu wa ta'ala), this win [ofmine] by that win [of yours] in the race". It is important tonote here that it is completely unlawful to reveal the secrets of marriage. Itis an unacceptable practice to talk about what takes place between a husband andhis wife in privacy.

Abu Horairah (may Allah be pleased with him) reported thatonce Allah's Messenger (peace and blessings of Allah be upon him) , after wefinished the prayer, turned to us and said, which read as follows:" Remainseated! Is there among you who comes out of his house, after he does whatever helikes with his wife, comes out and tells other: I've done such and such with mywife? Those who were present did not reply anything. Allah's Messenger (peaceand blessings of Allah be upon him) turned to the women and asked the samething, and they did the same. A young woman, who was present then, sat on herknee, stretched up to be noticed and her voice heard by Allah's Messenger (peaceand blessings of Allah be upon him) , and said: By Allah!

They all do, males andfemales. Allah's Messenger (peace and blessings of Allah be upon him) isreported to have said: Do you know the example of the person who does so? Hisexample is like that of a male and female Satans who meets one another on theroad, satisfy their sexual desire by getting their thrill while people arewatching".

In order to perpetuate the matrimoniallife, Islam sets forth certain rights and duties on each of the two spouses.This tends to protect family structure from disintegration at future time. Bothspouses must understand their relative rights and duties. The rights of wife over her husband It suffices here to list some verses ofQuran and traditions of Hadith of Allah's Messenger (peace and blessings ofAllah be upon him) that illustrate the rights of the wife in Islam.

1. Allah (subhanahu wa ta'ala) states in Quran Sura Nisa (4:19):" On thecontrary live with them on a footing of kindness and equity. If ye take adislike to them, it may be that ye dislike a thing, and Allah brings aboutthrough it a great deal of good".
2. Allah also (subhanahu wa ta'ala) states in Quran Sura Baqarah(2:228):" And women shall have rights similar to the rights against them,according to what is equitable; but men have a degree (of advantage) over them.And Allah is Exalted in Power, Wise".
3. Allah's Messenger (subhanahu wa ta'ala)is reported to have said:" Thebest among you is one who is best to his family [wife], and I as Allah'sMessenger am the best among you to my family".
4. One of the Companions (may Allah be pleased with him) asked Allah'sMessenger (peace and blessings of Allah be upon him), which read asfollows:" What is the right of the wife? Allah's Messenger (peace andblessings of Allah be upon him) is reported to have said: To feed her if youeat, clothe her if you clothe yourself, don't slap her on the face, don't benasty to her and don't be away from her [physically] except while both of youare at the same house".

5. Allah's Messenger (peace and blessings of Allah be upon him) is reported tohave said, which read as follows:" The most perfect Believers are thosewho are best in moral conduct, and the best among them are those who are best totheir women".
6. Allah's Messenger (peace and blessings of Allah be upon him) is reported tohave said, which read as follows:" Be mindful of Allah concerning women.You have taken them in by Allah's Trust and their private parts became lawfulfor you with Allah's Word".
7. Allah's Messenger (peace and blessings of Allah be upon him) is reported tohave said, which read as follows:" A [married male] Believer should nothate his Believing wife. He may dislike one of her attitudes, but he would[definitely] like another one of hers".

As such, we see that fullperfection is due to Allah (subhanahu wa ta'ala) alone. No man is perfect onehundred percent on this earth.

## The Rights of a Husband over his Wife

The following are only hints from theGlorious Quran and Hadith concerning the rights of a husband over his wife.

1. Allah (subhanahu wa ta'ala) states in Quran Sura Nisa [Women] describing therighteous women, (4:34):" Therefore the righteous women are devoutlyobedient, and guard in (the husband's) absence what Allah would have themguard".
2. Allah's Messenger (peace and blessings of Allah be upon him) is reported tohave said to mother (may Allah be pleased with him) when she asked him, whichread as follows:" Whose right is the greatest on a woman [wife]? He (peaceand blessings of Allah be upon him) replied: Her husband. She continued: Whoseright is the greatest on a man? He(peace and blessings of Allah be upon him)said: His mother".
3. Hossain bin Mohsen reported that his aunt once said to him, which read asfollows:" I went once to Allah's Messenger (peace and blessings of Allahbe upon him)

asking him about a certain matter. He (peace and blessings of Allahbe upon him) asked: Who is this woman? Does she have a husband? I repliedaffirmatively. He (peace and blessings of Allah be upon him) further asked: Howdo you treat him? I replied: I do my best serving him, until I can't. He (peaceand blessings of Allah be upon him) commented: You better take care of him as heis [your husband], either your Jannah, Paradise or your Fire".

4. Allah's Messenger (peace and blessings of Allah be upon him) is reported tohave said, which read as follows:" The best of women is the one whopleases you if you look at her, obeys you if you commands her [to do a lawfulitem], and protects your privacy and wealth if you are absent".
5. Allah's Messenger (peace and blessings of Allah be upon him) is reported tohave said, which read as follows:" If a woman [wife] maintains her fivedaily prayers, observes the fast of the month of Ramadan, protects her privateparts [by not committing adultery or fornication], and obeys her husband, shewould be given the choice to enter Jannah, Paradise through any gate shelikes".
6. Allah's Messenger (peace and blessings of Allah be upon him) is reported tohave said, which read as follows:" If I were to command someone toprostrate to another person, I would have commanded a wife to prostrate beforeher husband".

## Divorce in Islam

Islam regards marriage bond as sacred andblessed. As such, Islam is keen to strengthen the relationship between the twospouses. Allah (subhanahu wa ta'ala) indicates the great value of the marriagebond as He (peace and blessings of Allah be upon him) states in Quran Sura Nisa(4:21):" And how could ye take it when ye have gone in unto each other andthey have taken from you a solemn covenant".

In fact,Allah's Mssenger (peace and blessings of Allah be upon him) is reported to havesaid, which read as follows:" Iblis [Satan], places his throne on waterand sends his troops. The closest one [of his troops to him] is that who has thegreatest trail and temptation [to mankind]. As such, Satan would bring thatmember of his troop closer to him [in honor and respect for what he did]. One ofthe members of Satan's troops would come forward and reports what [evilactivities] he did. Satan would comment: 'You did not do anything.

Then anotherone of his troops would come forward and report: I did not leave that man [ahusband] until I separated him from his wife. Satan would bring that one of themembers of his troop closer to him [in honor and respect] saying: Yes indeed. Itis you [who deserves the honor]". Similarly, Allah'sMessenger (peace and blessings of Allah be upon him) demonstrated the respectand honor of the marriage bond by saying, which read as follows:" He isnot considered among us [Muslims], who turns a woman against her husband". Although Islam places a great importance on the marriageintegrity and declares it holy and honorable, yet Islam legalizes divorce thatbreaks this great bond. Nevertheless, Allah's Messenger (peace and blessings ofAllah be upon him) is reported to have described divorce, which read asfollows:" The most hatred lawful item in the Sight of Allah (subhanahu wata'ala) is divorce".

Islam reached this decision whenmarriage reaches a dead end between the two spouses and there is no othersolution except divorce. Islam is keen to protect the Muslim family and theIslamic society. The anti-social behavior of husband or wife can cause chaos inthe society. Such chaos may very well lead to mixed lineage, falsifiedinheritance, deprivation of genuine rights and spread of indecency in thecommunity. Although divorce is lawful, it is still wellrestricted. In fact, divorce is not a toy in the hand of the person, which hemay use it any way when he or she likes. Muslim scholars illustrate that divorcemust take one of the four following forms:

1. Divorce may be compulsorywhen the two assigned referees decide it inthe case of the disputed spouses. Allah (subhanahu wa ta'ala) states in QuranSura Nisa (4:35):" If ye fear a breach between them twain, appoint (two)arbiters, one from his family, and the other from hers; if they wish for peace,Allah will cause their reconciliation: for Allah hath full knowledge, and isacquainted with all things".

2. Divorce is unlawful, if there is no sound and visible reason orground for it.
3. Divorce is permissible, if the wife is vicious in terms of characterand attitudes.
4. Divorce is required, if the wife is not committed to the Islamicteachings, or if she is indecent or vulgar.

The same itemsalso apply to the husband as well. If a husband does not commit himself to theIslamic teachings, if he is indecent or if he has a bad character, or badpersonality, or if he has physical defects that make life miserable with him, awife is entitled to seek divorce from such a husband on such grounds.

### Khul'u in Islam

Khul'u is divorce on the instance of thewife's request in Islam, who must pay her husband compensation in order for himto accept divorcing her. If marriage were not based on love,affection, comfort, and agreement between the two spouses, life then would turninto misery rather happiness and comfort. Marriage, in such a case, would nolonger be a harmony, peace of mind and comfort, but rather hardship andadversity. If one of the spouses hated the other, or doesn't trust him, therewould be no hope for marriage continuation. Allah (subhanahu wa ta'ala) statesin Quran Sura Nisa (4:19):" On the contrary live with them on a footing ofkindness and equity. If ye take a dislike to them it may be that ye dislike athing, and Allah brings about through it a great deal of good". Islam legalized khul'u however when life with the otherspouse becomes unbearable. Of course, divorce normally is a right to thehusband; therefore, he can issue it when he feels fit. However, if the wifehates the life with her husband and could no longer take it, then, in such acase, she may demand divorce by the process of Khul'u, paying the husbandcompensation for what he had already paid her in order to terminate themarriage. This is the justice in the best form, we believe.A husband paid the dowry, bore the marriage expenses, and paid other expenses aswell. Allah (subhanahu wa ta'ala) states in Quran Sura Baqarah (2:229):"It is not lawful for you, [men], totake back any of your gifts (from yourwives), except when both parties fear that they would be unable to keep thelimits ordained by Allah. If ye [judges] do indeed fear that they would beunable to keep the limits ordained by Allah, there is not blame on either ofthem if she give something for her freedom. These are the limits ordained byAllah; so do not transgress them if any do transgress the limits ordained byAllah, such persons wrong [themselves as well as others]".

Islam aims at preserving people's honor and dignity. Islamalso aims to protect and secure the society by closing all doors for possiblesocial corruption. The presence of a husband with a woman whom he does not like,and vice versa; would very likely lead to suspicious and unlawful relationships.Therefore, Islam legalized divorce. Allah (subhanahu wa ta'ala) states in QuranSura Nisa (4:130):" But if they disagree [and must part], Allah willprovide abundance for all from His All-Reaching bounty: for Allah is He thatcareth for all and is Wise".

## Results of Sexual Freedom and Confusion

Islam bans adultery and all types offornication labeling it as one of the major sins in Islam. In fact, Islam bansall acts and means that may lead one to commit adultery or fornication. SayyidQutub illuminated in his book In the Shade of Quran:" Islam aims at eliminatingall forms of pure animalistic sexual behavior. Islam wishes to help establish aproper home and a caring family resulting of the proper and lawful sexualrelationship. Islam does not tolerate a mere sexual relationship that makes thehuman being very much like an animal, which is driven only by his mere sex formating and reproduction. Islam erects a loving and caring relationship betweentwo hearts and bodies of two human beings who live together and have the samehopes and common ground life. The proper "marriage nest" that is built on suchbasis would house the new generation under the custody, care, and guardianshipof both Muslim parents.

Hence, Islam instituted very strict and severepunishment for adultery and fornication. Islam considers adultery as animalisticbehavior that abolishes all human manners and principles. If a person is merelyinterested and concerned to satisfy his sexual desires, he would turn into ananimal in the shape and body of a human being. Such a person may not be trustedfor being in charge of the prosperity on earth. In fact, there is no realemotional satisfaction of the mere sexual relationship. Emotional relationshipis a continuous, everlasting, and caring one. It is not, in reality, what iscategorized to be in terms of a short-term materialistic love as a response forthe bodily attractions only, although some people may shed so many emotionalcharacteristics on it. Islam does not, at all, fight, or stand in the way of thenormal human behavior, but rather controls it, organizes it, purifies it, andelevates it above the level of the animalistic behavior. Islam promotes thehuman sexuality or lust to become the core of the personal morals, socialattitudes, and relationships. As for adultery and fornication, and moreprecisely prostitution, one feels that it is, in reality, empty of all thesefeelings, emotions, and sense of belonging and relationship. Islam looks atprostitution as one of the lowest ill acts of a human society. Such a poorpractice makes man below the level of animals in attitudes and behavior. Infact, there are many animals who live a decent and organized social life, awayfrom the mess and confusion that prostitution creates in some human societies".

It is useful to list some of the bad results and the chaossituation that sexual confusion brings to a human society and to the morals ofthe people. One of the inevitable results is the spread of adultery andfornication in the society. These are some of the results of the sexualconfusion in the human society:

*The spread of epidemic and fatal diseases*. Such diseases are notrestricted to the person who practices such unlawful activities, but it ratherspreads to others, whom he or she contacts. In fact, such diseases may, verylikely, spread very wide in the community. Allah (subhanahu wa ta'ala) states inQuran Sura Isra (17:32):" Nor come nigh to adultery: for it is a shameful[deed] and an evil, opening the road [to other evils]".

Allah'sMessenger (peace and blessings of Allah be upon him) is reported to have said,which read as follows:" Be mindful of adultery [and fornication] as itpossesses six traits. Three of these traits [are noticeable] in this world whilethe other three are felt in Hereafter. As for the worldly three traits, they areas follows: it would remove brightness from the face of the practicing person.It would also cause a person to feel poverty. In addition, it would shorten thelife span of a person. As for the other three traits that would be felt in theHereafter, they are as follows: it would entitle the practicing person toreceive the wrath and anger of Allah (subhanahu wa ta'ala). It would also causesuch a person to have poor results when he/she is held accountable for what hedid in this world. Lastly, it would entitle such a person to dwell eternally inthe Fire of hell".

Adultery and fornication would remove brightnessfrom the face of the practicing person because of the deprivation to enjoy fullpersonal satisfaction, physically and spiritually. Such a person would feel lowin morals and attitude. Thus, such a person would turn into an animal, in theshape of a human being. All what such a person cares for and interested in is tosatisfy his sexual desire, regardless of the means. Furthermore, adultery wouldalso cause a person to face poverty because of the huge amounts of money hewould spend on such unlawful sexual activities. Such a person would exert lot ofefforts and wastes lot of valuable personal energies as well, that he might haveutilized it in a better and more productive form. Thus, spending such wealth andenergy causes constant regret. Indulging in unlawful sexual activities wouldcause great harms to the health. In fact, adultery is a major health hazard.Thus, adultery and fornication would shorten the life span of a person becauseof the potential diseases that may endanger his life and possibly cut it short.

*Illegitimate children*: Such children are deprived the normal care andcustody of real loving parents. As a result, such children would lack theobjective and proper guidance and direction in their lives. No one, other thanthe real parents, could offer an honest, truthful, and meaningful guidance to achild. Consequently, such deprived class of children would grow up to beuncontrolled and full of hatred to the rest of the society members. Anna Freud,in her book Children without Families, comments on the psychological disordersthat can't be corrected by a psychiatric specialist except with greatdifficulties.

*Psychological disorders*:Unlawful sexual relationships would lead to alot of psychological diseases and disorders. People who practice and maintainsuch unlawful relationships would develop unease, lack of personal happiness andsatisfaction, inferiority complex, guilt, and self-discern as a result ofpracticing unlawful sexual relationships. Allah (subhanahu wa ta'ala) states inQuran SuraRum (30:21):" And among His Signs is this, that He created foryou mates from among yourselves, that ye may dwell in tranquility with them, andHe has put love and mercy between your [hearts]: verily in that are Signs forthose who reflect".

*Sexual confusion leads to moral confusion in the society.* It is awell-established fact that money could easily trap and lure people to doanything evil. Money also enables a person to get all what he likes in terms ofpleasures and satisfaction. Thus, if those who are practicing unlawfulsatisfactions lack the needed funds, they may commit any type of crime tosatisfy their needs. Such individuals may steal, cheat, molest, rape, lie,deceive, bribe, or even kill in order to get what they want. They do not carewhere, or how they get the needed funds, even if this is on the account ofothers.

*Descending of the Wrath promised by Allah (subhanahu wa ta'ala).*Allah (subhanahu wa ta'ala) promised the communities where adultery andfornication is practiced or condoned, to receive one of the severestpunishments. Allah's Messenger (peace and blessings of Allah be upon him) isreported to have said, which read as follows:" My Ummah, nation wouldcontinue to enjoy a blessed life so long as illegitimate children are notproduced in their society. When illegitimate children become available in thesociety, then the punishment of Allah (subhanahu wa ta'ala) would becomeimminent".

## CONCLUSION

We have presented in this book some of themajor highlights of Islamic standpoint on sex. We aim through this booklet tooffer some introductory remarks about this very important issue of human life,and the method Islam follows to govern it to become as one of the acts ofIslamic worships. A Muslim would be rewarded if he/she uses sex in the mannerdescribed and approved by Allah (subhanahu wa ta'ala) and His Messenger (peaceand blessings of Allah be upon him).

This booklet is hopedto urge a non-Muslim to further his knowledge about Islam; which offers the bestway of life. Islam encompasses all aspects of life, the private, and the publicas well. In fact, if a Muslim were serious about his Islamic practices, hisreward would continue reaching him, even after death. If a Muslim left a goodlegacy or guidance behind him, or if he even guided and directed people to acertain good practice, he would continue to receive the promised reward afterhis departure of this world. Allah's Messenger (peace and blessings of Allah beupon him) is reported to have said, which read as follows:" Upon the deathof a human being, his [rewards for his worldly] actions would discontinue exceptfor [the following] three items: a continuous charity, a beneficial knowledge heleft behind, or a righteous son [or daughter] wholeheartedly would continue topray for him". Allah's Messenger (peace and blessingsof Allah be upon him) is also reported to have said, which read asfollows:" Whoever calls people to a guidance [good practice] would receivethe same reward as they do. Their rewards would not be decreased. Whoever callspeople to a misguidance, [ill practice] would receive the same sin as they do.Their sins would not be decreased".

An indication to thefact that Islam pays attention to the minute details in the comprehensive lifeof a Muslim is the directive given to Muslims by Allah's Messenger (peace andblessings of Allah be upon him) while going to answer the call of nature.Allah's Messenger (peace and blessings of Allah be upon him) is reported to havesaid, which read as follows:" If a person wants to answer the call ofnature, upon entering the [bathroom], let him enter with the left foot saying:in the name of Allah. Oh Allah! I seek refuge with You against filth and evilthings. Then, when such a person leaves the bathroom should get out the bathroomarea with the right foot saying: All praise is due to Allah (subhanahu wata'ala) , [He is] Who removed the harmful things away from me and made mehealthy".

Allah's Messenger (peace and blessings of Allah be upon him)is reported to have said, which read as follows:" Don't face the Qiblah[Prayer] direction neither when you urinate, nor when you have bowlmovement". It is worthwhile mentioning the opinion ofone of the Western canonists concerning the Islamic system and laws and theircomprehensiveness to cover all aspects of life. Dr. Hopkins, the Professor ofPhilosophy in Harvard University, in his book The Spirit of International Policywrites:" The progress and development of the Islamic countries is not byfollowing the

Western styles, which claim that religion has no say over thedaily life of the individual, the laws and the political system. Man must findin the religion a source for growth and progress. At times, some people wonderwhether Islam is capable of generating new ideas and issue independent rulingsthat coincide with the requirements of the modern life. The response to this is:'Yes. Islam is internally ready to grow, or rather one may say, Islam is betterthan many other similar systems in its ability to develop. Nevertheless, thedifficulty is not in the ability of the religion of Islam because the lack ofmeans, but rather the lack of inclination and desire to use them. I do feel thatI can rightly decide that Islam possesses all the necessary requirements forsuccess". It is, therefore, safe to say that Islam is thegreatest religion that accompanies and guides man in every step of his life andaffairs.

A religion that can do this for the life of theBelievers, is definitely worth holding tight on and invite others to embrace. Non-Muslims are invited to study the pure realities of Islam and see forthemselves the benefits that can derive from Islam. Non-Muslims must not be partial in making a decision before learning the meritsand characteristics of Islam. Islam is a religion thatbrings all good and stops all evils. Islam has the solutions for the entireproblems of man on earth. The real problem, however, lies in the poor andincomplete commitment of its followers to apply its rules and spirit. Unfortunately, a great majority of Muslims tend to shun awayfrom the full application of the Islamic rules and regulations. They do that, attimes, to satisfy their own whims and desires, and at other times because therules of Islam conflict with their personal interests, which aim at fulfillingtheir goals even if this was by cheating or exploitation of others and by all means of corruption.

4

# THE ISLAMIC CODE

## IN THE NAME OF GOD, THE MERCIFUL, THE MOST COMPASSIONATE

In the introduction to this chapter it was stated that the Quran, the all-embracing source of the true concept of Islam, says that Islam is both a faith and a code. Up to this point we have discussed the beliefs that must be held with the head and the heart if one is to be a Muslim. The acceptance or rejection of these beliefs determines the dividing line between loyalty to Islam and infidelity. The Islamic code is the name given to the principles and laws which God revealed and which He requires all Muslims to adhere to strictly in all their actions, whether in their relations with Him or in their dealings with mankind.

The actions through which Muslims draw near to their Lord, recall His greatness, and show their trust in Him by their observance of His divine rules are known in Islam as *worship of God.* The actions through which Muslims uphold their interests and repel evils in themselves, between themselves and their neighbours, and between Muslims and non-Muslims, the actions through which they prevent maltreatment, preserve rights, fulfill the general good, and establish peace and security, are known in Islam as *dealings.* The great number of laws which make up the Islamic code are classified under these two headings: worship and dealings.

### *Worship of God*

The worship of God is made up of prayers, fasting, payment of religious tax, and pilgrimage. Basic to the worship of God is the acknowledgment of God's oneness and Muhammad's heavenly purpose in life, the cleansing of the heart and soul, the strict observance of obedience to God in all actions. This is the foundation, these are the pillars on which Islam is built. Therefore the Prophet (may God bless him) has said,

> "Islam is put upon five principles: belief In the single God and in Muhammad as His Messenger, performance of prayers, payment of religious tax, keeping of the month of Ramadan, and pilgrimage to the Holy Mosque by whoever finds the way clear to do it."

### Prayer

Prayer is a form of physical worship assigned to the Muslim five times a day at specified times. In prayer he stands wherever he happens to be at the appointed time and turns his face toward the Divine Mosque in Mecca. He begins his prayer by saying in a fairly loud voice, "God is the Most Great," praying reverently with profound intent to worship God. He then recites the Good Book's first Surah, along with a passage of the Quran which he has learned by heart, trying to understand its inner meaning. He then bows by bending until his back makes a straight horizontal line, holding his knees with his hands, and saying to himself as he bows, "Great God."

Then he lifts his head, saying, "God the Most Great," and kneels down, touching his forehead to the floor, saying as he goes down, "God the Highest." He then lifts his head, saying "God the Most Great," and sits comfortably on his heels. Then he touches the floor with his forehead a second time. This process is called one kneeling. There are five daily prayers: First is the morning prayer which the Muslim performs at the beginning of his day between the small hours of the morning and sunrise.

It is made up of two kneelings, at the end of which the worshiper sits to salute his Lord, admitting His oneness and the mission of His Prophet in a manner which has been universally copied from Muhammad (may God bless him). He then salutes the right side and the left side with the words, "Peace be upon you together with God's blessings." The second prayer is the midday prayer which is performed from noon until halfway between noon and sundown. The afternoon prayer comes between midafternoon and sunset. Each of those prayers is made up of four kneelings. The early evening prayer is three kneelings and is offered between sunset and the vanishing from the horizon of the twilight. The late evening prayer is performed after the twilight disappears; it is the last prayer of the day when the Muslim welcomes the night, and is made up of four kneelings.

With these prayers the Muslim thinks of his Lord five times during each day and night, appearing before his Lord repeatedly and saluting His name within his heart and soul, submitting himself to God, looking forward to His favour. Therefore he perseveres in obeying His commands.

The Muslim can perform these prayers anywhere—at the mosque, at home, in the field, at the factory, in the office—wherever he happens to be when the time falls due for prayer. He can pray alone, or he can pray with others standing in a line or lines arrayed closely in straight formation, like a highly-disciplined military parade, behind a leader who is followed by the congregation in all that he does. Congregational prayer in Islam is the best form of prayer because it encourages acquaintanceship, intimacy, cooperation, joint entreaty, remembrance, and cheerful submission to God, the Lord of all peoples.

Muslims are reminded of the time for prayer by the call to prayer which is given from the minaret of the mosque in the form taught by the Prophet, "God is Most Great. God is Most Great. I avow that there is no God other than Allah. I avow that there is no God other than Allah. I declare openly that Muhammad is the Messenger of God. I declare openly that Muhammad is the Messenger of God. Welcome prayer. Welcome prayer. Welcome good fortune. Welcome good fortune. God is Most Great. God is Most Great. There is no God but Allah."

Islam also has a weekly prayer, known as the Friday prayer because it is performed at noon on Friday. It is a congregational service with preaching before the prayer, which is made up of two kneelings. There are also two other prayers like the Friday prayer which are performed twice a year on the mornings of the two Islamic feasts, the first day following the month of Ramadan and the tenth day of the month of Dual Hijja. These two prayers are known in Islam as the prayers of the two feasts, Ramadan and al-Qurban. In addition to the daily prayers, the Friday prayer, and the prayers of the two feasts, there is in Islam the funeral prayer, a religious ceremony expressing the Muslims' loyalty toward their dead. Muslims are required to prepare their dead for burial by cleaning the body and wrapping it from head to foot in unstitched cloth; the body is then placed on a bed and the mourners stand in line and, led by one of them, join in the prayer for the dead person. They repeat four times the phrase "God is Most Great" and recite together the preface to the Quran; then they ask God's blessing on the deceased. The body is later buried. According to Islam the grave may be in the ground or on the surface level, but should not be elevated either for a member of the masses or for a prophet who has completed a heavenly mission.

In this connection it should be pointed out that Islam has no other funeral ceremonies than those mentioned above. The elaborate rituals, the special places for ceremonies, the special funeral processions which are sometimes seen, the domes built over graves, all these have nothing whatever to do with Islam. Nor is there any basis in Islam for the great respect paid to certain mausoleums with the object of securing blessings. Islam has nothing to say about visiting graveyards for inspiration or blessing. These customs have been copied by Muslims from others.

Islam is also opposed to the practice of withdrawing into monasteries or caves to repeat prayers. It looks upon the daily work to support one's family and to improve the life of the community as an obligation as important as prayer. Indeed, the daily prayers are assigned merely to fulfill the debt owed to God, and as a means of securing His aid in the daily struggle in the world. The Islamic code states clearly the everyday obligations of the Muslim which provide him with food for the soul through worship and further his material standing as an individual and promote the welfare of his community. Islamic law provides the best way for a man to maintain the right relationship with his Lord and a proper participation in the life of the world. This is not possible except for the Muslim. Except for the five daily prayers which distinguish the Muslim from the non-Muslim, the daily routine of the Muslim is like that of other men. He carries on the business for which his talents qualify him, earning his livelihood, guarding his family and his interests, and abstaining from sin in matters of food and drink and evil amusements. Then he retires at night to relax from work and fatigue. Islam does not prevent the Muslim from enjoying the beautiful things of life and the favours of God. "Say: Who has forbidden the adornment of Allah which He has brought forth for His bondmen, and the good things of His providing?" (Surah VII, 32).

### Fasting

Prayer is the first form of physical worship. The second is fasting—refraining from eating, drinking, and sexual intercourse all day from dawn to sunset during the whole month of Ramadan each year with the intention of showing submission to God's command. The act of fasting during Ramadan is the means by which the Muslim recognizes the favour God did to His subjects in the month of Ramadan when He began the revelation of the Quran to the Prophet Muhammad (may God bless him).

Fasting is the means by which the Muslim voluntarily abandons certain legitimate frivolous enjoyments as a means of putting his soul to a test and promoting its capacity for perseverance, thus strengthening his will to keep away from sins, both obvious and obscure. The Muslim thereby samples enough of starvation to make him a warm-hearted, hospitable person, sympathetic with the poor who are in constant want. This is precisely the spirit Islam endeavours to create in the Muslim's heart and mind by requiring fasting as a mode of worship. Therefore, Islam attaches no significance to the kind of fasting that does not inspire this great humanitarian spirit, and a person fasting for any other purpose has nothing to gain except hunger and thirst.

### Religious Tax

The third form of worship is the religious tax, *zakat*. This is a fiscal worship by which Islam requires the well-to-do to care for the needs of the poor and to pay a subsidy to maintain public benefits like hospitals, educational institutions, and a defense force. It is a sacred duty incumbent upon the rich to pay out of their possessions in excess of their requirements, and those of their dependents, portions which are universally recognized by Muslims as fair, and which in the aggregate meet the needs of the poor and the general interests of the community without adversely afflicting the owners. It is customary to give one-tenth of the product of the land if it is watered by rain and one-twentieth if it is irrigated by human effort; two and one-half per cent of savings is suggested, with equal proportions of the increase in cattle or in trade in goods. The motive for giving the religious tax is internal; there is no external pressure.

Worship through the giving of the religious tax is the best means of promoting the welfare of society, linking the classes of the community with reciprocal sympathy and compassion, and spreading throughout the people a sentiment of love and cooperation. Through the religious tax the nation protects itself from creating financial tyranny through the concentration of the bulk of the national income in the hands of a few individuals, or of the ruler who might claim it in the name of the state. The divine legislation which requires the religious tax preserves for the ordinary man freedom of choice as to his means of livelihood and at the same time provides the community with the aid and cooperation owed it by the individual. The Muslim who fails to pay the religious tax is failing in his religious duty and undermining one of the main pillars of Islam.

### Pilgrimage

Pilgrimage is also a form of physical, or external, worship in Islam. The pilgrimage is an annual form of congregational worship in which those Muslims who are able to make the trip assemble from all over the world at Mecca, the home of the revelation to Muhammad (may God bless him). There they visit the Holy Mosque and pray to God in Arafat, a narrow defile some thirteen miles from Mecca. It is a public worship expressing the full equality among Muslims gathered together from all over the world with a common objective—all performing the same actions, all seeking to gain God's favour. At Mecca all pilgrims stand on equal footing whether rich or poor, rulers or ordinary people, scholars or labourers. There all of them, wearing similar white, seamless robes and shorn of class distinctions, assemble around a single centre which inspires them with a strong sense of unity. There their views and aims are unified and their resolution is strengthened to work cooperatively for the fulfillment of the general good. This, then, is worship in Islam—based on the beliefs required of all Muslims, worship is performed through prayer, fasting, payment of the religious tax, and pilgrimages. These forms of worship are required by Islam as owed to God in order that Muslims may please Him, observe His commands, and show their gratitude to Him. As Muslims perform their worship they always think of God and of His gifts related to the body, wealth, and society. At the same time the Muslim realizes that these ceremonies performed in honour of God are of benefit to himself. Prayer and fasting give the Muslim discipline which he needs and further the development of his spiritual life; the religious tax encourages communal cooperation to meet the requirements of the poor and of society; and the pilgrimage widens the circle of acquaintances and increases mutual understanding and cooperation under the shadow of revelation and divine guidance.

### The Mosque

Although the prayers may be performed at the appropriate times wherever a Muslim happens to be, the mosque has since the dawn of Islam been the best environment for Islamic learning and the performance of religious ceremonies. It has been the centre for preaching and guidance, it has served as a court of law where disputes are reconciled, and has been like a social club where Muslims assemble to discuss topics of common interest. The mosque was not invented by Islam but is copied from ancient divine establishments. The Quran states that the first building set aside for worship for the people was the Holy Mosque erected by Abraham and his son Ishmael. The Good Book says of mosques in general, "He only shall tend Allah's sanctuaries who believes in Allah and the Last Day and observes proper worship and pays the poor-due and feareth none save Allah. For such (only) is it possible that they can be of the rightly guided" (Surah IX, 18).

The Quran mentions two mosques by name, the Divine Mosque in Mecca and the Aqsa Mosque in Jerusalem.

> "Glorified be He who carried His servant by night from the inviolable Place of Worship [Mecca] to the Far Distant

Place of Worship [Jerusalem], the neighbourhood whereof We have blessed" (Surah XVII, 1).

Among the first things the Prophet did on his return to Medina was to establish his own mosque as a means of bringing the Muslims closer together and forming the Muslim community, and as a place for performing the magnificent communal prayer.

Following the example of the Prophet, the Caliphs set up mosques where Muslims worshipped their Lord on an equal footing without any distinctions whatsoever. Today mosques are found throughout the Islamic world as the symbol of Islam, the centre for Islamic worship, teachings, and service.

## DEALINGS

Within the Islamic code, which provides guidance for all human activities, the distinction between worship and dealings is made for convenience in the exposition of Islam. We have seen the nature of the true worship of Islam; in considering the dealings we shall be concerned with the dealings within the Muslim community—the family, monetary affairs, relations with fellow Muslims, and government—and dealings with non-Muslims both as individuals and nations. Islamic law has clearly stated the obligations of the Muslims in all areas of life and the penalties to be inflicted for offenses and irregularities.

Under the guidance of its code of laws Islam preaches the one God and, by acknowledging the principle of equality, asserts the unity of the human race and denounces discrimination based on colour, racial, or regional differences. It aims at justice through the eradication of oppression and tyranny. It mistreats no stranger merely because he is a stranger in a strange land, nor the infidel because of his infidelity, nor the enemy because of his enmity; nor is a near relative given special treatment in Islamic law because of his relationship, nor is a friend shown partiality for his friendship, nor is a Muslim treated leniently because of his adherence to Islam.

"Be steadfast witnesses for Allah in equity, and let not hatred of any people seduce you that ye deal not justly. Deal justly, that is nearer to your duty" (Surah V, 8).

*The family.* Marriage in Islam requires the full agreement of both parties without compulsion being brought to bear on either person. A marriage which takes place forcibly is considered null and void. When an agreement is reached between the two, the man pays to the woman the bride money, which is a token of admiration, not a purchase price or a form of remuneration. The actual amount of the bride money is determined by agreement and is the exclusive property of the prospective wife; the husband is not entitled to use it in any way without her consent.

The marriage contract is repeated in the presence of two or more witnesses. The bride says, "I marry you to myself," and the groom replies, "I accept your marriage to me." It is quite in order for the two accredited agents for the bride and groom to repeat the phrases of the marriage contract also. If the contract is not authenticated by two witnesses it is unlawful, and no marriage exists between the two. Properly witnessed, this verbal contract completes the marriage and the man and woman may establish their home.

In Islam, the husband, by virtue of his physical strength and ability to secure means of livelihood, is given the responsibility of guardianship of the wife and of the home, within the framework of their reciprocal legal rights and obligations. Such guardianship is not an autocratic authority which excludes the wife from expressing her views or from the right of consultation; it is merely a rank of honour and control which must respect the wife's point of view.

Thus it is seen that the marriage in Islam is a simple agreement between two parties without any participation by religious or civil authorities. Nor does it curtail the wife's freedom of action or her control of property, so long as she lives up to the responsibilities of married life and cares for the home and children.

Islam authorizes a man to marry a second wife in special circumstances in which the objectives of the initial marriage, such as the begetting of children, cannot be fulfilled. There can be no doubt that marriage to a second wife is the best solution to the problem in cases in which the first wife, if divorced, might not be able to remarry or might have no one to look after her. Islam permits a man to have not more than four wives and stipulates that he may have not more than one wife unless he is able to discharge the rights of each wife and maintain absolute equity between them. Islam authorizes the woman to bring her case before justice if she believes that by marrying another wife her husband sought to injure her.

Islam permits marriage with Christians and Jews. In the Quran He says, "This day are (all) good things made lawful for you. The food of those who have received the Scripture is lawful for you, and your food is lawful for them. And so are the virtuous women of the believers and the virtuous women of those who received the Scripture before you" (Surah V, 5). But Islam forbids Muslims to marry disbelievers or polytheists, for He says, "Wed not idolatresses till they believe; for a believing bondwoman is better than an idolatress though she please you; and give not your daughters in marriage to idolaters till they believe, for lo! a believing slave is better than an idolater though he please you" (Surah II, 221).

Islam seeks to stabilize married life and reconcile differences between the husband and wife. It orders, for instance, that when there is a disagreement between husband and wife they should turn to their family or near relatives for arbitration. But if ill feelings gain such a hold on the married couple that their union is endangered, and no arbitration can succeed, and married life develops from a state of tranquillity, love, and compassion into one of anxiety, hardship, and boycott, and indeed is almost hell, then in such a situation, and only in such a situation, the husband is allowed by Islam, against its better judgment, to seek the remedy of divorce. Strictly speaking, divorce is a right bestowed on the husband in view of his ability to shoulder the marriage obligations and because of his aptitude for better self-restraint than the wife can display.

If the shock of divorce fulfills the purpose for which it is intended and both the husband and wife return to their senses, then they are permitted by Islam to resume their marriage within the terms of the Islamic code. Islam permits the husband to resort to the remedy of divorce twice, and to remarry each time if a satisfactory reconciliation is attained, but a third divorce is decisive and a woman so divorced cannot be made a legitimate wife a fourth time unless she first marries a different man and is then divorced by that man of his own free will, and there have been no consequences of that marriage. If that marriage had been arranged with the intention of divorcing him so that she might go back to her original husband, the contract for the second marriage was unlawful.

It is thus seen that Islam has not allowed divorce in order that a man may use the threat of divorce as a sword which he waves in the woman's face. On the contrary, Islam allows divorce as a bitter medicine to be used by a man to cure a situation or get rid of an association that defies remedy. Islam holds that if a man trespasses on a woman's rights by divorcing her without cause he is abusing his power and is therefore liable to be held responsible for committing a breach of duty. Islamic courts are allowed to censure the man for misusing the right of divorce.

The law of Islam permits the woman to ask the courts of law to look into her case if her husband maintains an unpleasant association with her, or causes real hardship to her unjustifiably, or if she finds that he suffers from a disease of the body or mind which prevents him from preserving her chastity. The court is authorized to order her to be divorced if she is justified in her contentions and her husband refuses to divorce her.

Just as Islam maintains equality between husband and wife in married life it insists on equality in the termination of the marriage. It does not allow the man in any circumstances to take undue advantage of the woman's innate weakness to deny her any of her rights or to abuse the rights which she owes to him. At the same time, it does not require a woman to go beyond her obligations to keep intact her purity and to preserve her husband's property and the home. The family bears a special responsibility for the education of the children in Islam. The training begins with teaching the child to repeat lessons concerning Islamic beliefs and to perform correctly the worship rites. The family is also responsible for seeing that the child receives further training in the school and the mosque where legitimate and illegitimate actions and beliefs are expounded so that when the child attains maturity he will have been guided along the way to a true understanding of Islam.

***Monetary Affairs:*** Inheritance in Islam is based on the blood relationship of parents, brothers and sisters, and children, and on the marriage relationship of husband and wife, without regard for sex or age in the right of inheritance. The parents, the children, and the consorts do not in any circumstances lose this right, though the amount of their share may be affected by the number of heirs. However, brothers and sisters are not entitled to inheritance in case the parents are living. If men and women are both heirs, the man receives twice as much as a woman except in the case of maternal half-brothers and half-sisters, who each get an equal share.

Islamic law has ruled that, since the man bears the support of the woman and the expenses of her children as well as the cost of her marriage, his share of the inheritance should be double that of the woman. Her share is allowed to stand her in good stead in case she loses the source of her livelihood. Islam has taken into consideration the fact that to allocate the inheritance among blood relatives and consorts strengthens bonds of affection and promotes among relatives a reciprocal interest in their common good. Jealousy would prevail and the family structure would be exposed to disintegration if favouritism were allowed among heirs of equal standing. Thanks to this system, Islamic society has been guarded against the threat of financial tyranny which may result when the entire inheritance goes to a single person. It is also guarded against the danger which would come from paying the inheritance into the state treasury, for that would deprive members of the family of the results of the efforts made by parents, children, relatives, husbands, and wives, and would be damaging to society.

Islamic law also sets the standards for financial dealings through its regulations governing such things as the terms of sale and lease, things liable to sale and lease and those liable to neither, ways to employ capital, conditions regulating deposits, authentication of debts, and like matters which could become sources of controversy. All these financial dealings must be based on truthfulness, fidelity, and a willingness to discharge obligations.

*Government:* The necessity for some sort of government in the Muslim community is indicated by many texts in the Quran, such as, "Retaliation is prescribed for you in the matter of the murdered" (Surah II, 178). "Lo! Allah commandeth you that ye restore deposits to their owners, and, if ye judge between mankind, that ye judge justly" (Surah IV, *58).* The obligations imposed upon the community by the Quran can only be discharged by the community deputizing a spokesman from its midst, a man possessing the mental qualifications, will power, and skills which enable him to secure unity of thought and cooperation in carrying out the tasks required for the common welfare. Such a man is known in Islam as the Caliph or Imam.

It is the duty of the Caliph or Imam, the leader in Islam, to consolidate public opinion, execute judgments, administer state machinery, encourage the faithful in the practice of their faith, such as prayers and the religious tax, and look after affairs of public interest with the guidance of a parliamentary democracy, the basis of government in Islam. The Caliph, in Islamic practice, is subject to control by the nation; he has no authority other than that given to him as a representative of the people and that which is required of him as the enforcer of supernatural laws. If he violates the terms of national representation or breaks God's orders, it is up to the nation to depose him and replace him. The Caliphate or Imamate in Islam is not based on a heavenly sanction which gives the Caliph power from God to rule the nation; he has no divine authority which makes it the duty of the people to obey him at any cost. The Caliph or Imam is only a member of the society whose actions are determined by divine laws and orders. The Caliph and the nation form an inseparable whole linked together by the strong tie of religious faith, worship of God, fair dealing, and interest in the public welfare. The Prophet (may God bless him) says, "The Muslims are equal before God." The first Caliph in Islam said, "Obey me so long as I obey God and the Prophet in dealing with you. Once I cease obeying them you are no longer obliged to obey me."

Thus in Islam we find no distinction in community life between that which is called religious and that which is outside religion. In Islam religion is concerned with faith and worship, and also with the upbringing, education, and guidance of the people, and with all economic and social dealings as to those which are legitimate and illegitimate, sound or corrupt; and religion is concerned with the government of the people and the administration of state machinery, with the operation of all the functions of the community or nation. Religion provides the guiding principles for the individual and for the state. There can be no state which has a separate framework for the government and for religion. Those Islamic regions which separate the state from religion are following a mere private school of thought, contrary to the teachings of Islam.

Islam recognizes equally the rights and responsibilities of the individual and the community. It has built its legislation on the recognition that a man has a personality independent of his compatriots and his community, a personality which forms an element in the social structure. He has rights and obligations as an independent individual and rights and responsibilities as a part of the nation to which he belongs. As an independent person, man is required by Islam to believe in God, worship Him, and to live in a manner which assures him a clear conscience; it is incumbent upon him to work for a living, to control himself and his children, and to realize his interests and maintain his existence without encroaching upon the life and welfare of other people. It is his right to own property and to enjoy the legitimate pleasures of life. As a member of the community it is the divine duty of man to contribute to the general good, to guide and aid his fellow men, to do his full share in furthering the social amenities of the community, and to take part in fighting the common enemy.

In return for the individual's fulfillment of his obligations, the community is required by Islam to protect the individual's life and property, and to safeguard the chastity of his womenfolk. Islam has legislated for this purpose, clearly defining the functions of the legitimate ruler who is representative of the community, and outlining the penalties which the ruler must enforce.

Within the Islamic framework the individual and the community have defined for them the rights and obligations which ensure life and happiness through cooperation and equity in assigning privileges and tasks without encroaching upon the rights of the individual or the community. Should the individual deny to the community any of the rights due to it, he deserves God's denunciation, and it is the duty of the ruler to censure him on behalf of the nation. And if the society, as represented in the ruler, fails to ensure the rights of the individual, then the individual is entitled to insist upon his rights, and the ruler deserves God's condemnation and anger. When the ruler does not protect the rights of the individual, the community is empowered to depose him and to replace him with a man who is able to live up to the functions of his high office.

***Dealings with non-Muslims:*** Islam does not hold any enmity or hatred toward non-Muslims. It stands for peaceful coexistence and cooperation in daily life with them. For thus the Quran says, "Say: O disbelievers! I worship not that which ye worship; Nor worship ye that which I worship. And I shall not worship that which ye worship. Nor will ye worship that which I worship. Unto you your religion, and unto me my religion" (Surah CIX). "Unto this, then, summon (O Muhammad). And be thou upright as thou art commanded, and follow not their lusts, but say: I believe in whatever Scripture Allah has sent down, and I am commanded to be just among you. Allah is our Lord and your Lord. Unto us our works and unto you your works; no argument between us and you. Allah will bring us together, and unto Him is the journeying" (Surah XLII, 15). When non-Muslims are resident in the same country with Muslims, the most important thing is to ensure freedom of belief and the opportunity for non-Muslims to worship God in their own sanctuaries and hold their religious ceremonies, and to maintain full equality between them and their Muslim compatriots in public rights and obligations.

As we have seen, Muslims are permitted to marry Christian or Jewish women, and such wives enjoy the same rights and duties as Muslim wives with full liberty to cherish their own religion and perform their religious duties.

Even if parents are polytheists and even if they strive to mislead their Muslim son to follow them, he is commanded by the Quran to be good to them and to treat them gently, for Allah says, "And We have enjoined upon man concerning his parents... But if they strive with thee to make thee ascribe unto Me as partner that of which thou hast no knowledge, then obey them not. Consort with them in the world kindly, and follow the path of him who repenteth unto Me" (Surah XXXI, 14-15). It is said in history that Abu Talib, the Prophet's uncle, who was a polytheist until his death, was a good helper and protector of Muhammad.

Islam is strongly averse to resorting to force to expound its cause or to compel people to embrace its faith. Islam's invitation to non-Muslims to embrace Islam is made by an explanation of its advantages—its easily understandable faith, its simple obligations in religious ceremonies and dealings, its tolerant ethical principles, freedom of research, deep understanding of the universe, and the fact that it makes no distinction between men except by virtue of piety and good achievements. It points out that in Islam no man has authority over another person's beliefs, and that only God has authority to introduce beliefs and to require or receive worship.

Islam bases its policy for relations between Muslims and other people of varying beliefs on acquaintanceship, cooperation, and working for the common good. Non-Muslims who live in the community in cooperation and peace are looked upon by Islam as equal to Muslims, each of them holding to his faith and preaching its aims with wisdom and friendly argument without bringing pressure to bear on anyone or encroaching on each other's rights. Islam requires of non-Muslims only abstention from hostility to Muslims and from sedition or opposition to the Islamic way of life.

In the relations between Muslim and non-Muslim states, Islam stands for "inviting the world to do good." Islam permits treaties and cooperation with non-Muslim powers in time of peace so long as the treaties do not contradict the basic principles of Islam. "Allah forbiddes you not those who warred not against you on account of religion and drove you not out from your homes, that ye should show them kindness and deal justly with them. Lo! Allah loves the just dealers. Allah forbiddes you only those who warred against you on account of religion and have driven you out from your homes and helped to drive you out, that ye make friends of them. Whosoever maketh friends of them—(All) such are wrong-doers" (Surah LX, 8-9).

Islam does not turn from friendly relations with non-Muslim countries unless it is the victim of an aggressive attack, or obstacles are placed in the path of Islam, or attempts are made to seduce the people. When Islam is exposed to such hardships, its believers are permitted, and indeed it is made incumbent upon them, to repel aggression, to restore peace, and to establish a just situation in which people can think and act freely. Islam forbids Muslims to launch aggressive war motivated by a spirit of cruelty, or a desire to drain the resources of a people, or to cause suffering, or to eject people from their homes. After an approved war breaks out, Islam rejects devastation or extermination as methods of war. It does not permit the killing of members of the civilian population who are not actively engaged in hostilities, such as women, children, the old, and the disabled. The Prophet said, "Do not exterminate the young ones." When he was asked, "Aren't they the children of the infidel?" he replied. "Are not the best among you children of infidels?"

Islam does not permit participation in war until after the causes are clearly known and the enemy has received a warning. Islam condemns maltreatment of prisoners of war, their persecution, or their murder. It is made clear in the Quran that the prisoners must be fed in order to win God's satisfaction. "And feed with food the needy wretch, the orphan and the prisoner, for love of Him" (Surah LXXVI, 8). The termination of an approved war does not require that the enemy forces embrace Islam. It is considered sufficient if the enemy stops his evil aggression and signs a treaty which preserves the rights of the people, and protects them from tyranny or sedition. Such are the principles which govern the relations of Muslim and non-Muslim nations and the code of *jihad*—the Holy Struggle. The basis for the Islamic code of war was laid in the Quran and it was carried out in practice by the Prophet and his foremost successors.

***Penalties and Rewards:*** Up to this point we have been discussing the Islamic code—worship and dealings. The code also states the rewards and penalties which are in store in this world and in the Second World. Islam has specified the death penalty for murder, the cutting off of the hand for theft, and flogging for adultery and slander. The punishment is definitely stated for these three categories of offences only; the penalties for other offences and irregularities are left to the ruler who is representative of the nation and who acts after consultation with the people.

Concerning the rewards and penalties in the next world, Allah has said, "Whoso obeys Allah and His messenger, He will make him enter Gardens underneath which rivers flow, where such will dwell for ever. That will be the great success. And whoso disobeys Allah and His messenger and transgresses His limits, He will make him enter Fire, where such will dwell for ever; his will be a shameful doom" (Surah IV, 13-14).

The penalty for the aggressor and the corrupt is stated in God's saying, "The only reward for those who make war upon Allah and His messenger and strive after corruption in the land will be that they will be killed or crucified, or have their hands and feet on alternate sides cut off, or will be expelled out of the land. Such will be their degradation in the world, and in the Hereafter theirs will be an awful doom" (Surah V, 33)

Thus we see that in both worship and dealings man stands before his Lord and receives rewards or punishment in the afterlife according to his merits. In Islam, both worship and dealings are religious ceremonies and the Muslim must answer for all his actions before God in the Second World just as he must answer before a court of law in this world.

If a Muslim commits a breach of divine law through intent and premeditation, it constitutes a dangerous sin for which he alone is responsible. Even an accomplice who seduces him to commit the sin cannot relieve him of responsibility; he must, as an accomplice, bear his own sin.

According to the Quran it is a law of God of long standing that it is only the sinner who bears responsibility, "That no laden one shall bear another's load" (Surah LIII, 38). One of the clearly established principles of Islam is that only God forgives sins, and that God has given no authorization to anyone whatsoever to pardon sins, "Who forgives sins save Allah only?" (Surah III, 135).

Another principle is that all sins are pardoned by God as he pleases except the sin of infidelity This is expressly stated in the Quran, "Lo! Allah pardones not that partners should be ascribed unto Him. He pardones all save that to whom He will" (Surah IV, 116). Infidelity includes doubt in God's oneness and divinity. Therefore those who denounce the Creator, and those who worship other than God, and those who disagree with God's legislation as to that which is legitimate or illegitimate are all infidels.

It is also a principle of Islam that if a sinner repents and abstains from committing further sins because of fear of God and a determination to uphold His orders, God has pledged to forgive the sin. "And He it is Who accepts repentance from his bondmen, and pardones the evil deeds, and knows what ye do" (Surah XLII, 25). And Islam holds to the principle that man is born free from sins and remains free of sin until he is mature and has heard God's teachings. If, then, he closes his eyes to God's teachings and refuses to observe them, only then is he regarded as a sinner, with exclusive responsibility for his sins.

**THE MORAL FRAMEWORK**

Thus far in this chapter we have dealt with Islamic beliefs, Islamic worship, and Islamic dealings. The moral framework of Islam is a fourth element of equal significance in the life of a Muslim, entailing reward or punishment in the afterlife according to its observances or neglect. The moral principles of Islam strengthen the Muslim's resolve to adhere strictly to Islamic teachings and rules of conduct for polite society. They consolidate the bonds of understanding and unify sentiment and common feeling among Muslims. Allah urges Muslims to speak the truth, forget and forgive, and display compassion, mercy, valor, and love in all their relations with others.

The moral framework of Islam states the principles of etiquette for polite society for the common people as well as for the most advanced. The Quran says concerning the etiquette of walking and modesty in one's bearing, "Turn not thy cheek in scorn toward folk, nor walk with pertness in the land. Lo! Allah loves not each braggard boaster. Be modest in thy bearing and subdue thy voice" (Surah XXXI, 18-19).

Concerning the etiquette of calling on one's neighbours, "Lo! those who call thee from behind the private apartments, most of them have no sense" (Surah XLIX, 4). And also, "Enter not houses other than your own without first announcing your presence and invoking peace upon the folk thereof" (Surah XXIV, 27).

And in closing the door to sexual irregularities, the Quran says, "Tell the believing men to lower their gaze and be modest. That is purer for them. Lo! Allah is Aware of what they do. And tell the believing women to lower their gaze and be modest" (Surah XXIV, 30-31). And concerning unkind conversations, "Lee not a folk deride a folk who may be better than they (are), nor let women (deride) women who may be better than they are; neither defame one another, nor insult one another by nicknames" (Surah XLIX, 11).

By these and similar rules of social etiquette Islam guided the steps of people in backward stages of development, urging them to rise to an appropriate standard and attain the level of the more advanced social classes. At the same time Islam invites men of all levels to live up to the highest point of ethical and spiritual progress. "Keep to forgiveness (O Muhammad), and enjoin kindness, and turn away from the ignorant" (Surah VII, 199). "The good deed and the evil deed are not alike. Repel the evil deed with one which is better" (Surah XLI, 34). "Those who spend (of that which Allah has given them) in ease and adversity, those who control their wrath and are forgiving toward mankind; Allah loves the good" (Surah III, 134). "If ye publish your alms-giving, it is well, but if ye hide it and give it to the poor, it will be better for you" (Surah II, 271).

In calling upon the people to guide their lives by these ethical principles, Islam insists, in the main, that they should be moderate in all things, sparing themselves misery and not lowering their status in life. Islam requires courage of Muslims and warns them against cowardice and extravagance. It demands forgiveness and renounces both submissive humbleness and revenge. It upholds hospitality and condemns spendthrift and miserly economy. It preaches perseverance and rejects panic and defeatism. It constantly urges, "Give the kinsman his due, and the needy, and the wayfarer, and squander not (thy wealth) in wantonness" (Surah XVII, 26). It praises moderation in all things, "And those who, when they spend, are neither prodigal nor grudging; and there is ever a firm station between the two" (Surah XXV, 67). These illustrate, briefly, the ethical principles which guide the actions of the Muslim.

## SOURCES OF ISLAMIC LEGISLATION

The fundamental source of Islamic legislation is the Quran, which has been proved beyond all doubt as God's own book brought down by His Prophet to guide the people to obey its commands and to refrain from actions which it prohibits. The legislation of the Quran is of two kinds: that which has a crystal clear and decisive meaning not open to debate, and legislation liable to have two or more meanings.

The secondary sources of Islamic legislation are the Sunnah and the schools of thought, dealing with those areas not decisively covered in the Quran, the areas of probable meaning. After the Quran, the chief interpretative authority for Islamic legislation is the Sunnah—Muhammad's own sayings, deeds, and legislative decisions which have been correctly and authoritatively transmitted. If a problem arises which is not dealt with clearly in the Quran or in the Sunnah, the answer is sought in the schools of thought, the theories worked out by "leaders of thought" who have been careful students of the Quran and the Sunnah, have thought profoundly about their inner meanings and understand their general principles, and who have special knowledge of virtue and the general welfare.

The order of merit of the three sources of Islamic legislation has been recognized by Muslims from the days of the Prophet. They will continue to be the basis of Islamic legislation to the end of time.

***The Quran:*** In the previous discussions of the Quran we have seen that it contains many specific passages calling upon the people to follow its teachings and be guided by its legislation. "Lo! We reveal unto thee the Scripture with the truth, that thou may judge between mankind by that which Allah shows thee" (Surah IV, 105). "These are the limits (imposed by) Allah. Transgress them not. For whoso transgresses Allah's limits: such are wrongdoers" (Surah II, 229).

The Quran legislates concerning worship, enjoining fixed hours for prayer; it prescribes fasting, the giving of alms, and pilgrimage. It lays down the regulations for family life—marriage and divorce. It gives clear directions concerning financial dealings, contracts and pledges, relations with the people of the scriptures and with infidels, holy war and fighters and non-fighters, the administration of community life, sources of legislation, and the penalties for disobedience.

Thus the Quran is established as the foundation of the faith and of the code of legislation. Although the legislation in the Quran which may have two or more meanings is the subject of theory and study, the legislation which is explicit and open to only one meaning is binding on all Muslims. Should the Muslim fail to follow such legislation in his practical affairs, he is looked upon as rejecting Islam. Whoever alleges that the Quran is the product of a particular people, or a special age, or a limited aspect of human life is a disbeliever in Islam and in God's Book.

***The Sunnah:*** There are two aspects to the Sunnah: legislation given by the Prophet on matters not specifically detailed in the Quran, and traditions based on the actions and utterances of Muhammad as a human being.

The legislation given by the Prophet is illustrated by the rules stating the form of prayer, the pilgrimage rites, and giving in detail the limits of legitimacy in marriage. For instance, marriage is illegitimate between two people who in their infancy fed from the same breasts, and a man may not be married at the same time to a woman and to her aunt. This type of teaching is based on the tradition of Muhammad's instructions on matters not specified in the Quran.

The second aspect of the Sunnah is not associated with legislation. It deals with the traditions based on the actions and teachings of Muhammad concerning the affairs left to man's discretion, affairs for which God has given no definite command as to their legitimacy or illegitimacy, such as when to stand up and when to sit, the etiquette pertaining to eating and drinking and sleeping, and matters to be dealt with on the basis of experience or expert knowledge like agriculture, industry, medicine, military discipline, and tactics. It is authentically related that the Prophet, in the course of one of his battles, ordered an army contingent to be dispatched to a particular point, but a group of his disciples objected, "Is it a position God commanded you to choose, or have you chosen it as a strategist?" He replied, "No, it is one of my own choosing." His disciples pointed out that it was not an ideal position and gave their reasons for preferring an alternate location. The Prophet was convinced and dropped his plan. At another time he expressed his views as to the proper way to fertilize palm trees, but the trees failed to produce fruit. When he was informed of the result, he said, "You are better acquainted with your own worldly affairs."

Knowledge which depends on human experience and traditions related to the Prophet concerning such matters are not the basis for Islamic legislation. Traditions attributed to the Prophet can only be a source of legislation that must be obeyed if they are based on revelations given to him to guide the people according to God's laws.

The Sunnah as a source of legislation is always subordinate to the principles and fundamental laws of the Quran; its importance lies in the fact that it expounds specific aspects of the general principles of the Quran. Sometimes the expounding may be done by the example of an action; in the case of prayer, the Prophet showed how it is performed, the number of kneelings required for each prayer, and the proper time limits for its performance. The expounding may also be done by adding certain ceremonies not expressly described in the Quran. Expounding is also done by the Prophet in expressing opinions concerning general rules, such as the opinion that the simpler of two possibilities should be chosen in following a general principle stated in the Quran.

Hence we may assert that the legislative Sunnah is an attempt on the part of the Prophet to teach the real meaning of the Quran, its inner implications and aims. Thus, the legislation based on the Sunnah really springs from the Quran.

God's policy in relation to the Prophet's endeavour to interpret the Quran was to endorse his endeavour if it was right and proper, and to direct his attention to the correct interpretation and even to censure him if he was in error. Once when the Prophet out of dutiful regard for his faith was wilfully denying himself certain good things allowable by God, He said, "O Prophet! Why bannest thou that which Allah has made lawful for thee, seeking to please thy wives?" (Surah LXVI, 1). This and similar instances in which the Prophet tried to get at the correct answer but failed provide the best proof that the Prophet used his discretion to determine things about which no revelation was forthcoming, and that whenever he made a mistake God directed him along the correct path.

Thus the Prophet used his discretion and received God's endorsement when he was right, and the result became law, binding on the people. So, also, his disciples copied his example and used their discretion when necessary, and on being informed of the outcome of their efforts the Prophet endorsed them if they were in order and God agreed with his approval. If they were in error, the Prophet directed his disciples' attention to the correct answer to which God guided him. In this way the results of his disciples' endeavours in his time were associated with his own efforts to interpret the Quran and became legislative Sunnah which it is incumbent on the people to respect. Thus we see that during the Prophet's lifetime there was no source of legislation other than the Quran and the Prophet's interpretation of it either through revelation or discretion.

The authenticity of the Sunnah is proved by the Quran, for it orders that the Prophet should be obeyed and it made obedience to him a form of obedience to God and a recognition of His love, "But nay, by thy Lord, they will not believe (in truth) until they make thee judge of what is in dispute between them and find within themselves no dislike of that which thou decides, and submit with full submission" (Surah IV, 65).

If the purpose of the legislation of the Sunnah is to expound the legislation of the Quran, and if God's policy with His Prophet was to endorse Muhammad's interpretation when it was correct and to guide him to what was right when he made a mistake, then the Sunnah legislation is the same as the legislation of the Quran, and equally binding on all Muslims.

*Schools of Thought:* In the time of the Prophet there were two sources of Islamic legislation: the fundamental source in the Quran, and the interpretative source in the Sunnah. After Muhammed's death his disciples found themselves in an expanding Islamic world, facing new issues for which they needed the guidance of explicit legislation. They would refer to the Quran and if they failed to find a satisfactory answer there they would turn to the Sunnah, which was preserved for them by reliable men who were fully acquainted with the Prophet's interpretations. If they did not find the answer to their question in either the Quran or the Sunnah, they pondered the points at issue—guided by their knowledge of the aims and guiding principles of Islamic legislation—and came to conclusions which are consistent with the Quran and the Sunnah, and have the authority of legislation. In this way the schools of thought, under carefully controlled conditions, became a third source of Islamic legislation.

The schools of thought, in their interpretations of the probable meanings of passages in the Quran and the Sunnah and in their rulings concerning issues not definitely dealt with in those sources, adopted certain general principles found in Quranic legislation as a guide. These are some of the principles on which the schools of thought based their decisions: all things are fundamentally allowable, unless specifically prohibited; toleration and the lifting of restrictions should be the aim of legislation; eradication of mischief is the aim of administration; necessity permits benefiting by things not otherwise allowable; necessity is given due appreciation; preventing mischief has priority over bringing about welfare; commit the lesser of two evils; mischief is not removed by mischief; one should suffer private damage to avert general disaster. Such general principles are the guides for the creation and interpretation of Islamic law.

Under the first two Caliphs: Abu Bakr and Umar, it was the policy when deciding public issues to consult with the leading disciples who were recognized for their accurate thinking, appreciation of the interests of the people, and grasp of the spirit of the legislation of the Quran and the Sunnah. When unity of view was achieved among those responsible leaders of the Muslim community, it was put into practice. In this way, the adoption of a law through consultation and a consensus *(ijma)* of the opinions of the leaders of Islam became a new source of Islamic legislation after the Prophet's death, covering all matters which were not expressly mentioned or clearly implied in either the Quran or the Sunnah.

The authenticity of the legislation of the schools of thought is assured by the Quran, for it says that the affairs of the people are matters of counsel and it orders that the people should obey the authority of those who are responsible for the common good and are known for sound interpretation. Such legislation is also authorized by the Sunnah, for the Prophet dispatched his lieutenants to remote regions with authority to use their discretion when guided by the consensus of opinion on all issues not defined in the Quran and Sunnah.

During the regimes of the first two Caliphs the differences of opinion were quite limited because of the trouble they took to ascertain the authenticity of the Sunnah and the importance they gave to consultations among the students of the law from among the Prophet's disciples, most of whom were resident at the Caliph's headquarters. It is important to note that the regimes of the two Shaikhs Abu Bakr and Umar are the only ones which define the correct use of discretion as a source of legislation. They show that discretion as a source of legislation must reach its conclusions through consultation which arrives at unity of view among Muslims of authority who are qualified to decide issues. Thus unity of view, considered by Islam to be a source of legislation in cases where neither the Quran nor the Sunnah is applicable, is the agreement reached by investigation and study by men of thought who understand the spirit of Islamic legislation and are responsible for guiding the interests of the people in the community.

Unity of view as a source of Islamic legislation is not the same as complete agreement among all members of the nation, whether men of thought or mere laymen, scholars or ordinary people. Such general agreement about Islamic principles definitely known to have been enacted is not the subject of thought and discretion and should be held equally by all Muslims. It is simply the general acceptance of the beliefs and code of legislation required of all members of the Islamic community.

For the unity of thought which is considered to be a source of binding legislation, the agreement or disagreement on the part of those not qualified to state views has no weight. Unity of view which can be the source of legislation must be attained through the use of methods of thinking and investigation which have been approved as valid; it must be reached by a limited number of men from among all classes of the nation, whose qualifications for the use of the approved methods are recognized; the views of all the qualified men must be ascertained; and unanimous agreement on a specific ruling must be sought. The unanimous agreement is difficult to attain because of the varying abilities of the men participating and the diversity of interests and regional circumstances influencing each investigator. Therefore it is recognized that unanimity can be achieved only on the basis of the principles that "there is no knowledge of any dissidents," or of "agreement by the preponderant majority." This is all that can be done to attain unity of view which can be a basis for legislation. "Allah tasks not a soul beyond its scope" (Surah II, 286). However, in seeking unity of thought as a basis for legislation, freedom of thought must be ensured for all those participating and no authority should bring to bear any pressure which would restrict the liberty of thought.

Islamic legislation based upon the consensus of opinion of the leaders qualified to decide is subject to review and alteration. The interests on which the leaders were called to rule vary in different areas, places, and conditions, making it allowable for the successors of the original leaders to review the position in the light of new circumstances and to make a new decision if the changed situation requires it. The new unanimity replaces the former legislation and becomes the new law which ought to be followed.

***Individual Private Discretion:*** In addition to the discretion employed in communal consultations concerning issues not specifically covered in the Quran or the Sunnah, there is the private discretion of the individual man in which decisions are reached by independent thinking. Private discretion *(ijtihad)* is not binding on anyone except the individual who uses it. Islam recognizes that the right of private discretion belongs to any individual who possesses the capacity for clear thinking and study, whether man or woman, ruler or subject, leading government civil servant or private citizen. Just as they have an equal right to engage in individual discretion, so do they have equal responsibility for making mistakes. Islam knows of no one who is immune from committing errors except the Prophet insofar as revelation was concerned. If the Prophet was liable to make mistakes in trying to find the correct answer—and indeed he did try and did make mistakes—then other Muslims, even those of great accomplishment or near relationship to Muhammad, are more liable to commit error.

The exercise of individual discretion was widespread after the time of the first two Caliphs, particularly after the great sedition arising out of the assassination of the third Caliph, Uthman. In its extreme form it transmuted Muslims into contending sects following their own private tendencies in determining schools of thinking and in conveying prophetic sayings.

It should be clearly understood that Islam does not set aside a specific person with the right to interpret the Quran or the Sunnah, nor does it make it a duty of the people to adhere to any person's individual views on questions which are open to private opinion. Every Muslim qualified to investigate questions has the right to do so.

Muslims who are not qualified ought to enquire concerning the qualifications of those who speak concerning the obligations of Islamic law. Islam does not bind any Muslim to follow a particular person, for no duty is owed other than those duties which were assigned by God and the Prophet. Nor did God or the Prophet order anyone to follow a given religious school of thought—with the result that since the dawn of Islam Muslims have been asking for right answers from any well-known students of religion they meet, without binding themselves to any specific teacher. Therefore Islam does not recognize as legitimate any tendency to imitate a given school of thought. All those who have legitimately used their discretion have warned others against copying their example unless they have been convinced by proof of the validity of their findings. They have said, "If this talk proves untrue, then it is just my own theory, and it is up to you to disregard all that I have said."

Thus it is understood that the men who hold religious positions in Islam, such as the Caliph or Imam, have no monopoly on thinking and understanding, nor are they immune from making errors, nor do they receive revelation or special inspiration. Such leaders can only advise, and guide, and administer justice within the limits of Islamic laws. The Caliph or Imam is elected to his office by the nation, and he represents the nation while in office. So long as he discharges his functions within the framework of God's orders, the nation aids and obeys him—and it deposes him if he deviates from the right course.

The position of the Judge (*Qadi*), or the *Mufti,* the *Shaikh of Islam,* and the *Mullak* is similar to that of the Caliph in matters of understanding and legislation. The Judge's responsibility is limited to passing judgment on disputes between parties in accordance with the laws of Islam. The Mufti's function is to explain questions put to him. If he happens to be a man of discretion, the Mufti expresses his own views; otherwise he copies someone else's opinions. However, his answers to questions are not binding on those who resort to him; they have the right to insist on proof that the answers are correct and his tradition is authentic, and they are entitled to ask the same or other questions of someone else in whose knowledge they have confidence.

*Shaikh* of Islam and *Mullah* are titles which gained popularity among Muslims in certain regions and eras, conferred on men who distinguished themselves in religious and legislative knowledge. Neither of them is depended upon for decisions in legislative matters, and they are not immune from committing mistakes. Islam does not recognize one Shaikh or one Mullah who has authority in Islamic knowledge, and certain religious sects which claim such leadership are deviations from Islamic teachings far from being in order.

Within the area in which private discretion is appropriate, whoever believed himself competent to think clearly did his best to understand the correct implications of Islamic teachings, each thinker following his own style of study and inference. Some thinkers confined themselves to a limited number of prophetic sayings, because of the spread of invented sayings which cast doubt on many widely accepted sayings. They preferred to rely upon general rules and the spirit of Islamic legislation. Such thinkers are known in the history of Islamic jurisprudence as rationalists, or men of thought. Others, known as students of the prophetic sayings, convinced themselves of the authenticity of the transmission of many more of the prophetic sayings and preferred to rely upon them for their decisions. Other thinkers based their judgments on the traditions prevailing in Medina because it was the environment where legislation was made at the time of the Prophet and during the first two Caliphates before the outbreak of the sedition.

Out of such varying uses of the right of private discretion there grew up schools of religious thought which in time gained popularity in Islam and were allowed to spread. In modern times there are four of these schools of interpretation, or schools of Islamic law, which are found living amicably together in the Islamic world. The Hanafi 'school was founded by Imam al-Numan Ibn Thabit, who died in Baghdad in the year 150 (AD. 767), based on the teachings of Abu Hanifah; the Maliki school was founded by Malik Ibn Anas, who died in Medina in 179 (AD. 795 the Shafii school was founded by Muhammad Ibn Idris al-Shafii, a native of Gaza who died m Cairo in 205 (AD. 820); and the Hanbali school was founded by Imam Ahmad Ibn Hanbal, a Persian who died in Baghdad in 241 (AD. 855).

These four schools of thought are still taught in most institutions of learning in Islamic countries. The Hanafi school is found chiefly in India, the countries which were under the Ottoman Turks, and China; the Maliki school is found today in North Africa and Upper Egypt; the Shafiis are found in Indonesia, southern Arabia, lower Egypt, and parts of Syria; the Hanbali school is influential in Saudi Arabia.

The fact that Islam has permitted individual as well as communal discretion—limited only by the original definite legislation of the Quran and the Sunnah, which define the roads to justice—enabled students of the Islamic code to choose freely the laws regulating the affairs of Islamic society. Such toleration has been the basis for the everlasting usefulness of the Islamic code and for its fitness to regulate the affairs of life everywhere and at all times.

# ISLAMIC BELIEFS AND CODE OF LAWS

## IN THE NAME OF ALLAH, THE BENEFICENT, THE MERCIFUL

Islam is the religion of Allah revealed to the Prophet Muhammad (Allah bless him and give him peace) in order that he might proclaim it to all mankind and men might be able to believe in it and put its teachings and regulations into practice.

The Apostle transmitted the Scripture precisely as it was revealed to him, explained its fundamental teachings, and in his own life followed the principles and regulations of the Holy Revelation.

Since the time of the Prophet, Muslims have for generation after generation received the Quran as it was given to the Apostle himself from Allah, passing it on precisely as it was taught at the beginning—whereof there is no doubt whatsoever. It has been definitely proved that the Quran could not possibly be the work of Muhammad or of any other human being, as is clearly seen when one considers its style, the treasures of teachings contained in it, and the environment in which Muhammad lived.

In the Scripture itself Allah defiantly stressed the impossibility of imitating the Quran when He said to the unbelievers, "And if ye are in doubt concerning that which We reveal unto Our slave (Muhammad), then produce a surah of the like thereof, and call your witnesses beside Allah if ye are truthful.

And if ye do it not—and ye can never do it—then guard yourselves against the fire prepared for disbelievers, whose fuel is of men and stones" (Surah II, 23-24). Such a final demonstration that the Scripture was revealed by Allah to Muhammad is the Muslim's authority for recognizing the Quran as the principle source of Islamic beliefs and the Islamic code governing practices. After the Apostle had been called by Allah, the *ulama*—those leaders who were well-versed in Islam—recognized that there were two types of texts in the Quran: those which are clear and definite and those which could have more than one meaning.

The Quranic texts which are clear and definite are concerned with the basic beliefs like belief in Allah and the Last Day. These texts also cover the origin of law, whether religious laws governing prayer, religious tax, and fasting, or prohibitions against such acts as manslaughter or attacks on the chastity of a woman, and laws governing the use of property. For them no freedom of interpretation is allowed. The texts which could have more than one meaning are concerned with subsidiary aspects of Islam, but not its fundamentals, and have given rise to a plurality of Muslim theories and attitudes which are more or less personal points of view and are far from being obligatory. Islam, except in matters concerning its basic beliefs and the principles of its code of practices, is not limited to one type of thinking or one specific legislative method. It is a tolerant religion which authorizes and permits wise liberality. As it has demonstrated throughout the Muslim world, Islam fits into all major cultures and constructive civilizations—and will continue to do so forever. The Quran, the principal basis of Islam, shows us that Islam cannot find its way into any heart or mind without the acceptance of its two basic branches: the beliefs and the code of laws.

Islam requires, first of all, a deep belief in it without any doubt or suspicion, as is made clear in many texts of the Quran and in the general agreement of the ulama of Islam. This emphasis on the primacy of belief was the first message of Muhammad to the Arabs, just as it was the message of all apostles and prophets; as the Quran says, "Say (O Muslims): We believe in Allah and that which is revealed unto us and that which was revealed unto Abraham, and Ishmael, and Isaac, and Jacob, and the tribes, and that which Moses and Jesus received, and that which the Prophets received from their Lord. We make no distinction between any of them, and unto Him we have surrendered" (Surah II, 136).

The code of laws provides the regulations which create the proper relations between man and God, such as saying prayers, fasting, and other religious duties; they guide man in his relations with his brother in Islam or the non-Muslim community, in organizing the structure of the family and encouraging reciprocal affection; they lead man to an understanding of his place in the universe, encouraging research into the nature of man and animals and guiding man in the use of the benefits of the natural world.

The Quran makes clear that the result of belief is faith, and the result of the code of laws is good behaviour, as is shown in many texts: "Lo! Those who believe and do good works, theirs are the Gardens of the Paradise for welcome, Wherein they will abide, with no desire to be removed from thence" (Surah XVIII, 108-9). "Lo! Those who say: Our Lord is Allah, and thereafter walk aright, there shall no fear come upon them neither shall they grieve" (Surah XLVI,13).

Islam is both belief and legislation which organizes all the relationships of man. Belief is the basis of the code of laws and the code of laws is the result of belief, for legislation without belief is a building without a foundation—and belief without a code of laws to put it into effect would be merely theoretical and ineffective. Thus, in Islam there is an intimate interrelation between belief and the code of laws governing all conduct, and those who deny this can by no means be considered to be Muslims.

Islam calls upon all people to accept its beliefs and code of laws regardless of race, sex, colour, rank, or any other difference. All people are equal before Allah and must bear their own responsibility to accept the revelations of the Quran: "O mankind! Lo! We have created you male and female, and have made you nations and tribes that ye may know one another. Lo! the noblest of you in the sight of Allah, is the best in conduct" (Surah XLIX, 13). "It will not be in accordance with your desires, nor the desires of the People of the Scripture [*i.e.,* Jews and Christians]. He who does wrong will have the recompense thereof, and will not find against Allah any protecting friend or helper. And whoso doeth good works, whether of male or female, and he (or she) is a believer, such will enter paradise and they will not be wronged the dint in a date-stone" (Surah IV, 123-24).

Those two verses make clear that the descendants or relatives of any of the apostles have no more rights in His sight than any common believer. They also emphasize that men and women bear equal religious responsibility, regardless of their sexual differences. The woman's responsibility is quite independent of that of her mate; his good behaviour will not benefit her and his bad actions will not harm her. Each will receive in the eternal abode the reward or punishment which his—or her—actions merit. "Allah citeth an example for those who disbelieve: the wife of Noah and the wife of Lot, who were under two of our righteous slaves yet betrayed them so that they (the husbands) availed them naught against Allah and it was said (unto them): Enter the Fire along with those who enter" (Surah LXVI, 10).

The son is also responsible for himself once he attains majority. The belief and behaviour of his parents neither benefit nor harm him, nor does his belief and behaviour benefit or harm his parents. Thus says the Quran, "O mankind! Keep your duty to your Lord and fear a Day when the parent will not be able to avail the child aught, nor the child to avail the parent" (Surah XXXI, 33).

Thus it is clear that it is the individual responsibility of each person to accept the revelation of Allah—the Islamic beliefs and code of laws governing conduct—regardless of sex, rank, race, or any other difference.

## The Fundamental Beliefs of Islam

A man announces his acceptance of the beliefs of Islam and his commitment to its code of regulations, he manifests the existence of Muslim beliefs in his heart, when he repeats the Word of Witness: *I witness that there is no God but Allah and that Muhammad is His Prophet.* To witness that Allah is One includes a perfect belief in Him as the source of creation and knowledge and the object of worship. To witness that Muhammad is His messenger includes a perfect belief in the Angels, the Scriptures, the messengers, the Day of Resurrection, and the principles on which the code of laws is based. This witness is the key to Islam, subjecting one to its beliefs and regulations. "The messenger believes in that which has been revealed unto him from his Lord and (so do) the believers. Each one believes in Allah and His angels and His scriptures and

His messengers—We make no distinction between any of His messengers—and they say: We hear, and we obey" (Surah II, 285). "It is not righteousness that ye turn your faces to the East and the West; but righteous is he who believes in Allah and the Last Day and the angels and the Scripture and the Prophets" (Surah II, 177).

We must believe in the existence and oneness of Allah, that He is the only creator and disposer of the universe, that He has no partner, that there is no comparable being, and that none but Allah is worthy of worship. "Say: He is Allah, the One! Allah, the eternally Besought of all! He begottes not nor was begotten. And there is none comparable unto Him" (Surah CXII). "Say: Shall I seek another than Allah for Lord, when He is Lord of all things?" (Surah VI, 165). "Say: Shall I choose for a protecting friend other than Allah, the Originator of the heavens and the earth, who feedes and is never fed?" (Surah VI, 14).

We must believe in all the messengers of Allah of whom we are informed by the Quran from Noah to Muhammad (Allah bless them and give them peace). Allah selects some of his slaves and prepares them through ideal education to be His messengers to mankind. Some of these apostles are mentioned in the Quran and other are not mentioned; we must believe in all of them.

We must believe in Angels, the ambassadors of the revelation from Allah to His apostles, and, of necessity, in the Scriptures, His messages to humanity. The principles of legislation of Allah are His laws that we must follow; we must not sanction that which Allah has forbidden, nor forbid that which He allows us to do. We must believe in the contents of all the messages concerning the code of laws which aims at the organization of human life in a way which meets the needs of mankind and promotes human welfare in accordance with His justice and mercy.

We must believe in the Day of Judgment and the Other World, which is the only eternal life and is the life of reward and punishment.

We have to believe in all of these facts.

Anyone who denies one of these Muslim facts cannot be treated as a Muslim nor subjected to the Muslim rules. Yet it does not follow that he who does not believe in any of these facts would be considered a nonbeliever by Allah and would therefore suffer eternal damnation. It simply means that he would not be treated as a Muslim; he would not be under any obligation to worship Allah according to Muslim rules. He would not be prevented from doing things prohibited by Islam—such as drinking wine or eating pork—and on death he would not be washed and prayed for by Muslims.

Man will, however, be considered to be an unbeliever if, after having been freely convinced of the truth of these beliefs, he rejects them, or any part of them, through obstinacy, pride, love of mammon or the pomp of power, or the fear of being criticized. But if these beliefs had not been presented to him at all, or were presented in a hateful way, or were presented in a true and right way but he was incapable of fully understanding them, or even if he were capable but died before being fully convinced—in such cases a man is not an unbeliever according to Almighty Judgment and will not suffer everlasting punishment. The only disbelief mentioned in the Quran for which man will suffer judgment is a disbelief arising from obstinacy and pride. Hence the distant peoples to whom Islam has not been introduced, or those to whom it has been introduced in a hateful way, or those who have not understood the evidence even though they tried, will not suffer judgment. But they will by no means be treated as Muslims for they have not adopted the Word of Witness; they have not said with conviction, "I witness that there is no God but Allah and that Muhammad is His Prophet."

Islam, when it invites one to adopt its beliefs, does not use any compulsion, for it detests compulsion. Faith cannot be attained by force; there can never be true faith through obligation. The Scripture says, "There is no compulsion in religion" (Surah II, 256). "And if thy Lord willed, all who are in the earth would have believed together. Would thou (Muhammad) compel men until they are believers?" (Surah X, 100). Not only is there no compulsion to adopt Islam, but Islam does not lead people to faith through spellbinding miracles which seek to convince without thought or the exercise of free choice. "If We will, We can send down on them from the sky a portent so that their necks would remain bowed before it" (Surah XXVI, 4).

Islam, in its invitation to accept its beliefs and to submit to its rules, rejects any methods which are not based on liberality and freedom of choice. Everyone has full liberty to embrace Islam voluntarily and through conviction. Thus Islam supports its beliefs through sound evidence and completely logical proofs. The Quranic evidence for the revelation of Allah-concerning belief in the One God, in Angels, the Scripture, the prophets, and the Last Day—is the Quran itself, the Word of Allah, whereof there is no doubt, as we have already seen.

The logic of this belief is that all that is mentioned in the Quran is a matter of fact because it is supported by a standing miracle which will never cease, the Quran itself. "And thou (O Muhammad) was not a reader of any scripture before it, nor dids thou write it with thy right hand, for then might those have doubted, who follow falsehood. But it is clear revelations in the hearts of those who have been given knowledge, and none deny our revelations save wrong-doers. And they say: Why are not portents sent down upon him from his Lord? Say: Portents are with Allah only, and I am but a plain warner. Is it not enough for them that We have sent down unto thee the Scripture which is read unto them? Lo! herein verily is mercy and a reminder for folk who believe" (Surah XXIX, 48-51).

## BELIEF IN ALLAH

The basic belief in Islam is belief in Allah—His existence, His unity, and His perfection. The evidence by which the Quran draws people's attention to the belief in Allah is based on reason and inner consciousness or intuition.

The rational evidence for belief in Allah is based on Islam's call to ponder on the nature of the universe—the earth, the heavens, the mysteries, the natural laws, the harmony and unity of the universe. Thus one comes to see that it is impossible that the universe could be self-created, or created by opposed or contradictory forces, or purposeless. This universe was created by an ultimate creative force; it was created by a supernatural force which guides and manages it through ultimate knowledge and wisdom. This universe is attaining its purposes through the will of the Almighty Creator. One of those purposes is its ultimate dissolution, after which comes the eternal abode, as we are told in many places in the Quran.

> When the heaven is split asunder, And attentive to her Lord in fear, And when the earth is spread out. And has cast out all that was in her, and is empty. And attentive to her Lord in fear! (Surah LXXXIV, 1-5)

> When the heaven is cleft asunder, When the planets are dispersed, When the seas are poured forth, And the sepulchres are overturned, A soul will know what it has sent before (it) and what left behind. (Surah LXXXII, 1-5)

> When the sun is overthrown, And when the stars fall, And when the hills are moved, And when the camels big with young, And when the wild beasts are herded, And when the seas rise, And when souls are reunited, And when the girl-child that was buried alive is asked, For what sin she was slain, And when the pages are laid open. And when the sky is torn away, And when hell is lighted, And when the garden is brought nigh, (Then) every soul will know what it has made ready. (Surah LXXXI, 1-14)

By such rational evidence we are instructed in the Quran as to the ultimate end toward which the universe is moving, the final destruction which awaits all created things. In almost every Surah we find rational evidence proving that the universe was created and is sustained by Allah. "Lo! in the creation of the heavens and the earth, and the difference of night and day, and the ships which run upon the sea with that which is of use to men, and the water which Allah sendes down from the sky, thereby reviving the earth after its death, and dispersing all kinds of beasts therein, and (in) the ordinance of the winds, and the clouds obedient between heaven and earth: are signs (of Allah's sovereignty) for people who have sense' (Surah II, 164). "And in the Earth are neighbouring tracts, vineyards and ploughed lands, and date-palms, like and unlike, which are watered with one water. And We have made some of them to excel others in fruit. Lo! herein verily are portents for people who have sense" (Surah XIII, 4). "We have built the heavens with might, and We it is who made the vast extent (thereof) And the earth have We laid out, how gracious was the

Spreader (thereof)! And all things We have created by pairs, that happily ye may reflect" (Surah LI, 47-49). These are only a few examples illustrating the many texts which give rational evidence of the creative power of Allah.

The intuitional evidence for belief in Allah, the belief based upon the recognition of Allah by our inner consciousness, is brought to our attention in the Quran by pointing out the important psychological fact that there is an instinctive feeling of faith in Almighty Allah, the Creator of the universe, which comes to men when they are free from inclinations, or the distractions of dull routines, or when surprised by the question of the origin of the universe, or when faced with hardships or misfortunes which they cannot overcome by themselves. These facts are illustrated by many texts of the Quran. "And if thou (Muhammad) ask them: Who created the heavens and the earth, they will surely answer: The Mighty, the Knower created them" (Surah XLIII, 9). "When We show favour unto man, he withdraws and turnes aside, but when ill touches him then he abounds in prayer" (Surah XLI, 51). "And if a wave enshrouds them like awnings, they cry unto Allah, making their faith pure for Him only. But when He brings them safe to land, some of them compromise. None denies Our signs save every traitor ingrate." (Surah XXXI, 32).

The Quran illustrates this sudden, instinctive faith in Allah by describing in detail Pharaoh's feeling when he was faced with death by drowning and realized the impossibility of escape, "And We brought the Children of Israel across the sea, Pharaoh with his hosts pursued them in rebellion and transgression, till, when the (fate of) drowning overtook him, he exclaimed: I believe that there is no God save Him in whom the Children of Israel believe, and I am of those who surrender (unto Him). What! Now! When hitherto thou has rebelled and been of the wrong-doers? But this day We save thee in thy body that thou may be a portent for those after thee. Lo! most of mankind are heedless of Our portents" (Surah X, 91-93). Thus we see that the belief in Allah is based on both rational evidence and intuitive insight, evidence which is available to all men who are not heedless of the Divine portents.

The Scripture also guides us to the Names and Qualities of Allah, all of which refer to His power, His wisdom, and all His perfections. Many of the Names are difficult to translate from the Arabic, for example, Allah is the One, the Eternally Besought of All, the First, the Last, the Beneficent, the Powerful, the Almighty, the Wise, the Knower, the Creator, the Shaper out of Naught, the Fashioner, the Guardian, the Majestic, the Superb, the Glorified. The Creator names Himself in this manner, "He is Allah, than whom there is no other God, the Knower of the invisible and the visible, He is the Beneficent, the Merciful. He is Allah, than whom there is no other God, the Sovereign Lord, the Holy One, Peace, the Keeper of Faith, the Guardian, the Majestic, the Compeller, the Superb. Glorified be Allah from all that they ascribe as partner (unto Him). He is Allah, the Creator, the Shaper out of naught, the Fashioner. His are the most beautiful names. All that is in the heavens and the earth glorifies Him, and He is the Mighty, the Wise" (Surah LIX, 22-24).

These names which show His superiority, mercy, and perfection are recognized by wise men to be true and justly applicable, because a true understanding of the nature of the universe indicates that these are the qualities of Allah. The wise man recognizes also that no other being in the universe is worthy of such names, for all these beings are creations—changeable, needy, and deficient. In the Quran the proper and comprehensive name which emphasizes His individuality is the *Ultimate Being*, known to Muslims as Allah, or the name of the Almighty and the Sublime.

Muslims call Him and worship Him by such names. For thus He says: "Allah's are the fairest names. Invoke Him by them. And leave the company of those who blaspheme His names. They will be requited what they do" (Surah VII, 80). It is forbidden for a Muslim to invoke Him by a name or an adjective that is not mentioned in His Scripture or by His Apostle.

The Ultimate Being can be described, but not conceived by man. When the Quran guides men to belief in Allah, it aims at turning man's thought from the fruitless attempt to know the essence and reality of His Ultimate Being and instead to guide men to know His creative ability and the activities which reveal His qualities, His might and perfection. The Quran shows that He is above all qualities possessed by His creation, that His qualities are divine and superior and that attempts to know His essence, to describe Him by such concepts as monism or pantheism, will fail. For He says, "Such is Allah, your Lord. There is no God save Him, the Creator of all things, so worship Him. And He takes care of all things. Vision comprehends Him not, but he comprehends (all) vision. He is the Subtile, the Aware" (Surah, VI, 103-4).

The story of Moses (the Blessing of Allah be upon him) when he asked his Creator to show him Himself, is a good illustration of the impossibility of knowing the essence of the Ultimate Being. "And when We did appoint for Moses thirty nights (of solitude), and added to them ten, and he completed the whole time appointed by his Lord of forty nights; and Moses said unto his brother: Take my place among the people. Do right, and follow not the way of mischief-makers. And when Moses came to Our appointed tryst and his Lord had spoken unto him, he said: My Lord! Show me (Thy self), that I may gaze upon Thee. He said: Thou wilt not see Me, but gaze upon the mountain! If it stand still in its place, then thou wilt see Me. And when his Lord revealed (His) glory to the mountain He sent it crashing down. And Moses fell down senseless. And when he woke he said: Glory unto Thee! I turn unto Thee repentant, and I am the first of (true) believers" (Surah VII, 142-43). It is by such texts that the Quran makes clear that Allah can be described, His qualities can be partially known, but His essence cannot be conceived of by man.

One final point should be stressed in relation to the Islamic belief in Allah. Islam rejects all forms of polytheism. Allah is One. The Quran often reprimands those who believe in the existence of two gods, or in Trinitarianism, and those who worship any part of His creation such as the sun, the moon, or idols. The Quran calls upon such polytheists to consider the numerous evidences of His ultimate Unity. "If there were therein Gods beside Allah, then verily both (the heavens and the earth) had been disordered" (Surah XXI, 22). "Allah has not chosen any son, nor is there any God along with Him; else would each God have assuredly championed that which he created, and some of them would assuredly have overcome others. Glorified be Allah above all that they allege" (Surah XXIII, 91). "Say: O People of the Scripture: Come to an agreement between us and you: that we shall worship none but Allah, and that we shall ascribe no partner unto Him, and that none of us shall take others for lords beside Allah" (Surah III, 64). "Lo! I have turned my face toward Him Who created the heavens and the earth, as one by nature upright, and I am not of the idolaters" (Surab VI, 80). Thus it is seen that Islam clearly rejects all polytheism, Trinitarianism, and idolatry and worships only the One.

## Belief in Angels, Jinn and the Soul

The first of the basic beliefs of Islam is the belief in Allah, as we have said. The second basic belief is the belief in Angels. The Scripture describes Angels as supernatural and says that such is their real nature that they do not appear in the material world generally, but only by divine command. The Quran says, "And they say: The Beneficent has taken unto Himself a son. Be He glorified! Nay, but (those whom they call sons) are honoured slaves; They speak not until He has spoken, and they act by His command" (Surah XXI, 26-27).

The Angels' functions are concerned with spirits and souls. Some of these functions, through which they carry out His orders and His will, are recorded in the Quranic texts. Some of the Angels carry His revelations, His orders, His messages to His prophets and apostles: "And lo! it is a revelation of the Lord of the Worlds, Which the True Spirit has brought down Upon thy heart, that thou may be (one) of the warners" (Surah XXVI, 192-94).

Other Angels support the prophets and make the believers stand firm. "And we gave Jesus, son of Mary, clear proofs (of Allah's sovereignty) and We supported him with the holy Spirit [*i.e.*, the angel Gabriel]" (Surah II, 253). "When thy Lord inspired the angels, (saying:) I am with you. So make those who believe stand firm. I will throw fear into the hearts of those who disbelieve" (Surab VIII, 12).

Other Angels are preachers who preach the true and the good and encourage believers by His good tidings of His eternal Paradise. "Lo! those who say: Our Lord is Allah, and afterward are uptight, the angels descend upon them, saying: Fear not nor grieve, but hear good tidings of the paradise which ye are promised. We are your protecting friends in the life of the world and in the Hereafter.

There ye will have (all) that your souls desire, and there ye will have (all) for which ye pray" (Surah XLI, 30-31). Others are Angels of Death, such as Azrad. "Say: the Angel of death, who has charge concerning you, will gather you, and afterward unto your Lord ye will be returned" (Surah XXXII, 11). "Those whom the angels cause to die (when they are) good. They say: Peace be unto you! Enter the Garden because of what ye used to do" (Surah XVI, 32).

"Lo! as for those whom the angels take (in death) while they wrong themselves, (the angels) will ask: In what were ye engaged? They will say: We were oppressed in the land. (The angels) will say: Was not Allah's earth spacious that ye could have migrated therein? As for such, their habitation will be hell, an evil journey's end" (Surah IV, 97). Other Angels are registers of the deeds of human beings, preserving the records until the Day of Judgment when they are shown to man. "Lo! there are above you guardians, Generous and recording, Who know (all) that ye do" (Surah LXXXII, 10-12).

Such exemplary functions, like all other functions of the Angels, are supernatural. The Quran describes Angels as "Messengers with wings and force." "Allah chooses from the angels messengers, and (also) from mankind" (Surah XXII, 75). "Praise be to Allah, the Creator of the heavens and the earth, who appointeth the angels messengers having wings two, three, and four. He multiplies in creation what He will. Lo! Allah is Able to do all things" (Surah XXXV, 1). As has been demonstrated previously, the Quran is the basic resource of Islam and therefore the Muslim's belief in Angels must be fully limited by definite Quranic texts, which are the only source of such supernatural facts. Another kind of supernatural creature is the Jinn. The Quran differentiates between Jinn and Angels in several ways. Concerning the substance of the Jinn, the Quran states several times that He created them from fire. "And the Jinn did We create aforetime of essential fire" (Surab XV, 27).

Some of the Jinn are virtuous, others are wicked. According to the Quran, speaking of the Jinn, "And there are among us some who have surrendered (to Allah) and there are among us some who are unjust. And whoso has surrendered to Allah, such have taken the right path purposefully. And as for those who are unjust, they are firewood for hell" (Surah LXXII, 14-15). In contrast, we have seen above that the Angels are "honoured slaves." Angels, as we mentioned previously, are the messengers of Allah to His prophets and apostles, but Jinn, like mankind, receive the revelations through His apostles. This is shown in the Quranic text, addressed to Muhammad, "And when We inclined toward thee (Muhammad) certain of the Jinn, who wished to hear the Quran, when they were in its presence, said: Give ear! and, when it was finished, turned back to their people, warning. They said: O our people! Lo! we have heard a Scripture which has been revealed after Moses, confirming that which was before it, guiding unto the truth and a right road. O our people! respond to Allah's summoner and believe Him. He will forgive you some of your sins and guard you from a painful doom" (Surah XLVI, 29-31).

Jinn share with mankind the responsibility of hearing and believing Muslim teachings. On the Judgment Day, both mankind and Jinn will be called by Allah in the same way and will be responsible in the same degree. "In the day when He will gather them together (He will say): O ye assembly of the Jinn! Many of humankind did ye seduce. And their adherents among humankind will say: Our Lord! We enjoyed one another, but now we have arrived at the appointed term which Thou appointed for us. He will say: Fire is your home. Abide therein for ever, save him whom Allah wills (to deliver). Lo! thy Lord is Wise, Aware" (Surah VI, 129). But the Angels do not share with mankind the same responsibilities. The Quran makes it clear in many passages that Angels possess all the spiritual virtues and none of the shortcomings of human beings, while the Jinn are described as sometimes being whisperers and provocators—evils which are sometimes found in men.

Concerning the soul, or spirit, the Quran says very little. "And (remember) when thy Lord said unto the angels: Lo! I am creating a mortal out of potter's clay of black mud altered, so, when I have made him and have breathed into him of My spirit, do ye fall down, prostrating yourselves unto him" (Surah XV, 28-29). There is another text in which He says, "Why, then, when (the soul) comes up to the throat (of the dying) And ye are at that moment looking" (Surah LVI, 83-84). All that we can deduce from such texts is that the soul is the source of life, and that it is the vital force of existence without which beings become lifeless. As to the precise nature of the soul, the Quran says nothing. However, there is no Quranic text which prohibits searching for such a supernatural spirit, whether or not such researches might be fruitful. His saying, "They will ask thee concerning the Spirit.

Say: The Spirit is by command of my Lord, and of knowledge ye have been vouchsafed but little" (Surah XVII, 85), indicates that the identification of the soul is His own concern and that the human mind is too limited to understand such a supernatural reality. This has been a subject of scientific research, but up to now those who have studied the problem have not reached a clear understanding about the soul. Concerning the soul after death, the texts of the Scripture and the sayings of the Prophet say nothing except that the soul remains after death, either living in ease and comfort or in torment. Thus He says, "Think not of those, who are slain in the way of Allah, as dead. Nay, they are living. With their Lord they have provision. Jubilant (are they) because of that which Allah has bestowed upon them of His bounty" (Surah III, 169-70).

### Belief in the Apostles

Belief in Angels is the highest stage of belief which leads to the right way, the belief in Allah. Belief in apostles is not a belief in the supernatural, for they are men with the same human nature that other men have. They differ from other men in that they have been selected by Allah and authorized to receive His revelations through His Angels in order that they may proclaim them to mankind and lead men in practising their teachings. Such a divine selection preserves them from error in all that they proclaim of His divine messages. At the same time, their very human nature and qualities make it easy for believers to accept what they say and imitate what they do. He says, "And We sent not (as Our messengers) before thee other than men whom We inspired. Ask the followers of the Reminder [*i.e.*, the Jewish Scripture] if ye know not? We gave them not bodies that would not eat food, nor were they immortals" (Surah XXI, 7-8).

It is a divine fact that in all ages Allah has sent His messages to men through His apostles to direct and strengthen human beings toward good. Since the dawn of creation it has been the aim of the divine will to further the spiritual progress of man by providing the guidance which enables man to arrange his daily affairs so that he lives wisely and correctly, "and there is not a nation but a warner has passed among them" (Surah XXXV, 24). Thus messages have been revealed again and again with the one purpose of guiding man to perfection. Each age had its message and each generation had the chance to hear His words. In all these messages, the principles taught were the same. "He has ordained for you that religion which He commanded unto Noah, and that which We inspire in thee (Muhammad), and that which We commanded unto Abraham and Moses and Jesus, saying: Establish the religion, and be not divided therein" (Surah XLII, 13).

The Messenger Muhammad(Pbuh) illustrated the unity of divine messages by saying that all the apostles are builders of one house, the earlier apostles laying the foundation for the later ones who build upon their foundation. The Quran calls upon mankind to believe in all His messengers as well as in the scriptures revealed to them. To believe in some apostles and reject others is a fallacy from the Islamic point of view. The Quran says, "Say (O Muslims): We believe in Allah and that which is revealed unto us and that which was revealed unto Abraham, and Ishmael, and Isaac, and Jacob, and the tribes, and that which Moses and Jesus received, and that which the Prophets received from their Lord. We make no distinction between any of them, and unto Him we have surrendered" (Surah II, 136). "And who believe in that which is revealed unto thee (Muhammad) and that which was revealed before thee, and are certain of the Hereafter" (Surah II, 4).

Those who believe in some apostles and reject others will be punished, for the Quran says, "Lo! those who disbelieve in Allah and His messengers, and seek to make distinction between Allah and His messengers, and say: We believe in some and disbelieve in others, and seek to choose a way in between; Such are disbelievers in truth; and for disbelievers We prepare a shameful doom" (Surah IV, 150-51). On the other hand, those who believe in all of His apostles will receive their reward. "But those who believe in Allah and His messengers and make no distinction between any of them, unto them Allah will give their wages; and

Allah was ever Forgiving, Merciful" (Surah IV, 152). The message of the Apostle Muhammad(Pbuh) includes the foundations of all the previous messages which guide humanity to perfection and open the way to human progress, both materially and spiritually. Islam calls mankind to believe that Muhammad is the last of all prophets and apostles, as is made clear in the Quran, "Muhammad is not the father of any man among you, but he is the messenger of Allah and the Seal of the Prophets; and Allah is Aware of all things" (Surah XXXIII, 40). "This day have I perfected your religion for you and completed My favour unto you, and have chosen for you as religion AL-ISLAM" (Surah V, 3).

Muhammad's(Pbuh) message, or Islam, is addressed to every human being in all ages and all over the world, regardless of colour, race, nationality, or any other difference. "Say (O Muhammad): O mankind! Lo! I am the messenger of Allah to you all" (Surah VII, 158). The messages of the apostles before Muhammad differed from his in that they were limited to the apostle's people or tribe, as the Quran shows. "We sent Noah (of old) unto his people, and he said: 0 my people: Serve Allah. Ye have no other God save him" (Surah VII, 59).

"And unto (the tribe of) A'ad (We sent) their brother, Hud" (Surah VII, 65). "And to (the tribe of) Thamud (We sent) their brother Salih" (Surah VII, 73). And the Quran reveals concerning Jesus (the Blessings of Allah be upon him): "Allah createth what He will. If He decreeth a thing, He says unto it only: Be! and it is. And He will teach him [Jesus] the Scripture and wisdom, and the Torah and the Gospel. And will make him a messenger unto the children of Israel" (Surab III, 47-49). Thus we see that Muhammad(Pbuh), the last of the prophets, brought a message which was unique in that it was addressed to all men everywhere.

It should be clearly understood that, according to the Quranic texts, the function of the apostles is limited to guiding and educating people through revelation. They are worthy of the highest degree of honour and respect, for they are fully authorized to assume spiritual and educational leadership for all men, but they have no authority over people's beliefs, minds, or hearts. They are in no way responsible for the unbeliever. They have no power to confer any benefit or to inflict any punishment on themselves or other human beings. He says, "We have not sent thee (O Muhammad) as a warden over them" (Surah XVII, 54). "Thy people (O Muhammad) have denied it, though it is the Truth. Say: I am not put in charge of you" (Surah VI, 66). "Say: For myself I have no power to benefit, nor power to hurt, save that which Allah wills" (Surah VII, 188).

## THE APOSTLES ARE HUMAN BEINGS

The Quran asserts that the fact that their messages were divine revelations did not change their human nature or make them into supernatural beings. They were highly honoured to be selected as messengers, but they remain human; their only infallibility is that given them by Allah concerning the religious facts revealed through them.

The Quran says, "Say: I am only a mortal like you. My Lord inspireth in me that your God is only One God. And whoever hopes for the meeting with his Lord, let him do righteous work, and make none share of the worship due unto his Lord" (Surah XVIII, 111). As human beings, in all matters other than the messages of Allah, apostles can be right or wrong like any other human beings. It is recorded in the Quran that Allah admonished His Apostle Muhammad for some of his actions, as for instance when the Apostle was distracted from his responsibilities to the Muslims by his honourable aim to preach to the idolators (Surah LXXX, 1-10).

We have seen that worship may be offered only to Allah. Islam states that no Angel or human being is entitled to any kind of worship. No human being can be of any assistance in the Day of Judgment, nor can a human being remit any sins, for himself or for others. Only Allah has the power to pardon or punish, only Allah is entitled to worship. And just as no Angel or prophet is entitled to worship, so also no worship may be offered to any of the educated believers, the leaders in Islam, no matter how distinguished. Islam has no saints in the sense of beings with intercessory powers who may be worshipped. Rather than saints in that sense, Islam has Allah's *Aoulia*, that is, His constant obeyers, His favourites. According to the Quran they have no special distinction which gives them any sort of saintliness or supernatural ability such as the authority to intercede or remit sins. The constant obeyers, or favourites of Allah, are true believers who follow the apostles in all that is revealed to them by Allah, obeying the divine commands and avoiding that which He prohibits.

Some people, influenced by non-Muslim sources, say that Allah has, in addition to the apostles, His distinctive slaves who are authorized by Him to rule the universe and to respond and fulfill the people's demands. It is even said that when such "saints" die they should have distinctive tombs, high domed, and lighted at night; that one should seek their blessings, offer them pledges, and bow before them. Such errors have become popular among some Muslims and in other religious congregations, but all such errors are entirely rejected by His religion in all His messages.

### Belief in the Scriptures

To accept and believe in the messages of Allah is a mere logical consequence of belief in Angels and apostles. The messages are the contents of all His scriptures, which include instruction concerning true beliefs and the fundamental principles for codes of law which guide men in distinguishing the approved from the forbidden in human actions. Islam calls mankind to believe in all His scriptures which have been revealed through the apostles—such as Abraham's Books, Moses' Bible, Jesus' Gospel, and Muhammad's Quran. From the Muslim point of view, no one who denies any of these scriptures is considered to be a believer.

It also follows that if Muhammad is the final Apostle, the Quran is the final Scripture. The Quran, as is known to anyone who is thoroughly acquainted with its contents, States the basic beliefs, the basic principles of worship and of human dealings, and the ideals of morality. The Quranic texts do not give in detail the code of laws regulating dealings—human actions—but they give the general principles which guide people to perfection, to a life of harmony—to an inner harmony between man's appetites and his spiritual desires, to harmony between man and the natural world, and to a harmony between individuals as well as a harmony with the society in which men live. The means of establishing harmony which are revealed in the Quran are based on faith and justice, and a wise understanding of human nature.

It is not the function of the Quran to explain in detail the facts of the universe, its secrets and the useful ways in which it can serve mankind. It does, however, urge men to use their minds and skills to gain understanding of the universe, its secrets and its wonderful phenomena.

It opens the way for man to use his mind and powers in whatever vocation falls to his lot, to increase his knowledge, and to strengthen his faith in the Almighty. It guides mankind to individual and social welfare and establishes justice among men. The Quran limits the human mind only in basic beliefs and principles of legislation, a wise limitation which is necessary to guide the people's faith and bring them to submission to Allah.

## Belief in the Last Day

The fifth principle of faith in Islam—after faith in Allah, Angels, apostles, and the scriptures—is belief in the Day of Resurrection, the Judgment Day. It is the end of man and His goal in the creation of man. "And that man has only that for which he makes effort, And that his effort will be seen, And afterward he will be repaid for it with fullest payments (Surah LIII, 39-41). What happens to a man on the Last Day—his reward or punishment, his pleasure or pain,—is determined by what he has chosen to do in this world. The Other World is the world of judgment for what man has done. "On the day when We shall summon all men with their record, whoso is given his book in his right hand—such will read their book and they will not be wronged a shred.

Whoso is blind here will be blind in the Hereafter, and yet further from the road" (Surah XVII, 71-72). Thus the belief in the judgment of the Last Day is the strongest motive for man to seek perfection and progress in this world in order that he may be accepted and favoured by Allah in the Other World.

The Quran mentions in various places the rewards and sufferings which will come to men in the Other World. Although it uses phrases that are commonly used by man in his daily life, Islamic sources emphasize that life in the Other World is a new life that differs from life in this world in everything except the names.

> But for him who feareth the standing before his Lord there are two gardens. Which is it, of the favours of your Lord, that ye deny? Of spreading branches. Which is it, of the favours of your Lord, that ye deny? Wherein are two fountains flowing. Which is it, of the favours of your Lord, that ye deny? Wherein is every kind of fruit in pairs. Which is it, of the favours of your Lord, that ye deny? Reclining upon couches lined with silk brocade, the fruit of both gardens near to hand. (Surah LV, 46-54)

Concerning the sufferings in the Other World, He says, "The guilty will be known by their marks, and will be taken by the forelocks and the feet" (Surah LV, 41). "While the reward of disbelievers is the Fire" (Surah XIII, 35). "And lo! for all such, hell will be the promised place" (Surah XV, 43). Thus in many passages does the Quran describe the blessings and sufferings of the Other World in a way which urges men to believe according to the teachings of Allah's messages and to act in accordance with the principles of dealings laid down in the Quranic texts.

A Muslim never doubts, nor hesitates to hold a firm belief in, the eternity of the blessings of the Other World. He knows that those who obstinately continue to be disbelievers will be punished for that disbelief which contradicts the natural disposition of man. That punishment, according to the Quran, will continue eternally.

It is not definitely stated in the Quran whether Hell is everlasting or not, but it is clearly stated that Paradise and its blessings are eternal. In all matters of belief concerning the Last Day and the Other World, the human mind is subject to the definite Quranic texts and the sayings of the Apostle.

These, then, are the beliefs of Islam: belief in Allah the One God, in Angels, in the apostles, in the scriptures, and in the Day of Judgment. These beliefs are, according to Islam, the basis of every divine religion; therefore, the religions which are not founded on them are false religions. Allah rejects the disbelievers, those who are polytheists, who do not believe in Angels, or in the apostles, or in the scriptures, or in the Last Day—and He invites them all to believe in Islam through logical thought and acceptance of the evidence revealed to men.

Man was called by Allah to adopt these beliefs. As an expression of His mercy and His goodness to His slaves, He has made man master of the earth, God's deputy on earth to make use of its blessings by using and developing its natural resources.

Allah has called upon man to study the universe in order that he may see and understand the wonders of His creation which confirm man's faith and lead him to spiritual and material progress. The Quran says, "He it is Who created for you all that is in the earth" (Surah II, 29).

"See ye not how Allah has made serviceable unto you whatsoever is in the skies and whatsoever is in the earth and has loaded you with His favours both without and within?" (Surah XXXI, 20).

"Allah it is Who has made the sea of service unto you that the ships may run thereon by His command, and that ye may seek His bounty, and that happily ye may be thankful; And has made of service unto you whatsoever is in the heavens and whatsoever is in the earth; it is all from Him. Lo! herein verily are portents for people who reflect" (Surah XIV, 12-13).

Islam states that Allah created man with a disposition which leads him sometimes to choose the good and sometimes to choose the evil way of life. His good deeds lead him to his own happiness, to social welfare, and to his being acceptable to Allah, while his evil deeds lead him to unhappiness and to destruction in this life and damnation in the next. For thus says Allah,

> Did We not assign unto him two eyes, And a tongue and two lips, And guide him to the parting of the mountain ways? But he has not attempted the Ascent—Ah, what will convey unto thee what the Ascent is!—(It is) to free a slave, And to feed in the day of hunger, An orphan near of kin, Or some poor wretch in misery, And to be of those who believe and exhort one another to perseverance and exhort one another to pity. (Surah XC, 8-17)

The purpose of Allah's messages and revelations is to strengthen the good tendencies of men and guide them to perfection in this life, thus laying the foundations for the next life. Islam points out that each man must choose for himself the way to happiness through good deeds or the way to unhappiness and punishment through wickedness.

Islam, in placing the responsibility on each individual, makes no distinction between human beings; each is given the same rights and responsibilities regardless of his sex, race, colour, or other differences.

Blessed are faithful and true believers. The Quran says, "Whosoever doeth right, whether male or female, and is a believer, him verily We shall quicken with good life, and We shall pay them a recompense in proportion to the best of what they used to do" (Surah XVI, 97).

In the eyes of Islam a man chooses either good or evil by his own free will and is rewarded or punished according to his deeds. He is only guided and advised by the messages of Allah and by the apostles but is still completely free to choose as he wishes.

It is quite clear that if Allah wanted to He would have created man wholly good and completely ignorant of all evil. Since man has been created free to choose between good and evil, he will be rewarded or punished on Doomsday according to what he has chosen.

There is no supernatural force which limits a man or compels him to adopt any mode of behaviour. What is called fate, or testing, is nothing but the operation of natural laws, such as the principles of cause and effect and of the freedom of man.

In former times, disbelievers excused themselves by saying that they had been predestined to certain actions by His will. But the Almighty rejected such an excuse and made it clear that full responsibility is thrown on each man because of his free mind and the guidance given by the apostles.

"They who are idolaters will say: Had Allah willed, we had not ascribed (unto Him) partners neither had our fathers, nor had we forbidden aught. Thus did those who were before them give the lie (to Allah's messengers) till they tasted of the fear of Us. Say: Have ye any knowledge that ye can adduce for us? Lo! ye follow naught but an opinion. Lo! ye do not guess. Say—For Allah's is the final judgment—Had He willed He could indeed have guided all of you" (Surah VI, 149-50). It is true enough that the Almighty foresees how man will act; but this foresight is nothing other than divine knowledge of the freedom of choice, which is a natural law.

Therefore, Islam does not allow a man to wander from the rightful faith and then offer the workings of fate as his excuse. For if that were so, His commandments, the missions of the apostles, the scriptures, and the promise of reward and punishment would all be null and void, impossible to reconcile with the Almighty's Wisdom and Justice.

6

# THE RATIONAL AND MYSTICAL INTERPRETATIONS OF ISLAM

No account of Islam is complete if it does not take into consideration the extraordinary efforts which the various Muslim sects have made to understand Islam, and the results which they have achieved. Islam is not merely a body of doctrines expressed in the Quran and the prophetic Traditions; neither is it best represented by the orthodox school at any particular time. It is a living religion which has received and is still receiving its vitality from the people who confess it; it is a great movement which has passed through various stages of development over its long and complicated history, influencing and being influenced by the religious and cultural forces in its environment. Through the interaction between Islam in its original form and those external forces some of the fundamental concepts of Muslim dogmas and practices were reinterpreted and reshaped.

Some of these interpretations are not orthodox, it is true, but they are nevertheless Islamic, at least insofar as they are based on Islamic texts, even though the texts are examined under a different light. It is the purpose of this chapter to discuss the interpretations gleaned from the writings of the old schools of Muslims—mystics and rationalists, including both the theologians and the philosophers—who are not usually regarded by the orthodox school as strict Muslims, but whose influence on Muslim thought and practical religious life is felt even today.

The earliest rationalists were known as Mutazilites, and the mystics of Islam are the Sufis. The discussion in this chapter will be limited to the theological, philosophical, and mystical attitudes toward certain of the fundamental problems of dogmatic beliefs and religious practices in Islam.

## THE THEOLOGICAL ATTITUDE

Islam, like all other great religions, has a theology of its own which aims at the establishment of its fundamental articles of faith and the refutation of heresy and innovation. The Prophet Muhammad was no theologian—nor was any prophet before him. In fact, the revelations that prophets have brought into the world defy any serious attempt at a systematic theology. The systematization of religious dogmas in Islam was a task undertaken by the followers of Muhammad when the need for the establishment of a Muslim theology was felt. The criterion for the early theology was taken by writers such as Ibn Khaldun and Adud al-Din al-Iji to be the teachings of the early Muslims and the orthodox party. In the opinion of these writers the Mutazilites (rationalists) and the Shias and many other theological schools are heretical. This is too narrow a view to be adopted, and in dealing with Muslim theology here the term "theology" is used in a wider sense to include the speculative thinking of orthodox and non-orthodox theological schools.

The fundamental principle which Muslim theology has always endeavoured to establish is the principle of the unity of God. On this principle Muslim theologians know no compromise. It is the keynote of Muslim faith and the root from which all other dogmas of Islam are derived. Hence Muslim theology is also called the science of unification (of God), because its object is to determine the nature of God and His attributes, and to explain the relation between Him and His creation, all of which follow as corollaries from a definite concept of Allah as the Absolute One. The Quran, though not itself a book on theology, contains the rudiments of almost all theological problems.

It speaks of God as the only one to be served, the Supreme Master and Ruler of the world. It asserts His absolute transcendence in these words, "Say: He is God alone. God the eternal: He begettes not, nor is begotten; and there is nothing like unto Him" (Surah CXLI). The Quran contains a long list of the attributes of God over which there has been much discussion and disputation among the Muslim theologians. It condemns polytheism, atheism, and deism; and it emphatically denies the eternity of the world. Although on the whole it is sympathetic to Christianity, it rejects the Christian Trinity and all its implications.

In discussing these theological problems the style of the Quran varies considerably. Sometimes it takes the form of a logical argument—a syllogistic proof or an argument based on analogy—but more often it adopts the rhetorical style, calling on man to reflect upon himself and the wonderful world around him so that by means of such reflection he might know his Lord. When dealing with moral precepts the Quran appeals to man's own conscience and bids him reflect upon his actions and the actions of his fellow men.

Such were the seeds from which, under favorable conditions, an elaborate theology developed in the Muslim world. There was no science of theology during the lifetime of the Prophet and the first four Caliphs. The early Muslims accepted the word of the Quran literally. They raised no metaphysical or theological questions. When they were in doubt about a Quranic verse dealing with God or any of His attributes they were told to accept it as it was stated in the Quran with no further explanation or interpretation. The idea was to have faith in Islam, to propagate it, and to defend it, rather than to inquire into its nature. The orthodox party represented by Ahmad Ibn Hanbal (died 241; AD. 855) adhered strictly to tradition and opposed any form of independent thinking.

Later on they even rejected the theological investigations made on strict Quranic lines, and iooked with suspicion upon the teaching of the ascetics of their time. They would only allow discussion of questions related to the law (sharia) and the practical affairs of everyday life. But soon after the death of Muhammad political questions relating to his rightful successor were raised, and with them arose certain theological questions concerning the nature of the true Imam (Muslim head of state), the meaning of faith, sin, infidelity, punishment in the Future World, and so on. The interest was primarily political, but the contending parties gave their views a religious colouring, and there was much persecution and bloodshed in the name of religion. Political, or rather political-theological, parties appeared on the scene—the Kharijites, the Qadarites, the Shiites, the Murjites, and the Umayyads, who were the state party and the bitterest opponents of Ali and his followers. This was a period of strife and dissension within the Muslim community during which the whole future of Islam was at stake.

What interests us here is their discussion of faith, sin, and retribution. The Murjites—literally those who postpone; here, those who postpone judgment until it is pronounced by God on the Day of Judgment—were more tolerant than the others in their political views and more liberal-minded on theological questions. They believed that faith alone is sufficient for man salvation. The sinful believer who professes the unity of God and acknowledges His Prophet thus will not suffer everlasting punishment in Hell, a view which was diametrically opposite to that of the Kharijites. They even went so far as to say that a believer need not be a professed Muslim, for faith is a confession of the heart while Islam is an outward or public confession of the tongue.

The question was taken up more seriously later when it lost its political significance and became a theological problem of academic interest. What is the real nature of faith, and what is its relation to religious practice? Does faith admit any degrees? That is, can one man be more faithful than another, or can one and the same person ascend higher and higher in the scale of faith? The Murjites denied the quantitative evaluation of faith, while the rest of the theologians held the view that faith admits increase and decrease. Faith is more nearly perfect when it is accompanied by actions, or better still, when it is so deeply rooted in the heart that it becomes the principle from which righteous actions necessarily follow.

Faith which is not accompanied by good works is like a tree which bears no fruit, but true faith becomes a "faculty of the heart"—as Ibn Khaldun calls it—which urges the faithful to perform their religious obligations and to abstain from sin. "A true believer," the Prophet says, "commits no adultery and no theft." In other words, to have real faith and to sin is a contradiction in terms. The theory that faith increases and decreases has its roots in the Quran in such passages as this, "The believers are they whose hearts thrill with fear when God's name is mentioned, and whose faith increases at each recital of His words, and who put trust in their Lord" (Surah VIII, 2).

Such were the beginnings of the era in which Muslim theology was being formed. But these rudimentary and altogether primitive speculations on certain religious problems soon assumed larger proportions when Muslim scholars who were skilled in the art of dialectic and tolerably conversant with Greek philosophy appeared on the scene. There were now two Important factors which helped the development of the new theology, one internal and the other external.

The internal factor is the nature of the Quran itself. As has been pointed out in previous chapters, the Quran contains two different types of verses, those which form the main substance of the Book and are clear and definite in their meaning, and the comparatively few verses which are dubious or less definite. This is admitted in one of the Medina revelations which runs as follows, "He (God) it is who has sent down to thee the Book. Some of its verses are of themselves perspicuous; they are the basis of the Book; and others are dubious. Those whose hearts are inclined to error follow the dubious verses, thereby seeking discord and seeking interpretation. But none knows its interpretation save God. Those who are firm in knowledge say: We believe therein-it is all from our Lord. But none will bear this in mind save men endued with understanding" (Surah III, 7).

The reason for the presence of these dubious verses in the Quran has been discussed by theologians. The majority incline to believe that they are purposely given as a trial in order to test the strength and validity of man's faith. Those whose faith is firm accept them unquestionably, while others whose hearts are inclined to error—as the Quran says—reject them or interpret them in such a way as to cause discord in the Muslim community. Whatever the real reason may be, the fact remains that these dubious verses played an important role in stirring up dispute among Muhammad's followers of the second generation. Out of these disputes emerged different parties, each supporting a different point of view. It is worth while quoting Ibn Khaldun on the subject. He says, in his *Prolegomena:*

In the Quran there are passages which describe God as an absolutely transcendent Being. Their meaning is clear and admits of no interpretation. They are all negative statements; and, on account of their clarity, are accepted by all believers.... The other passages which are comparatively few are suggestive of anthropomorphism [these are the dubious passages]. They were accepted [by the early Muslims] without any enquiry into their meaning. But the innovators of their time resorted to a different method, by subjecting the dubious passages to critical examination. Some exaggerated their anthropomorphic side and attributed to God hands, face, feet, and so on, thus falling into gross corporealism and violating the absolute transcendence of God which is explicitly mentioned in numerous other passages and with such undoubted clarity.... Others admitted anthropomorphism with regard to the attributes of God such as occupying a place, sitting on the Throne, coming and going and speaking in words, and so on. They, like the others, also drifted into corporealism.

The disputes centring around such passages had a far-reaching effect on the course of the development of many theological doctrines which occupied the minds of Muslims for generations. We can even find some traces of these theological disputes in modern times.

The second, or external, factor in the development of Muslim theology is the cultural influences which were brought to bear upon Islam from without. Up to the second half of the second century we meet only the individual men who expressed their opinions on some religious problems. There was no general or recognized system of religious thought; there were no real theological schools, although there were what we might call semi-theological parties.

The course of development changed when foreign influence came into play. Some ethical problems were raised, particularly the problem of determinism and free will. Such metaphysical problems as were inspired by the Quran also came to the fore—the problem of the attributes of God, the divine attribute of speech and the Quran as the eternal word of God, the problem of beholding the vision of God in the next world, and so on. It is significant that most of the major issues in religion were discussed in Syria, which was an important centre of Christian theology. We know that John of Damascus the great doctor of the Greek Church, was a Vizier (Minister) under the Umayyads, and that he and his pupil Theodorus Abucara wrote polemic treatises on Islam summarizing discussions between Christians and Muslims. Some of these treatises were written in a catechetical form: If a Muslim asks you such and such a question, answer so and so. This is taken as an evidence that direct contact between Muslim and Christian scholars must have taken place at an early stage. But while the possibility of such contact is admitted, there is no justification for the exaggerated view put forward by such scholars as De Boer, Von Kremer, and D. B. Macdonald that the development of Muslim theology was largely influenced by Christian thought.

The other foreign factor which influenced Muslim theology, particularly in its mature form, is Greek philosophy. We can see traces of it in almost all the leading theological theories—either in the bearing of some Greek concepts on such theories, or in the way they were presented and discussed. Yet, here again, Greek ideas never remained unaltered; they were given such a turn as to harmonize with the fundamental concepts of Islam.

A consideration of the two major issues in Muslim theology—God and the problem of divine attributes, and man and the problem of free will—will illustrate the significant trends in the development of Islamic theological thought.

## The Theological Conception of God

A variety of concepts of God, ranging from crude anthropomorphism to absolute transcendentalism, have their roots in the Quran. V/hen the Muslim theologians began to reflect on the nature of God, they found themselves faced with two types of Quranic verses: those which describe God in relation to His creation, and those which describe Him in Himself. According to the former, God sees, hears, speaks to His people, creates with His hands, sits on His Throne, comes with His Angels, and will be seen on the Day of Judgment. They also ascribe to God typically human qualities such as pleasure and displeasure, love and hatred, and the like. These attributes are some of the ingredients, so to speak, of the personality of the one God who speaks to His servants and hears their call, loves the righteous, and hates the wicked. The Prophet says, "Pray to God as if thou sees Him, for if thou sees Him not, He sees thee." That is, picture God as a person, for you cannot address yourself in prayer to the Absolute.

The second set of Quranic verses, those which describe God in Himself, refer to the divine attributes of transcendence by which God is distinguished from created beings. The question is: Can we predicate attributes of God at all? The Quran certainly does. God is described as omnipotent, as omniscient, as knowing and willing, as eternal, infinite, everlasting, and unlike all created beings. Some of these attributes are positive, others are negative. Can they all be predicated of God in the same way? The orthodox party maintain that they can, but they do not go into what such predication logically implies. The Mu'tazilites examine the implications of such predication. The negative attributes present no difficulty and are therefore admitted by them. The positive ones are either reduced to negations or denied as separate entities distinct from or added to the divine Essence. They do not deny that God knows, wills, and does things, but deny that His knowledge or will or action is different from and coeternal with His Essence. They are all identical with the Essence. To assert the separate existence of the divine attributes which are eternal because they belong to God is to assert a plurality of eternal beings, which is contrary to the oneness of God. Some Mu'tazilites went so far as to deny all positive attributes. To say that God knows such and such a thing, they say, means that He is not ignorant thereof, and the same with the rest of the attributes.

It is interesting to notice that the first Muslim thinker to deny the divine attributes in the above sense was Wasil Ibn Ata (died 131; AD. 748) in his refutation of the Christian doctrine of the Trinity, which he considered a plurality of eternal attributes in one Essence. His view received more elaboration in the later circles of the Mu'tazilites who gave it a more philosophical turn. God was reduced by them to a simple monad stripped of all attributes and qualities. Hence they were called by their opponents *Muattila,* that is, those who render the divine attributes useless or functionless.

The opposite view was held by the orthodox party and later by the Asharite school. Their argument on the whole is not very convincing, and most of it is quibbling with words. God, they say, has attributes, but they are neither identical with His Essence nor different from it. They are "states" which though distinguishable from the Essence are yet inherent in it. The whole trouble, it seems, rested on one fundamental misconception: they personified the attributes but went on thinking they were dealing with the ordinary simple attributes of God. To talk about an eternal attribute which is different from the divine Essence but coexistent with it is to personify it and give it the status of a substance—a position very similar to that of the Christian Trinity. Had these theologians said that the attributes were mere intelligible relations qualifying the Essence, or mere names with which God has described Himself, the question as to their identity or nonidentity with the divine Essence and the other question as to their eternity or temporality would not have arisen.

The failure to realize the significance of describing the attributes of God from two different aspects is responsible for most of the disputes and futile arguments with which Muslim books on theology abound. The two contending parties—the traditionalists and rationalists—concentrated on one set of attributes to the comparative neglect of the other. The result was two extreme views, with corporealism or moderate anthropomorphism on the one side and absolute transcendentalism on the other.

The Mu'tazilites, who were the champions of transcendentalism, resorted to a method of interpretation which explained away all the anthropomorphic passages in the Quran, and they discarded the anthropomorphic Prophetic Traditions as invalid or not authentic. This was necessary to preserve their conception of the absolute unity and transcendence of God. The traditionalists wavered between immanence and transcendence but were more inclined toward immanence. The rational interpretation of the Mu'tazilites had its advantages as well as its disadvantages. In one respect it helped to liberate Islam from the materialistic and mythological concepts of God by insisting on the more spiritual and abstract attributes. But it was carried to an extreme by some of the rationalists who reduced the Godhead to an abstraction void of all content.

The enquiry into the nature of the divine attributes naturally led to a discussion on the nature of the Quran as the revealed word of God or the external manifestation of the attribute of divine speech. The orthodox, who held the doctrine of the eternity of the attributes, said the Quran was eternal. The rationalists said it was created, or there would be something eternal other than God, and this would be a violation of His oneness. The Prophet to whom the Quran was revealed did not hear the words of God, but heard a voice which God created in a material medium and which conveyed to him the content of the divine mind. The Quran as we know it is therefore created. This was the doctrine of the Mu'tazilites which was championed by the Abbasid Caliph al-Mamun.

When the triumphant days of the Mu'tazilites were ended, the orthodox party saw their opportunity once again and declared that all was uncreated, even the very Word written in the Book and recited in man's prayer. The Asharite school took up the problem later and discussed it on a higher level. They were influenced by older speculations on a similar subject, particularly the Christian and Jewish theories of the Logos, which in their turn were influenced by ancient Greek theories.

The Asharites held that God's speech was eternal. The Quran, the divine command, and the creative Word *Be*, were all forms of the eternal attribute of speech. "The command of God," says the Quran, "is such that when God wills a thing, He says to it: Be; and it is" (Surah XXXVI, 81). The creative command and the creative Word *Be* are therefore prior to all phenomenal existence. The Quran also says, "One of His signs is that the heavens and the earth are sustained by His command" (Surah XXX, 25). Thus the divine command is not only the instrument of creation, it is also the sustaining principle of the created world. Such verses were originally meant to emphasize the absolute sovereignty of God as the supreme Creator and Maintainer of the universe, but a new meaning was read into them by the Asharites in support of a Logos theory comparable in many respects to the Christian and Stoic theories. The divine command and creative Word were personified and given power to create and sustain that which they create. Moreover, the Word, or Logos, is in one respect identical with God, in another different from Him and coeternal with Him. Thus the Word of God gradually took a place similar to that of the Memra in Jewish theology, and the Second Person in the Christian doctrine of the Trinity.

The Asharites went a step further. They distinguished between two kinds of speech, the external and the internal. The external, which consists of words and sounds and can be put down in writing, is created. The internal, which is expressed by such words and sounds, is identical with the divine consciousness and is therefore eternal. This distinction is certainly borrowed from the philosophy of the Stoics who spoke of potential and actual, or internal and external Logoi. It is also in line with the Christian theory of the Logos which distinguishes the Word which was from eternity with God and was God from the Word which appeared in a temporal manifestation in the form of Christ. Perhaps the earlier Asharites did not express themselves in such plain words. They did not work out the metaphysical implications of their theory. They were more concerned with the problems of the eternity of the Quran which they thought they had proved. What they actually proved is the eternity of the divine mind or the divine knowledge, and the temporal manifestation of this knowledge when revealed to the Prophet. This position was taken up by al-Ghazali and later Asharites.

## DETERMINISM AND FREE WILL

The ethical problem of determinism and free will has its roots in the much wider metaphysical problem of the conception of God in His relation to the world in general and mankind in particular. The pessimistic attitude of the Semitic mind toward the world as a fleeting shadow, the notion that it has value only as a place in which man prepares himself for a more permanent life, led to the conception that God is the absolute sovereign power which rules all things, including man and his actions. We have a definite trace of this conception in the Quran. God is the supreme King of Heaven and earth whose authority is not to be challenged. The following examples are typical of a large number of similar texts in the Quran. "He should not be asked concerning what He does" (Surah XXI, 23). "He createth what He will" (Surah XXX, 54) "He it is Who created you from dust" (Surah XL, 67). "He alone misguides whomever He pleases and guides whomever He pleases" (Surah XXXV, 8). And in talking to his people, Noah says, "Nor shall my counsel profit you if God wills to misguide you, though I fain would counsel you aright. God is your Lord, and unto Him shall ye return" (Surah XI, 34). This is one side of the picture; in its theological aspect it emphasizes the absolute authority of God over His creation, and in its ethical aspect suggests a deterministic theory of man's actions.

The other side of the picture shows the same two aspects closely related to one another. God, who is described as supreme power and will, is also described as just. The following typical passage from the Quran illustrates the justice of God. "We will not burden a soul beyond its power; with Us is a Book which speaks the truth, and they shall not be unjustly treated" (Surah XXIII, 62). "These are the signs of God: we recite them to thee in truth and God wills not injustice to mankind" (Surah III, 108). "God does them no injustice; it is they who are unjust to themselves" (Surah III, 117). "In truth has God created the heavens and the earth that each soul shall be rewarded for what he has earned, and that they shall not be wronged" (Surah XLV, 22). Thus, according to the Quran, justice is an essential attribute of God, and it is inconceivable that God can be the absolute despot who wills and acts as He pleases even if His actions are contrary to justice.

It is obvious that the two opposite theories, determinism and free will, can be traced back to a conflict between two conceptions of the nature of God—God as absolute power and God as just.

The early Muslims who were the true sons of the desert preferred to think of God after the pattern of a tribal God with unlimited authority, a conception from which they derived their ethical theory of determinism. Their God can do everything, even that which is unjust or unreasonable. On the ethical side they taught that man was nothing but an instrument in the hands of his Lord, subjected to the strictest laws of determinism. This theory, known as oriental fatalism, has caused Islam to be stigmatized as a fatalistic religion, but nothing could be farther from the truth, for Islam attaches the greatest importance to the role which man plays in the sphere of his actions. The Mu'tazilites, on the other hand, emphasized man's responsibility for his own actions. They argued against the despotism of God as well as against determinism and fatalism and put their whole trust in human reason, which to them was sacred. They taught that appeal should be made to reason first, rather than to the religious law. Reason tells us that we are the authors of our own actions and that some of them are right and others are wrong. Perception of right and wrong is an innate power of the human mind not due to knowledge taught by religion. Man therefore is a free agent and the maker of his own destiny. He is also the maker of his own moral law which must coincide with the religious law because the religious law is rational. There can be no religious injunction which is contrary to reason.

Man, however, is not purely rational, according to the Mu'tazilites. There is an irrational element in man to which he sometimes yields. This is why he sometimes goes astray and falls into error and sin, and this is why religion is needed as a reminder to the forgetful and to those whose rational will is thwarted by carnal desires. The Muslim rationalists were certainly on the road to Kant. The good will is the only thing that has intrinsic value in moral life, and it is man's own. Without freedom of the will and personal responsibility, retribution, punishment and reward, and the Future Life with its. Heaven and Hell are all empty words void of meaning.

Rationality is not only the guiding principle in man's actions and beliefs, according to the Muslim rationalists; it is also the ruling principle in the cosmos. This world is the best of all possible worlds because it is the work of a supreme Mini The so-called evil in the world is an integral part of the goodness of the whole.

The root of the doctrine of free will is to be found in the Quran itself and there is no justification for seeking an external source for it. In fact, the Quranic passages in favour of free will by far outnumber those which are suggestive of determinism. "And say: The truth is from your Lord: let him then who will, believe, and let him who will be an infidel" (Surah XVIII, 30). "This truly is a reminder: and whosowills, takes the road to his Lord" (Surah LXXVI, 29). "Say: Everyone acts after his manner; but your Lord knows who is best guided in his path" (Surah XVII, 84). "He who does evil or acts unjustly against himself, then asks pardon of God, will find God forgiving, merciful. And he who commits a crime, commits it to his own hurt" (Surah IV, 111-12). According to the Quran man is free to choose his actions and beliefs, and he merits punishment or reward according to whether his choice is right or wrong. It is for God to show the right path, and for man to follow it or not follow it. Everything is predestined in the sense that it is predetermined by man's nature and known as such to God from eternity. The eternal knowledge of God does not interfere one iota with man's choice. Only in this sense can any meaning be attached to moral and religious obligations. Man alone works out his salvation, and this by faith and good deeds. Faith is rarely mentioned alone in the Quran; it is usually coupled with good deeds as the necessary prerequisites for entering paradise. "Bring good tidings to those who believe and do the good things that are right, that for them are gardens 'near which rivers flow" (Surah II, 25). "Those who have believed and done the good things that are right, they shall be the inmates of Paradise" (Surah II, 82).

## THE PHILOSOPHICAL ATTITUDE

The attitude of the Muslim philosophers toward Islam is somewhat different from that of the theologians. The main object of the theologians was to defend, in their own way, Islamic dogmas. The philosophers sought to reconcile Islamic dogmas with philosophic ideas, to arrive at a conception of God which would satisfy the requirements of free thought as well as those of religious beliefs. The conception of God as the ultimate ground of all phenomenal existence had, somehow or other, to be brought into harmony with the conception of the personal God of Islam. To what extent the attempt was successful we shall see later.

The first Muslims to philosophize about the simple ideas of Islam were the Mu'tazilites. They were followed by the philosophers al-Kindi, al-Farabi, and Ibn Sina (Avicenna). The philosophers were on the whole contemptuous of their predecessors. Even al-Ghazali could not conceal his disappointment with the method of the theologians.

"Their method," he says, "is right only insofar as it accomplishes their own objective; but it is of no avail to anyone who admits nothing but self-evident truths."

Generally speaking one can say that the theological method had no philosophic basis, though this applies more to the school of the Asharites than the Mutaziites. The Asharites were skeptical in their attitude toward sense data. They denied causality and causal necessity and even refused to call God the First Cause. They taught that natural phenomena appear to be uniform not because they are subject to necessary laws but because the human mind reads sequence into them. At any moment God may interrupt such uniformities and cause miraculous things to happen. Nothing takes place as a result of interrelations between natural phenomena. Everything is fresh creation. Their whole conception of God and the natural world was different from, and directed against, the Aristotelian philosophy which forms the basis of the thinking of the Muslim philosophers.

It is impossible to give an account of the individual systems of all the philosophers of Islam here. In this general treatment of the subject the aim will be to set forth the attitude of the school of al-Farabi and Ibn Sina, who represent Muslim philosophy in its strict and more limited sense. Ibn Sina in particular represents this philosophy in its mature and final form in a clear and well-reasoned manner. His object, like that of all Muslim philosophers before and after him, was to find a formula by which religious dogmas and philosophic principles can be reconciled. In this he was the faithful follower of al-Farabi. For both of them Greek philosophy was almost infallible, yet they acknowledged, in their own way, the basic theological principles of Islam. Their philosophy therefore is a mixture of ideas often irreconcilable except with the help of the drastic method of explaining away the opposite concepts. It is also highly eclectic in character, but eclecticism was not entirely the work of the Muslim mind as some scholars maintain. Two of the most important sources from which the Muslim thinkers drew considerable material reached them in an already eclectic form—Neoplatonism and Hermetic philosophy. Plato and Aristotle had already been brought into some harmony and their ideas interpreted in the light of the ancient wisdom of the Orient with its characteristic religious sentiment. This made them all the more appealing to the Muslim philosophers whose aim was to philosophize Islam.

When Greek thought found its way into the Muslim world, the philosophers found themselves faced with a problem which they attempted to solve. On the one hand Islam called them to a simple faith in God who is the sole creator and sustainer of the world. It offered them no philosophy or even a basis for one. On the other hand, Greek philosophy in the form in which it came to them represented the final achievements reached by the Greek mind in its search for a solution of the problem of existence. It was impossible for Muslims to accept without alteration any religious teaching which, outwardly at least, contradicted their philosophic ideas. But it was equally impossible to go the full length with Greek philosophical theories and accept their necessary consequences. Therefore, the only way left open to them was to reconcile the two. The question was—which of the Greek philosophical theories should they accept? Aristotle's theory of a Prime Mover who set the whole world in motion, then left it to its own fate? Or Plato's theory of God as the supreme Idea of Good—whose relation to the existing world he left unexplained? Or the Stoic's theory of pantheism? Or the Neoplatonic theory of emanation?

Those were the chief Greek theories of the nature of God known to the Muslims, and none of them could possibly be accepted by them without serious modification. The pantheistic view of reality never appeared in the Muslim philosophy of the type we are discussing here, but a full-fledged theory of pantheism was put forward later by the greatest of all Muslim mystics, Muhy al-Din Ibn Arabi. We shall say more about him later. The Muslim philosophers made use of Platonic, Aristotelian, and Neoplatonic ideas in constructing their own metaphysics, in which Islamic ideas also play an important part. But even the Islamic concepts were interpreted in such a way as to make them more philosophical, thus narrowing the gulf between Islamic and pagan thought.

The problem with which Muslim philosophers were faced was that of the relation between the external world, with its multiplicity of spatio-temporal and changeable phenomena, and an ultimate, immutable, and unchangeable First Principle. In philosophical language, the problem was that of the relation between the one and the many, or the noumenon and the phenomena; in theological language it was the problem of God and the universe. The Greek thinkers were far from the idea of the Godhead as explained in revealed religions. Aristotle's philosophy is one of strict determinism in which both the material world and God are subject to a supreme law of self-necessity. The metaphysical-poetical conception of Plato reduces God to a mere abstraction. It was the Neoplatonists who, though in the main adhering to their pagan tradition, put forward some sort of a philosophy of religion. It is no wonder therefore that they paved the way for establishing Christian and Muslim philosophy of religion, and that their influence in Muslim religious thought in particular was predominant.

The attempt to reconcile Islam with Greek philosophy in general and Neoplatonism in particular was an honest but a very daring one. Whether the Muslim philosophers succeeded or failed is another matter, but the fact remains that through making the effort they made their genuine contribution to the history of human thought. They also exposed themselves to the severest criticism of their adversaries. Ghazali's vehement attacks on their views will be referred to later.

Ibn Sina is generally regarded as a true representative of the philosophy which sought to reconcile Islamic and Neoplatonic thought. His metaphysical views are regarded by no less an authority than Ghazali as being the most typical of his school, and when Ghazali launches his attacks against the philosophers he has Ibn Sina in mind all the time. Al-Farabi is also an excellent type, but he lacks the clarity and comprehensiveness of his successor. Al-Kindi is more of a logician, natural philosopher, and theologian. Ibn Rushd's (Averroes) greatness is to be found more in his commentaries on Aristotle than in independent philosophical thought. The rest of the Muslim philosophers of the West are mere satellites moving around al-Farabi and Ibn Sina.

## GOD AND THE WORLD

Ibn Sina prefers to call God the Necessary Being, or the Self-Subsistent Being, rather than Allah. His intention is to bridge the gulf between the religious and philosophical concepts of the Deity, and thus to be able to follow up his analysis of being and necessity, or self-subsistence, to their logical conclusions. The name Allah has some Muslim associations which make it unphilosophical.

Ibn Sina starts his analysis of the relation between God and the world with a consideration of the notion of being—a purely ontological procedure—which he divides into necessary and contingent being. The necessary being is that being whose existence is self-necessitated; it exists *per se*; its essence and existence are identical; the supposition of its nonexistence involves contradiction. The contingent being is that which has no essential or necessary reason for its existence; its being or nonbeing are equally possible; its essence is different from its existence. This is the phenomenal world; it is all that is "other than God." Ibn Sina says that the mere fact that we have a notion of the Necessary Being proves that He exists. Existence is a positive quality of perfection, and if we have an idea of the Perfect Being, that Perfect Being must exist, or our idea would be self-contradictory. This is the ontological argument used in modern philosophy by Descartes and Leibnitz, though the consequences which Ibn Sina draws are different.

Ibn Sina also makes use of the Aristotelian distinction between necessity and contingency, but goes far beyond what Aristotle has said in the subject, both in his proof of the existence of God and in his explanation of the relation between God and the universe. He criticizes the cosmological argument of the theologians by which they infer the existence of an eternal Creator from the existence of the phenomenal world. Contingency, he says, not origination in time, is the cause of the dependence of the world upon God. To say that it is origination in time—that is, creation—leads to these absurdities: that God's will and creative power were idle for an infinite time before the creation of the world; that to choose the creation of the world at a certain time, and not before or after that time, must have been due to circumstances outside God's nature, which means that some sort of change must have taken place in Him; and that the world after it has been created could very well be independent of its Creator, since its need of Him is only for creation and not for preservation after creation.

A contingent universe, on the other hand, has no temporal beginning and is dependent for its existence and the continuity of its existence on God. It is an eternal being which derives its existence every moment from God. There is only logical—not temporal—priority between them, the priority of cause to effect. The cause has never existed in time before its effect in this case. We can also call it priority of rank since the cause is usually regarded as superior to the effect. Here Ibn Sina is in complete agreement with Aristotle and in complete disagreement with the theologians who insist on the idea of creation, which is one of the principle dogmas of Islam.

The world, they hold, was created out of nothing by the will of God and at the time He appointed. No question should be asked as to why it was not created before or after, because such relations as before and after have no application within the domain of the eternal Will. This is the argument adduced by Ghazali in his refutation of the philosophers' doctrine of the eternity of the world.

In spite of his theory of the eternity of the world, Ibn Sina describes God as the Maker, the Fashioner, and sometimes the Creator of the world. These epithets occur in the Quran and have one definite sense in common—bringing the world into existence from nothing. Ibn Sina, who believed in the impossibility of creation out of nothing, explains these terms in such a way as to deprive them of their temporal significance. That which comes into being need not always have a temporal beginning, nor need it be the result of an act of will. It can be the result of a spontaneous and necessary overflowing of being from an original source, like the overflowing of the rays from the sun. This is the case with regard to the world in its relation to God. If eternity and necessity are essential attributes of God as the Primary Cause, so must they be attributes of His actions, which are His effects.

Thus we see how far Ibn Sina went in his deterministic philosophy. Necessity is the fundamental law to which both the phenomenal world and God Himself are subjected.

## THE ATTRIBUTES OF GOD

The conception of God in Muslim philosophy, in spite of all that has been said, is not quite the same as the Aristotelian conception. God, according to al-Farabi and Ibn Sina, is not a mere principle of action within the material world but is an independent and transcendent Being over and above the material world, forever producing it and preserving it.

Their conception of the Godhead is both theological and philosophical. God has two different kinds of attributes: metaphysical attributes, which can be inferred directly or indirectly from the definition of God as the Necessary Being; and theological attributes with which God describes Himself in the Quran. Even the metaphysical attributes are often tinged with a religious colour and explained in a way which makes them partly ethical and partly theological. This is because these philosophers are forever oscillating between philosophy and religion, although their loyalty on the whole is to philosophy.

According to Ibn Sina the divine attributes are simplicity, oneness, absolute perfection, pure goodness; God is the contemplator and the contemplated; God has no equal nor opposite.

Simplicity logically follows from the definition of God as the Necessary Being; for complexity, whether material, quantitative, or even intelligible, is contrary to necessity and self—subsistence. The complex, whatever it is, is dependent on its constituent parts and on something else to make it a whole. It follows, therefore, that God is not a material substance, is not divisible, is not a compound of two or more substances, and is not definable.

Oneness is an attribute of God, for God is one m every He has no partner who participates either in His or in His attributes. This is the first article of the faith. Plurality of gods contradicts the notion of self-necessity.

Absolute perfection is an attribute of God. God is perfect and complete. In Aristotle's language, God is pure actuality; there is nothing that is possible in Him which is not actually realized—His will, His knowledge, and His action, the whole of His nature. Everything else is in the process of becoming. The perfection of everything other than God is a potentiality which God brings into an actuality.

Pure goodness is an attribute inferred from God's being free from matter and potentiality. Goodness here is equivalent to positive being, the opposite of evil or not-being. All other things possess the two aspects of being and not-being, because in one respect they are actual and in another they are potential. God is not only the pure good, He is also the fountainhead from which good—positive being—is forever flowing into everything in the world. The whole realm of existence turns toward Him in love-like fashion for the good it receives from Him, for the qualities of being through which the world advances along the road to perfection. The world in fact does love God, because it loves the good, and good is the only thing that is loved for its own sake. Through love, therefore, God sets the whole world in motion, and whatever takes place in existence is the fruit Sf this love.

Ibn Sina, who is nOt so successful in his theory aZout God as the Active Cause, adMirably succeeds in portraying Hum as the Final Cause. His argumunt here is potent, clear, and fnee from verbal quibbling. In fagt, it is the most beautiful par| of his metaphysics; it is here•that his philosophy and mysticiOm meet. The relation between GoT and the external world is here(expressed in terms of love and ~evelation—love on the part of t\e world, and revelation on the lart of the Beloved. The divine ict of bestowing being on things is the very act of self-revelatqon. God reveals Himself to His Kreatures in a manner suitable t{ the requirements of their innef nature, which is fixed and immAtable, or in proportion to the @egree of perfection which they Yspire to achieve. The divine Prcvidence is the work of a mind wDich comprehends an orderly systEm gradually unfolding itself. The self-unfolding of the phenomefal world is paralleled in the ehernal self-revelation of God, avd the two processes are inseparable. Ibn Sina's theodicy, aesthetics, and optimistic theory of the nature of the world branch off from this mystical philosophy. It is here that he seems to be more under the influence of Plato and Plotinus than Aristotle.

For Ibn Sina, God is essentially an intellect whose sole activity is to contemplate Himself. He is the contemplator and the contemplated, the subject and the object in one. There is no duality in Him as there is in other minds. Duality of any kind is contrary to His absolute unity and simplicity.

There is a great deal of discussion about the knowledge of the Divine Mind. The theologians, following the Quran, hold that God knows everything past, present, and future, seen and unseen. They say that He is omniscient, that nothing takes place in the world which is not in accordance with His prior knowledge. The philosophers, on the other hand, maintain that God's knowledge is primarily of Himself and that, knowing Himself, He knows the world in a general way. He is the Ultimate Cause of things, as we have explained, and knowledge of the cause entails knowledge of the effect. They argue that knowledge of individual happenings in the world depends on a temporal relation between the knower and the known and therefore involves change in the knower, but God's knowledge is above time and change.

Ibn Sina also maintains that God has neither an equal nor an opposite. He has no equal because it is impossible for two necessary beings (gods) to be. He has no opposite because two opposites must be similar in one respect and dissimilar in another respect, in which they are said to be opposites—and God has no similar in any respect whatsoever. Therefore He has no opposite.

The Muslim philosophers do not omit the Quranic attributes of God such as omnipotence, omniscience, justice, generosity, and the like, but they interpret them philosophically or explain them away. We have already given the attributes of knowledge and will as examples. So it is quite evident that their concept of God is neither the pagan conception of the Greek philosophers nor the strictly orthodox Islamic conception. The denial of creation in its ordinary sense and the doctrine of the eternity of the world are definitely non-Islamic. In their view, however, they have shifted the problem to a higher plane by maintaining that the world is the outcome of God's inner necessity and the eternal urge within Him to give an outward manifestation of His bounty and generosity.

Although on the theoretical side the Muslim philosophers certainly seemed to be anti-Islamic, at least in some of their views, on the practical side they were true Muslims, insofar as we can gather from their biographies. Al-Farabi is said to have led a saintly life of religious devotion and contemplation. Ibn Sina, though allowing himself some bodily indulgences, is not reported to have neglected his religious duties. It is true that his conceptions of Heaven and Hell and the Resurrection are somewhat unorthodox, but he does not completely deny the orthodox concepts. We will conclude this section with his own words, taken from his *Nine Epistles:* The ultimate object of man wherein lies his greatest happiness in future life is to gain knowledge of the realities of things so far as his nature allows, and do what is incumbent upon him. Only in this way does man's soul become more honourable and perfect, an intelligible microcosm comparable to the existing Macrocosm, and become ready to enjoy the greatest happiness in the world to come.

## THE MYSTICAL ATTITUDE

The mysticism of Islam is known as Sufism, a name said to be derived from the Arabic word *suf* which means wool, referring to the woollen mantles worn by the Sufis. With Muslim mysticism we see the climax of the development of religious life and teaching in Islam. Neither the philosophers nor the theologians nor the canon lawyers have contributed so much as the mystics toward deepening the meaning of their religion and enriching its teachings. It is due to them that Islam, in the way they understand it, can be compared with other great religions of the world, for mysticism is the only ground on which the great religions meet.

Muslim mysticism has, from the time of its inception, been a spiritual revolution against a variety of forms and systems, both social and religious. After a long period of hard struggle, Sufism established itself in two quite different ways: as a religious philosophy and as the popular religion of Islam. During some of its flourishing periods, the Sufis were counted by the millions all over the Muslim Empire and in some countries their influence was so great that the heads of their orders were the practical rulers, with supreme authority in every major problem concerning the religious or secular institutions. Such influence can be found even now in some Muslim communities.

As an ideal mode of spiritual life, Sufism has passed through various stages. At some times it was thoroughly orthodox, at others so far removed from orthodoxy as to become a mere system of religious philosophy. It has also undergone some periods of stagnation and corruption during which its followers completely lost sight of the noble and lofty ideals of the original founders, preserving an outward appearance of ritual with nothing to correspond to it in the heart. But these remarks belong more to the history of Sufism. Our immediate object here is to try to set forth the mystical attitude toward Islam so far as it can be gleaned from the lives and teachings of the great Sufi masters, leaving everything else out of our account.

The special attitude of the Muslim mystics toward Islam was quite clear from the time their movement started. Until the end of the second century (eighth century AD) religious laws were based on the literal texts of the Quran and Prophetic Traditions, and scrupulously carried out. They were thoroughly studied and strictly adhered to in practice. Knowledge of the canon law—jurisprudence—was the most venerated of all knowledge, and adherence to its rules was the ultimate aim as well as the true mark of every pious Muslim. When the Sufis appeared on the scene, they came with another religious ideal. To them the examination of the esoteric meaning of the law was a more worthy objective than the study of the law in its esoteric sense. Hence arose the distinction between the outward expression of the law and its inward significance, and with it the distinction between the study of jurisprudence on the one hand and Sufism on the other. The jurists became known as the externalists and the Sufis as the internalists. Gradually the opposition between the two camps grew more and more intense as they realized that they stood for two different conceptions of Islam and its teachings.

The differences between the legalists and the Sufis were apparent in their interpretations of the meaning of religious law and the ways in which it should be derived and justified. They differed as to the nature of worship and the way it should be performed. They did not agree as to which actions are lawful or unlawful or what parts of the law are basic to Islam. Nor did they agree as to the object and value of obligatory and supererogatory religious devotions. Is God the object of formal worship or of love? They differed on many points of Islamic dogma, especially concerning the conception of God in His relation to man, and the meaning of the unity of God.

It is obvious that such disputes touch the very core of Islam, and it is no wonder that the Muslim theologians and jurists became the bitterest enemies of the Sufis and fought them on all fronts for centuries. The first opposition to their movement came from the traditionalist Ahmad Ibn Hanbal (died 241; AD. 855). He could not conceal his admiration for a Sufi like al-Harith al-Muhasibi (died 243; AD. 857), but admitted that al-Muhasibi spoke in his sermons a language unknown to him, the language of the Sufis. He did not doubt his sincerity but was full of suspicion and apprehension. Relentless persecution of the Sufis was carried on by Ibn Hanbal's party and other theological sects in order to put an end to their growing influence.

Gradually the new mysticism of Sufism—or rather, the new religious spirit—gained ground. It was realized that Islam as understood by the jurists was ultimately reduced to formal ritual which consisted in the performance of certain bodily movements. Prayer, fasting, and pilgrimage were well-defined and measured physical movements, almost void of genuine feeling. Such an attitude toward Islam was sure to satisfy the externalists whose main concern was to give precise definitions to religious terms, lay down general laws, and see that they were strictly observed. It did not satisfy the religious sentiment of the Sufis, who looked for a deeper meaning behind the outward forms. Qushayri tells us that Ruwaym of Baghdad (died 303; AD. 915) said, "All people hold fast to external appearances [of religion], but this community [the Sufis] holds fast to realities. All people consider it their duty to observe the external aspect of the religious law; the Sufis consider it their duty to strive after piety and unremitting sincerity." In these few words Ruwaym sums up the whole situation by pointing out the real difference between the Sufis and the rest of the Muslims in their respective attitudes toward Islam. For the Sufis, Islam is *haqiqa,* a reality hidden behind words and forms, while for the rest of the Muslims it is principally words and forms.

Such a distinction was practically unknown to the early Muslims. The idea started with the Shia who taught that the Quran, like everything else, had two aspects, one external and the other internal. The latter is what the Sufis call the esoteric meaning of the Quran, which is only revealed to the chosen people of God. They extended the idea to everything in Islam. A real contrast was made between the sharia (religious law) aspect of a religious principle or usage and its haqiqa aspect, that is, between the religious law as such and its real meaning.

It is true that the great teachers of Sufism agree that sharia should be strictly observed, and that the abandonment of sharia on the pretext that haqiqa, the reality or spirit of the law, has been obtained is not only impiety but infidelity. Haqiqa without sharia, they say, is baseless, and sharia without haqiqa is meaningless. A reasonable balance between the two is essential for a truly religious life. Such a balance is described by Ghazali in these words,

He who says that haqiqa is contrary to sharia, and the internal [side of religion] is contrary to the external is nearer to infidelity. Every haqiqa that has no root in sharia should be rejected. Sharia is the law enjoined upon people; haqiqa is seeing the work of Divine Providence. Sharia is worship of God; haqiqa is to behold him. Sharia is to obey the Divine Command; haqiqa is to know by mystic vision what God has predestined, what He has revealed and what He has concealed.

So, according to Ghazali, haqiqa is the spiritual justification and proof of religion. The true meaning of religious teachings is seen by the mystic in his heart. Its real nature is revealed to him. When, for instance, the mystic is called upon to worship God, the meaning of the Godhead and of worship is freshly perceived by the inner light. This is the general attitude adopted by the majority of orthodox Sufis and ardently defended by such men as Tustari (died 273; AD. 886), Kharraz (died 277; AD. 890), Junayd (died 297; AD. 909), and Ghazali (died 505; AD. 1111). But some Sufis went too far in emphasizing haqiqa and minimizing the importance of sharia and were eventually led into various degrees of the erroneous belief that the awareness of inner reality frees one from the moral obligations of the law. They represent the other extreme of Sufism which is condemned by the genuinely pious Muslims. Others among the Sufis held fast to sharia, but understood it in ways which were much wider and more liberal than the interpretation of the orthodox, looking upon the law as either a system of self-discipline or as a set of symbols representing hidden religious meanings.

Those Sufis who regarded the law as essentially a system of self-discipline rejected the claim that the sharia is a collection of norms and codes divided and subdivided into more norms and codes. For them it must not be understood within the narrow limits and strict definitions of the lawyers and theologians. The value of any religious work should not be judged on the basis of its compliance with the law; its value should be determined by the degree to which it fulfills the ideal of the lawgiver.

Voluntary acts of devotion are considered superior to obligatory acts because they fulfill a higher ideal—the love of God—while obligatory acts of devotion only show submissive obedience to God's commands.

The Sufis quote the following Tradition in which God says, "In no way does My servant so draw nigh unto Me as when he performs those duties which I have imposed on him; and My servant continues to draw near to Me through works of supererogation, until I love him. And when I love him, I am his eye, so that he sees by Me, and his ear, so that he hears by Me, and his tongue, so that he speaks by Me, and his hand, so that he takes by Me."

This means that in the act of devotion he becomes completely absorbed in God and loses every vestige of his individual being and feels himself to be one with his Beloved. Such a state is not attained by the ordinary performance of religious duties. The Sufi seeks the attainment of the spiritual benefits which he gains through his acts of devotion, not the mere performance of outward acts as such. Thus the real essence of religion is that which resides in the heart, not that which is performed by the body. The religious command should be addressed to the heart, not to the bodily organs.

This attitude, noble as it is, seems to have paved the way to antinomianism in some Sufi circles. Religious duties, they argued, are a means to an end, and if the end is reached we can very well dispense with the means.

Haqiqa, religious truth, is for them the end and sharia, religious law, is the means. That there were such men even in the golden age of Sufism who allowed themselves all sorts of license and indulgences under the pretext that they had reached their goal is evident from the scathing remarks which we read in the opening chapters of the treatise on Sufism by Qushayri (died 465; AD. 1072).

He attacks most mercilessly the men of his time who believed that haqiqa frees one from the moral obligations of the law, and appeals for a revision of Sufism in the light of the teachings of the old masters, calling upon the Sufis to lead a true religious life in accordance with the Quran and the example of the founders of the Sufi path.

Qushayri's warning was not in vain, for fifty years later it found a remarkable response in the writings of Ghazali who took upon himself the task of reconciling Sufism with Islam. He interpreted the principles of Sufism in the light of Islam and showed their interdependence.

It is true that Ghazali was primarily concerned with the solution of his own spiritual problem when he was in search of the truth, but in solving his own problem he solved the problem for thousands of others who were and still are searching for the same truth. This truth he found in the Sufi way of life lived according to strict Muslim law. Religious truth is the inner meaning of the law revealed in the heart of the Sufi by the Divine Light.

In addition to the Sufis who looked upon the law as a means of self-discipline there were those who looked upon the sharia as a set of symbols standing for hidden religious meanings. Those symbols are of value only as a reminder or an occasion in which the hidden meanings are realized. The pious Muslim should perform the acts of worship prescribed by the sharia with his heart set on their spiritual meanings, otherwise his worship is merely an empty mechanical action.

This attitude takes into account the external, physical acts of worship as well as the internal acts of the heart. The danger is that it might lead to discarding the external acts altogether on the ground that they are superfluous.

The Sufis who insisted on the observation of both the external and internal acts of worship read into the external teachings of Islam meanings undreamed of by canon lawyers. Prayer, for instance, is not regarded as a set of words to be uttered and movements to be performed but is looked upon as essentially a spiritual discourse between man and his Creator. All movements and words are symbols whose meanings form a part of that inner discourse.

Similarly, pilgrimage is not a mere trip to the Holy Shrine of Mecca; it is the spiritual journey of the human soul to God. Each step of the journey, each of the rites of the pilgrimage—such as circumambulation of the Kaaba, the kissing of the Black Stone, the standing on Mount Arafat—is a symbol of great spiritual significance. Each bodily movement of the pilgrimage has a corresponding movement of the heart.

The mention of God, known as *dhikr,* is another example of the symbolic interpretation of Islamic worship. It is not a mere repetition of the name Allah, but is the silent recollection and contemplation of God, done in such a way that the heart of the contemplator becomes occupied with nothing but Him and the lover becomes completely absorbed in his Beloved.

The Sufis go through the rest of the forms of worship in the same way. The man who performs religious rites without observing their hidden meanings is, according to them, like a child who reads the words of a book without understanding them. His religious life is void because his heart is void. In the case of prayer and dhikr, such a man's heart is occupied merely with the name of God, not with God Himself.

## THE SUFI CONCEPTION OF GOD

Just as the attitude of the Sufis toward the religious teachings of Islam was a revolt against the jurists who stifled the true spirit of religion in order to preserve its form, their attitude toward God was also a revolt directed against the theologians and the philosophers.

The barren speculations of the Muslim rationalists deprived the Godhead of its positive content, and God was reduced to a logical abstraction. The orthodox theologians made of Him a despot whose absolute power could do everything, even the impossible and the irrational.

The philosophers, in their attempt to reconcile Islamic dogmas with Greek philosophy, were obliged to abandon many of the theological attributes of God, or explain them away, and put an active or final cause in place of a creator of the world. To the majority of the Sufis, God is essentially a personal being endowed with attributes which determine His relations with the world in general and man in particular. The outline of their picture of God is taken from the Quran, but the details which bring out the main features of the pictures are supplied by them, each in his own way.

God, they say, is the Creator of the world, the Maintainer, the sole Doer of everything, the Light of heaven and earth, the Merciful, the Compassionate, but above all He is the God who abides in the hearts of men. "Neither My heaven nor My earth contains Me," He says in a Tradition often quoted by the Sufis, "but I am contained in the heart of My servant who is a believer." So the Sufi does not look afar for his God, for the kingdom of God is in his heart if he can only see it.

The ultimate goal of the Muslim mystics is to bring this state into full realization, to feel the presence of God in the heart in such a way that nothing else is allowed to occupy it. Their aim is the complete absorption of the individual self in the contemplation of God.

If we pass in review over the long and complicated history of Sufism, we find that three different conceptions of God—ethical, aesthetic, and pantheistic—appear in successive stages of its development. They all had their roots directly or Indirectly in the Quran and Prophetic Traditions, or were brought into relation with such texts by means of interpretation.

The ethical conception of God was predominant in the earliest period of Muslim asceticism. The essence of God was regarded as absolute power and will. God was the supreme author of all things, including men's actions.

The present life was essentially evil and therefore should be abandoned if the everlasting happiness of the Future World was to be attained. The early Sufis had an exaggerated sense of guilt and of the terrible torments that awaited the sinners in Hell. Consequently an overwhelming fear of God and His wrath seized their hearts, and their pious devotions were regarded as a means of escape from the judgment to come.

They had almost forgotten the words of God in which He says, "My mercy embraces all things," and, "God pardons everything except associating other gods with Him." This fear coloured the moral and religious life of the early ascetics, and determined their attitude toward God, the world, and their fellowmen. The aesthetic conception of God in Sufi metaphysics was based on the idea of reciprocal love between God and man. The root of this doctrine is to be found in the Quran, but further elaborations of it were due to foreign influences coming from Manichaeanism and Neoplatonism.

The first note in this direction was struck by the woman saint of Basra, Rabia (died 185; AD. 801). From the third century onward, the doctrine of divine love became the dominant feature of Sufism. God was the Beloved of the Sufis, and loving Him for His own sake was the end of all their endeavour. It was no longer the fear of Hell or the hope of Paradise, but the hope of obtaining a glimpse of the everlasting beauty of God which motivated the Sufis. Rabi'a says in one of her prayers, "0 God! if I worship Thee in fear of Hell, burn me in Hell, and if I worship Thee in hope of Paradise, exclude me from Paradise. But if I worship Thee for Thine own sake, withhold not Thine everlasting beauty." Also attributed to her is the following verse:

> Two ways I love Thee: selfishly, And next, as worthy is of Thee. 'Tis selfish love that I do naught Save think on Thee with every thought. 'Tis purest love when Thou dost raise. The veil to my adoring gaze. Not mine the praise in that or this. Thine is the praise in both I wis. (Translated by R. A. Nicholson in *Legacy of Islam*, pp. 213-14)

As time went on, the idea of divine love went deeper and deeper into the life and thought of the Muslim mystics. On the practical side it became the sole motive of their actions. Moral ideas centred around it, just as they centred around the fear of God in the earlier period. Altruism or selflessness became the highest virtue. This meant the abandonment of worldly pleasures and the absolute denial of selfishness for the sake of God.

"The essence of love is self-denial," says Ghazali. "It is the ultimate end of all mystic stations. Every state that comes after it is a fruit thereof; and every station that precedes it is a step toward it." Jalal al-Din Rumi, the great Sufi mystic, says, "Love is the remedy of our pride and self-conceit, the physician of all our infirmities."

The Sufis devoted their lives to the worship of God because they loved Him and were anxious to win His love. On the theoretical side, divine love was regarded as the sole reason for the creation of the world. Creation is an expression of God's love, it is His eternal Beauty reflected in an external form. The Sufis quote the following Tradition in which God says, "I was a hidden treasure and I loved to be known, so I created the creation that they might know Me."

Moreover they maintain that love is the key to all Heavenly mysteries, and the essence of all true religion. It brings with it, not reasoned convictions, but convictions based on the infallible proof of immediate intuition. It is the celestial light that guides the traveller on his way to God.

Pantheism did not appear in Muslim mysticism—or at least not in a systematic form—before Muhy al-Din Ibn Arabi (died 638; AD. 1240), the greatest of all Arabic-speaking mystics of Islam. Pantheistic tendencies were seen as early as the third century, for instance in some of the utterances of Bayazid of Bistam (died 261; AD. 875), but they were not worked out into a consistent pantheistic doctrine.

Ibn Arabi, on the other hand, was the first to produce a full-fledged pantheistic philosophy which left its indelible marks on the whole of Sufism ever since his time.

The fundamental principle of this philosophy is the principle of the unity of all Being. His understanding of this principle is best summed up in his own words: "Glory to God who created all things, being Himself their very essence." In his *Fusus* he says,

> O Thou who created all things in Thyself, Thou unitest that which Thou createst. Thou createst what existeth infinitely. In Thee, for Thou art the narrow and the All-embracing.

In Islamic pantheism the phenomenal world is reduced to a mere shadow of reality, and God is regarded as the only real Being who is the ultimate ground of all that was, is, and will be. There is no actual duality of God and the phenomenal world, but there is an apparent duality asserted by the unaided intellect, which is incapable of comprehending the essential unity of the whole.

It is at most a duality of aspects of One Being—not of two independent beings. Looking at the two aspects within one whole, reality is both God and the universe, the One and the many, the transcendent and the immanent, the internal and the external. If we think—as we usually do—in terms of duality, we predicate of Reality all pairs of opposite attributes. But mystic intuition asserts that God is the only Real Being who is above all description and qualifying attributes, and the world is a mere illusion.

There is therefore a definite place for God in this philosophy, although in some respects He is far removed from the God of Islam. Ibn Arabi makes a distinction which is the dividing line between his metaphysical theory and his theology; it is a distinction between God as the unknowable and incommunicable Reality, and God as the object of belief, worship, and love. His conception of God as the object of belief comes very close to that of the ordinary monotheist, but the gap between pantheism and strict Muslim monotheism was too great for him to bridge.

God is the object of worship not in the sense that He is exclusively the God of the Muslims, the Christians, or the adherents of any other religion, but in the sense that He is the Essence of everything that is worshipped.

He is not to be confined to any particular form of belief or creed. Everything that is worshipped is one of the infinite number of forms in which He reveals Himself. To confine Him to one particular form to the exclusion of all other forms is infidelity, and to acknowledge Him in all forms of worship is the true spirit of religion.

This is the universal religion which the pantheistic Ibn Arabi preaches, a religion which comprises all religions and unites all beliefs. In his *Tarjumanu al-Ashwaq* he expresses this conviction,

> My heart has become a receptacle of every form; It is a pasture for gazelles and a convent for Christian monks, And a temple for idols, and pilgrims' Kaaba, And the Tablets of the Torah and the Book of the Quran. I follow the religion of love whichever way its camels take; For this is my religion and my faith.

The religion of love, according to Ibn Arabi, is religion in its widest and most universal sense. All worshippers do in fact worship God, although they appear to worship their particular gods. And since love is the essence of worship—for to worship is to love to the extreme—and since the objects of worship are nothing but the external manifestations of God, it follows that God is both the supremely beloved and the supremely worshipped One.

This brief discussion shows some of the ways in which the interpretations of Muslim theologians, philosophers, and mystics have contributed to the vitality of Islam throughout its long history, making their varied contributions to the development of Muslim thought and influencing Islamic practices.

Although they have often been considered as unorthodox by the leaders of Islam, their attempts to provide a rational basis for Islamic beliefs and a mystical basis for Islamic worship have for centuries enriched and stimulated the Muslim community.

7

# ISLAMIC BELIEFS

## MONOTHEISM: THE ONENESS OF ALLAH (TAWHID)

Allah, or God, is the centre of Muslim belief. Whereas certain religions focus on individuals, like Christianity focuses on Jesus (peace be upon him), Islam focuses solely on Allah. Although Muslims respect the divine prophets, the prophets-including Prophet Muhammad (peace be upon him and his family)-are still only servants of Allah.

> The Quran itself speaks of the oneness of God: "Allah has borne witness that there is no God but Him-and the angels, and those with knowledge also witness this. He is always standing firm on justice. There is no God but Him, the Mighty, the Wise." (3:18)

The oneness of Allah is not only a philosophical argument but is an affirmation that all human beings declared before their souls came into their bodies:

> [Remember] when your Lord brought forth the children of Adam from their loins and made them testify over themselves, saying, "Am I not your Lord?" They said, "Yes! We testify," lest you should say on the Day of Resurrection, "Verily, we were unaware of this." (7:172)

Such was the covenant that Allah made with all people at the time of creation regardless of whether these same people now claim to believe in God or not. At that time, they proclaimed His majesty, His sovereignty, His power, and His absolute oneness and transcendence.

Likewise, all people today, regardless of their origins, are naturally inclined towards the idea that God is one and without partner. The Quran tells Prophet Muhammad (peace be upon him):

> Set your face to the true religion [Islamic monotheism], the natural inclination (fitra) with which Allah has created mankind. [Let there be] no change in what Allah has made; that is the straight religion, but most people do not understand. (30:30)

## Describing God

One of the shortest chapters of the Quran, "The Oneness of God", ummarizes the nature of God in five verses:

> In the name of Allah, the most Gracious, the Most Merciful
>
> Say, He is Allah, the One
>
> Allah, the Eternal
>
> He begets not, nor was He begotten
>
> And there is nothing at all comparable to Him.

The most fundamental Islamic teachings about God are contained in these verses, i.e. that there is only one God Who is eternal, unique, and has no blood relation to any human beings. Different prophets also gave their own descriptions of God which are also related in the Quran. Prophet Abraham (peace be upon him) says: "My Lord is He Who gives life and causes death." (2:258) After him, Moses (peace be upon him), when confronting the Pharaoh, says: "Our Lord is He Who gave each thing its form and nature then guided it aright." (20:50) These two verses both describe Allah in His relation to human beings, but of course Allah's being extends far beyond His relation to mankind.

Imam 'Ali (peace be upon him) has also described Him thus:

> He who assigns to Him different conditions does not believe in His oneness, nor does he who likens Him grasp His reality. He who illustrates Him does not signify Him; he who points at Him and imagines Him does not mean Him. Everything that is known through itself has been created, and everything that exists by virtue of other things

is the effect of a cause. He works, but not with the help of instruments; He fixes measures, but not with the activities of thinking; He is rich, but not by acquisition. Time does not keep company with Him, and implements do not help Him. His being precedes time, His existence precedes non-existence, and His eternity precedes beginning. By His creating the senses, it is known that He has no senses. By the contraries in various matters, it is known that He has no contrary, and by the similarity between things it is known that there is nothing similar to Him. He has made light the contrary of darkness, brightness that of gloom, dryness that of moisture, and heat that of cold. He produces affection among inimical things.... He is not confined by limits nor counted by numbers. Material parts can surround things of their own kind, and organs can point out things similar to themselves.... Through them, the Creator manifests Himself to the intelligence, and through them He is guarded from the sight of the eyes.... He has not begotten anyone lest He be regarded as having been born. He has not been begotten, otherwise He would be contained within limits. He is too high to have sons.... Understanding cannot think of Him so as to give Him shape....

Allah expresses His own eternity and perpetuity Himself: "Every thing on earth shall perish, but the face of Allah will remain, full of majesty and honour." (55:26-27)

## THE 99 NAMES OF ALLAH

"And to Allah belong the most beautiful names, so call on Him by them." (7:180) Islamic tradition says that Allah has many different names representing different aspects of His being, and 99 of them are commonly recited together:

| English | Arabic |
|---|---|
| The Merciful | ar-rahim |
| The Beneficent | ar-rahmaan |
| The Sovereign | al-malik |
| The Holy | al-quddus |

| | |
|---|---|
| The Peace | as-salaam |
| The Guardian of Faith | al-mumin |
| The Protector | al-muhaymin |
| The Mighty | al-'aziz |
| The Compellor | al-jabbar |
| The Majestic | al-mutakabbir |
| The Creator | al-khaaliq |
| The Evolver | al-baari' |
| The Fashioner | al-musawwir |
| The Forgiver | al-ghaffar |
| The Subduer | al-qahhar |
| The Bestower | al-wahhab |
| The Provider | ar-razzaq |
| The Opener | al-fattah |
| The Knowing | al-'alim |
| The Constrictor | al-qaabid |
| The Abaser | al-khaafid |
| The Expander | al-baasit |
| The Honorer | al-muizz |
| The Exalter | ar-raafi' |
| The Hearing | as-sami' |
| The Dishonorer | al-mudhill |
| The Judge | al-hakam |
| The Seeing | al-basir |
| The Subtle | al-latif |
| The Kind | al-halim |
| The Just | al-'adl |
| The Aware | al-khabir |
| The All-Forgiving | al-ghafur |
| The Great | al-'azim |
| The High | al-'aliy |
| The Appreciative | ash-shakur |
| The Preserver | al-hafiz |
| The Immense | al-kabir |
| The Reckoner | al-hasib |
| The Maintainer | al-muqit |

| | |
|---|---|
| The Generous | al-karim |
| The Majestic | al-jalil |
| The Responsive | al-mujib |
| The Wise | al-hakim |
| The Watchful | ar-raqib |
| The All-Surrounding | al-waasi' |
| The Glorious | al-majid |
| The Loving | al-wadud |
| The Witness | ash-shahid |
| The Resurrector | al-baaith |
| The Truth | al-haqq |
| The Trustee | al-wakil |
| The Strong | al-qawi |
| The Firm | al-matin |
| The Praiseworthy | al-hamid |
| The Guardian | al-wali |
| The Originator | al-mubdi |
| The Reckoner | al-muhsi |
| The Giver of Life | al-muhyi |
| The Restorer | al-muid |
| The Creator of Death | al-mumit |
| The Living | al-hayy |
| The Self-Subsisting | al-qayyum |
| The Finder | al-waajid |
| The Noble | al-maajid |
| The Unique | al-waahid |
| The One | al-ahad |
| The Eternal | as-samad |
| The Able | al-qadir |
| The Powerful | al-muqtadir |
| The Expediter | al-muqaddim |
| The Delayer | al-muakhkhir |
| The First | al-awwal |
| The Last | al-aakhir |
| The Manifest | az-zaahir |
| The Hidden | al-baatin |

| | |
|---|---|
| The Governor | al-waali |
| The Exalted | al-muta'ali |
| The Source of Goodness | al-barr |
| The Acceptor of Repentance | at-tawwab |
| The Avenger | al-muntaqim |
| The Pardoner | al-'afuw |
| The Compassionate | ar-rauf |
| The Owner of Soverignty | maalik al-mulk |
| The Lord of Majesty Bounty | dhul jalaali wal-ikraam and |
| The Equitable | al-muqsit |
| The Gatherer | al-jaami' |
| The Self-Sufficient | al-ghani |
| The Enricher | al-mughni |
| The Preventer | al-mani' |
| The Distresser | ad-darr |
| The Benefitor | an-naafi' |
| The Light | an-nur |
| The Guide | al-haadi |
| The Incomparable | al-badi' |
| The Everlasting | al-baaqi |
| The Inheritor | al-waarith |
| The Guide to the Right Path | ar-rashid |
| The Patient | as-sabur |

## DIVINE JUSTICE ('ADL)

Anyone who believes in Islamic monotheism must believe in the Almighty's justice. Because Allah is just, He never wrongs His creatures, for injustice is an evil deed while He is far from doing evil. Because He is omniscient, He does not neglect anything, and because He is self-sufficient, He has no cause to wrong others. Since He owns everything, He does not need the actions of anyone. His wisdom also transcends the universe.

Thus, unlike some human beings, He has no cause for injustice:

> "He is always standing firm on justice. There is no God but Him, the Mighty, the Wise." (3:18)

"And your Lord does not deal unjustly with anyone." (18:49)

"We did not wrong them, but they wronged themselves." (16:118)

Just as Allah encourages human beings to emulate some of His attributes, such as being patient and forgiving, He also tells us to follow the way of justice. "Say: 'My Lord has enjoined upon me justice.'" (7:29) Although common people may falter in this area, none of the prophets of God or their successors ever committed any act of injustice.

Allah's justice embraces the entire universe. Whoever ponders over the existence of the universe and the order therein will not only observe the spread of Allah's justice over His entire creation but also each of its signs apparent in all aspects of nature--from the physical world to the biological world, and from the microcosmos to the macrocosmos. The justice of God is particularly visible in the fate and destiny of human beings, and in their freedom of choice.

Although Allah's justice encompasses everything, people should pray to Allah to treat them not with His justice but rather with His mercy, for if He treated people solely with His justice and punished them immediately for all of their sins, humanity would have perished a long time ago.

### Predestination or Free Will?

The question of man's predestination or freedom of choice has preoccupied mankind throughout the ages and continues to be discussed by Islamic philosophers and scholars. Ultimately, two schools of thought regarding this question have emerged. One, called the Compulsionists, holds that human beings have no freedom of choice whatsoever in life. Every decision people make, every word people say has been predestined since the time of creation. If someone is faithful, it is not he who decides to embrace the faith; if someone is unfaithful, it is not he who rejects the faith. All has been written.

The second school of thought, the Free Will school, declares that human beings are masters of their own acts. This notion is in concordance with the Quran, which states: "None will be wronged in anything, nor will you be requited anything except that which you used to do," (36:54) as well as: "The truth is from your Lord. So whomever wills, let him believe, and whoever wills, let him disbelieve." (18:29) From these two verses, it is clear that human beings have the freedom to act but must bear the moral responsibilities for their own actions. Furthermore, the acknowledgement of divine justice itself forces people to accept that their every action is not predestined.

The beginning of guidance is always from Allah, but the beginning of man's destruction is in his own erroneous opinions. "Whatever good reaches you is from Allah, but whatever evil befalls you is from yourself." (4:79)

## PROPHETHOOD (NUBUWWA)

The prophets were the people who received divine revelation. Allah has sent numerous prophets and messengers to humankind since the dawn of history. These prophets were of two types: "local" and "universal." While the local prophets were sent with specific messages to specific groups of people, the universal prophets were sent with messages and books for all of humankind. There were only five universal prophets, and their names were Noah, Abraham, Moses, Jesus, and Muhammad (may the peace of Allah be upon all of them).

A unique characteristic of all the prophets and messengers is that they were infallible-that is, they never committed any sin. The easiest way to see this is to consider that these people were the examples sent for humanity to follow, and so if they committed errors, people would be obliged to follow their errors, thereby making the prophets and messengers untrustable. Infallibility means protection, and, in Islamic terminology, means the spiritual grace of Allah enabling a person to abstain from sins by his own free will. This power of infallibility and sinlessness does not make a person incapable of committing sins; rather, he refrains from sins and mistakes by his own power and will.

Infallibility is essential since the job of the prophets and messengers is not only to convey the divine scriptures of Allah but also to lead and guide humanity towards the right path. Therefore, they have to be role models and perfect examples for mankind. This has basis in both the Quran and conventional wisdom; the Quran mentions infallibility 13 times. Allah says to the Satan: "Certainly you shall have no authority over My servants except those who follow you and go astray." (15:42) The Satan then says to Allah: "By Your might, then I will surely mislead them all, except Your chosen servants among them [the messengers and imams]."(38:82)

Not only did Prophet Muhammad (peace be upon him and his family) not commit any sins, but he was also never harsh to human beings or animals. Allah says: "And by the mercy of Allah you dealt with them [people] gently, and had you been severe and harsh-hearted, they would have broken away from you." (3:158)

In most societies, people with bad records would be ineligible to be presidential, governmental, or mayoral candidates since they would be expected to lead society and be good examples of righteousness and honesty. Unfortunately, as a campaign of distorting the image of the prophets of God, many distorted stories exist today, such as the stories in the present-day version of the Old Testament accusing Prophet David (peace be upon him) of adultery with Baathsheba, Prophet Noah (peace be upon him) getting drunk, Prophet Lot (peace be upon him) committing incest, and Prophet Moses (peace be upon him) committing adultery with the Ethiopian women. These are examples of the ethical wrongdoings and moral weaknesses that the enemies of Allah tried to ascribe to His pure messengers.

The Holy Quran speaks of the sins attributed to certain prophets such as Adam (peace be upon him). These verses should not be understood literally in the sense that Adam was committing a sin; allegorical verses are common in the Quran. Adam (peace be upon him) did not disobey the obligatory commands of Allah; the command that he did not honour was a recommended command, and, therefore, in the Islamic law, he cannot be considered to have committed a sin.

Although Allah preordained who the prophets were going to be, the prophets nonetheless had to strive for this position. The foremost example of this testing that the prophets had to endure can be seen in the life of Prophet Abraham (peace be upon him), the father of the prophets. Abraham (peace be upon him) was born into an idolatrous society, but by the purity of his nature he recognized that the idols his people worshipped were capable of nothing, neither harm nor good. So one day, when no one was present, he smashed all of them but the largest, and when the people came to him and asked who had destroyed their gods, he told them to ask the remaining statue if they really believed that their stone idols had power.

Although the people realized at that point that their idols were powerless, they didn't know how to respond, so out of shame and anger they cast Abraham (peace be upon him) into a huge fire. But Allah protected Abraham (peace be upon him) from the fire and confounded the plots of the polytheists.

After being tortured for and then saved by his faith in Allah, Abraham (peace be upon him) still had to undergo the hardest test of obedience to Allah-the direct order, from Allah, to sacrifice his son Ishmael.

This order came to him in a dream, and although sadness overwhelmed him, he was a strong believer in Allah and did not question it. Ishmael too accepted the command of Allah unquestioningly and allowed his father to lead him to a mountaintop to be sacrificed. His only request was that his father place him face down so that his father would not see his expression as he was being killed.

Abraham (peace be upon him) raised his blade, still ready to comply with the command of Allah. But just then came the revelation that this had only been a test, that God would not order Abraham (peace be upon him) to sacrifice his son, and that Abraham (peace be upon him) could sacrifice a sheep in his stead. This event is commemorated every year on a holiday called the Feast of Sacrifice ('eid al-adhaa) on which animals are killed and the meat distributed to the poor.

After passing these tests, Abraham (peace be upon him) became the leader of humankind as well as the father of the prophets of the three main monotheistic religions-Judaism, Christianity, and Islam. Although Allah sent prophets to every group of people on the earth, the Quran only mentions the names of 25 of them.

The first of them was Adam (peace be upon him), the father of humanity, and the last of them and the seal of the prophets was Prophet Muhammad (peace be upon him and his family).

### Why did Allah send different Prophets and different Religions?

The way of Allah is one, and because the final messenger, Prophet Muhammad (peace be upon him and his family), has come, there should be no dispute as to what is the right way to follow.

However, throughout history, different messengers with slightly different messages were sent to different peoples because the religious needs of humanity were growing and developing just as the human race was itself growing and developing, and also because different civilizations needed different types of guidance. Nevertheless, the source and basic message behind them was the same-namely, Allah the Exalted and Glorious.

Allah sent Moses (peace be upon him) with the Torah as a light and guidance for the Children of Israel (the Jews) along with many other prophets such as David, Solomon, and so on (peace be upon them). 1,500 years after Moses, Allah sent Jesus (peace be upon him), the son of Mary (peace be upon her), confirming the Torah and bringing the Gospel which has also been likened to guidance and light.

Finally, 600 years after Jesus (peace be upon him), Allah sent Prophet Muhammad (peace be upon him and his family) with the Quran to confirm all the messages before him and to complete the revelation of religion to mankind.

Since all the Judeo-Christian-Islamic prophets were sent sequentially, the question arises as to why Judaism, Christianity, and Islam now exist as separate religions.

The answer is that the followers of these religions, particularly Judaism and Christianity, corrupted the original teachings given to them and ended up making sects of their own rather than following the pure word of God. But as the Quran says:

For each of you, We have made a Law and a clear way. If Allah had willed, He would have made you one nation but that

He may test you in what He has given you. So strive as a race in good deeds. Your return is to Allah; then He will inform you about that which you used to differ. (5:48)

## THE LIFE OF PROPHET MUHAMMAD (PEACE BE UPON HIM AND HIS FAMILY)

In 6th-century CE Arabia, the majority of people were pagans. They lived in tribes, each with its own leader. Some were farmers, others traders, but many reared camels and raided other tribes for booty. It was into this society, in CE 570, that Prophet Muhammad (peace be upon him and his family) was born in Mecca. His parents died and he was looked after first by his grandfather and then by his uncle. As he grew up, Prophet Muhammad (peace be upon him and his family) became known as Prophet Muhammad (peace be upon him and his family) al-Amin, 'the trustworthy'. He worked for a wealthy older widow, Khadija, who, impressed with his honesty, asked him to marry her. He was twenty-five, and they remained married until her death twenty-five years later.

Prophet Muhammad (peace be upon him and his family) often used to go from the bustle of Mecca for periods of reflection in a cave outside the city. During one such time, when he was forty years old, he heard the voice of the angel Jibril giving him a command:

> Recite in the Name of your Lord who creates, Creates man from a clot. Recite! Your Lord is the Most Bountiful, Who taught the use of the pen, Taught humankind that which they knew not. (96:1-5)

Prophet Muhammad (peace be upon him and his family) repeated the words until he had learned them by heart. He rushed home and related his experience to his wife, who comforted and reassured him. Khadija and the Prophet's young cousin 'Ali (peace be upon him) were the first people to understand and accept that Allah had chosen 'the trustworthy one' to deliver his final guidance.

Prophet Muhammad (peace be upon him and his family) continued to receive revelations for over twenty years.

As time passed, it became clear to ever-increasing numbers of people that Prophet Muhammad (peace be upon him and his family) was indeed a Messenger of Allah. The least receptive were those powerful Makkans who trafficked in idols and slaves and benefited most from idol worship and the pilgrim trade. They treated Prophet Muhammad (peace be upon him and his family) with derision. Despite this, he continued to deliver the revelations of Allah's mercy and justice, which were welcomed by the poor and oppressed.

The Prophet (peace be upon him and his family), his family, and followers were driven from Mecca. For three years they sheltered in a valley outside the city in conditions of hardship and hunger. Narrowly escaping assassination in Mecca, the Prophet (peace be upon him and his family) traveled to Medina in CE 622. The migration from Mecca to Medina, known as the Hijrah, became the starting point of the Muslim calendar.

Prophet Muhammad (peace be upon him and his family) was very well received in Medina where he became head of what was to become the first Islamic state. In CE 630, Prophet Muhammad (peace be upon him and his family) and his followers entered Mecca. At the Kaaba, Prophet Muhammad (peace be upon him and his family) cleared the hundreds of idols from inside and proclaimed that truth had come and falsehood had vanished. He was 63 when he died, and by the time of his death the majority of people in Arabia had accepted Islam as their way of life.

The final verse of the Quran to be revealed to Prophet Muhammad (peace be upon him and his family), a few days before his death, was this: "Today I [Allah] have perfected for you your religion, completed my favour upon you, and have chosen for you Islam as your religion." (5:3)

## SUCCESSION TO THE PROPHET MUHAMMAD (PEACE BE UPON HIM AND HIS FAMILY) (IMAMA)

All of the prophets and messengers of God had successors, and just as Allah appointed His prophets and messengers for the guidance of mankind, He also appointed successors to the prophets and messengers as a matter of necessity. Abraham (peace be upon him) was succeeded by two of his sons, Isaac and Ishmael (peace be upon them), while Moses (peace be upon him) was succeeded by his brother Aaron (peace be upon him) and Jesus (peace be upon him) by two prophets whom the Quran mentions in the chapter called "Ya Sin". (36:13-14) Likewise, Prophet Muhammad (peace be upon him and his family) was succeeded by twelve distinguished successors, one after another. These successors were called imams and were appointed by Allah, not by humankind. The right to ordain imams belongs only to Almighty Allah, and the Quran speaks about this in many verses:

> "And remember when your Lord said to the angels, 'Verily I am going to place a successor (khalifa)." (2:30)
>
> Allah addressed Prophet David (peace be upon him) as such: "O David! Verily We have placed you as a successor on earth." (38:26) "And remember when the Lord of Abraham tried him with certain commands which he fulfilled; Allah said to him, 'Verily I am going to make you a leader (imam) of mankind.'" (2:124)
>
> Allah also attributes the right of appointing leaders to Himself: "We made from among them leaders, giving guidance under Our command." (32:24)

During his lifetime, Prophet Muhammad (peace be upon him and his family) specifically mentioned the names of the leaders that would come after him, that there would be twelve of them, and that all of them would be descended from a particular Arab tribe called Quraysh.

The twelve successors to Prophet Muhammad (peace be upon him and his family) are as follows:

Imam 'Ali ibn Abi Talib (600-661) Imam 'Ali (peace be upon him) was the Prophet's cousin and son-in-law and the one about whom he said: "I am the city of knowledge and 'Ali is its gate." He also said, "Whoever considers me his leader, 'Ali is also his leader." 110,000 people heard the Prophet (peace be upon him and his family) say this at a place called Ghadir Khum. Muslims and non-Muslims alike recognized Imam 'Ali (peace be upon him) for his wisdom, bravery, and justice. Many of his sayings and speeches have been preserved in a book called The Peak of Eloquence (Nahj al-Balagha). He was assassinated by members of a fringe movement while he was praying.

Fatima az-Zahra (562-580) Although not one of the successors, Fatima al-Zahra (peace be upon her) is included in this list because of her high status and importance. Fatima al-Zahra (peace be upon her) was the daughter of the beloved Prophet of Islam (peace be upon him and his family) from his respected wife Khadija. She was born in Mecca on the twentieth day of Jumaada al-Thaani (the sixth month of the Islamic calendar). Although he had several children, Fatima was his favourite, for she was carrying the light of the message of the Prophet (peace be upon him and his family) to the generations to come through her offspring. A chapter of the Quran was revealed about her:

> Verily We have granted you [Prophet Muhammad] al-kawthar. Therefore, turn in prayer to your Lord and sacrifice for Him. And he who makes you angry-he will be cut off from offspring.

She and her father had a mutual attachment; 'Aisha, one of the wives of the Prophet (peace be upon him and his family), has said: "I never saw a person who so resembled her father in speech, movements, and gestures more than Fatima, and once she goes to visit her father, he stands, takes her hand, kisses it, and places her in his own seat." Fatima was so emotionally and spiritually close to her father that he declared: "Fatima is part of me. Whoever angers her angers me, and she is the mother of her father." Fatima proved to be the best daughter to her father, mother for her four children (Hasan, Husain, Zaynab, and Um Kalthoum), and the ideal wife for her husband Imam 'Ali (peace be upon him). She was the perfect example of a virtuous, righteous lady in Islam. She set many examples in her social and political life. As a result of the conflict over power after the demise of the Holy Prophet (peace be upon him and his family), Fatima al-Zahra (peace be upon her) died at the age of 18 years.

### Imam Hasan ibn 'Ali (625-670)

Imam Husain ibn 'Ali (626-680): Imam Husain (peace be upon him) revolted against the tyrant of his time, Yazid the son of Muawiyah. He left his hometown of Medina to go to the city of Mecca and then with 72 of his followers and close family members to Iraq where he was brutally massacred on the day of Ashura in the city of Karbala, 60 miles to the south of Baghdad. Imam Husain (peace be upon him) stood for truth, sacrificed himself for truth and justice, and fought corruption and aggression. The battle of Karbala represents the battle between truth and falsehood, good versus evil, and justice versus aggression, oppression, and tyranny. Therefore, he became the beacon of light for all free people in this universe, shook the foundations of the Muslim nation with his martyrdom, and steered the consciousness of the Muslim people at that time. Hundreds of revolutions and revolts followed his martyrdom until the corrupt empire of Bani Umayyah collapsed. Imam Husain (peace be upon him) still plays a very significant role in the life of the Muslims in their endeavour to fight injustice and deviation in all societies.

### Imam 'Ali Ibn al-Husain (659-713)

### Imam Muhammad Al-Baqir (676-733)

Imam Jafar as-Sadiq (702-765): Imam Jafar al-Sadiq (peace be upon him) was the son of Muhammad al-Baqir (peace be upon him) and was the sixth imam of the school of the ahl al-bayt. He was born on the seventeenth day of Rabi' al-Awwal (the third month of the Islamic calendar) in the city of Medina. He learned from his father the sciences of religion and the teachings of Islam and became the authority of jurisprudents, scholars, and preachers after the martyrdom of his father.

He made the mosque of Medina a university from which to spread Islamic ideology and graduated hundreds of scholars versed in Islamic sciences and prophetic traditions.

Scholars and preachers gave their testimonies acknowledging his great standing and abundant knowledge. One of them, Sibt al-Jawzi has said, "Never have I seen scholars less knowledgeable in the presence of a man like al-Sadiq." The men of knowledge and piety saw in Imam Jafar al-Sadiq (peace be upon him) a leader, a scholar, and an unmatched educator. He was also a great social personality and an effective political force in the leading political circles.

Imam al-Sadiq (peace be upon him) taught two of the leaders of the other Islamic schools of jurisprudence: Abu Hanifa (Nu'man ibn Thabit) and Malik ibn Anas. Imam al-Sadiq (peace be upon him) uttered thousands of hadith (Prophetic traditions) regarding every facet of life.

He extensively discussed Islamic ethics, mannerisms, integrity, goodness of character, and acts of worship in addition to jurisprudence and debated with leaders of other schools of thought.

Imam al-Sadiq (peace be upon him) was poisoned by the caliph of his time and was buried in the cemetery of al-Baqi' in Medina.

*Imam Musa al-Kazim (746-799)*

*Imam 'Ali ar-Rida (765-818)*

*Imam Muhammad al-Jawad (811-835)*

*Imam 'Ali al-Hadi (827-868)*

*Imam Hasan al-Askari (846-874)*

Imam Muhammad al-Mahdi (869-present): Imam al-Mahdi is the last of the imams of the people on earth, and with him the line of succession to the Holy Prophet (peace be upon him and his family) ends. Because of the necessity of having a representative from Allah present on the earth, he still-by the will of Allah-lives in this world, but he does not live in public view. He will, however, reappear towards the end of human civilization at a time when the world has been filled with evil and injustice to restore order and make justice prevail.

These imams were the authorities of Allah among mankind. Like the Holy Prophet (peace be upon him and his family), they were all special personalities in matters of knowledge, forbearance, morality, and justice.

## The Family of the Prophet (Ahl al-Bayt)

The ahl al-bayt are the immediately family of the Prophet Muhammad (peace be upon him and his family), namely: his daughter Fatima al-Zahra; his cousin, son-in-law, and first successor Imam 'Ali; and his grandchildren Hasan and Husain (peace be upon them). The purity of these five is spoken of in the Quran: "Allah only wishes to remove all uncleanliness from you, O People of the House (ahl al-bayt), and to make you as pure as possible." (33:33) Like the prophets and the prophets' successors, these five were infallible, free from all sin or error.

Near the end of his life, Prophet Muhammad (peace be upon him) said: "It is probable that I will be called soon, and I will respond. So I leave behind me among you two weighty things: the Book of Allah [the Quran], and my Ahl al-Bayt. Verily, Allah, the Merciful, the Aware, has informed me that these two will never be separated from each other until they meet me at the fountain in Heaven called Kawthar." The Prophet (peace be upon him and his family) has also said: "The parable of my ahl al-bayt is similar to that of Noah's ark. Whoever embarks on it will certainly be rescued, but whoever opposes the boarding of it will surely be drowned." The necessity of taking hold of both things that the Prophet (peace be upon him and his family) left behind cannot be overemphasized; those who choose to follow the Quran but not the guidance of the ahl al-bayt will invariably go astray.

As a rule, the prophets of Allah did not ask any reward for the pain and suffering they endured while attempting to guide mankind. In fact, this refusal to accept compensation can be seen as the mark of a prophet: "Obey those who ask no reward from you and who have themselves received guidance." (36:21) However, by the command of Allah, Prophet Muhammad (peace be upon him and his family) made one slight exception; although he refused to accept anything for himself, he was commanded to say: "I do not ask you for any reward except love for my relatives [the ahl al-bayt]." (42:23) Love for the Prophet's ahl al-bayt does not benefit the Prophet himself (peace be upon him and his family) so much as it does the one who approaches them with kindness and loyalty and in return derives knowledge, guidance, and blessings from Allah.

Imam 'Ali (peace be upon him) has spoken about the ahl al-bayt:

> We, the ahl al-bayt, possess the doors of wisdom and light of governance. Beware that the paths of religion are one and its highways are straight. He who follows them achieves and secures the aim and objective. And he who stands away from them goes astray and incurs repentance.

The example of the descendants of Muhammad-peace and blessing of Allah be upon him and his descendants-is like that of stars in the sky. When one star sets another one rises.

We are lights of the heavens and the earth and the ships of salvation. We are the repository of knowledge, and towards us is the homecoming of all matters. Through our Mahdi (the final successor to the Prophet) all arguments shall be refuted, and he is the seal of the imams, the deliverer of the ummah (the Muslim nation), and the extremity of the light. Happy are those who hold onto our handle and are brought together upon our love.

## THE DAY OF JUDGEMENT AND THE RESURRECTION (QIYAMAT)

Approximately 1,200 verses of the Quran speak of life after death and the Day of Resurrection, as do a vast number of sayings related from Prophet Muhammad and his successors (peace be upon all of them). This number reveals the importance and significance of life after death and emphasizes that the life of the human being does not end at death but in fact continues afterwards towards a new life-indeed, its true life. Allah placed human beings on the earth to test them, and so different people live for different lengths of time before they die and their souls are separated from their bodies. Their souls then live on, facing the grave and the questioning therein. After that, the souls return to their bodies which will be resurrected on the Day of Judgement, on which day they will receive whatever they deserve according to their beliefs and deeds in life.

Some people will go to Heaven, also called the Garden, or the Paradise. Others will go to Hell, oftentimes called the Fire. And a select few will be brought into a state of nearness to God. Both Heaven and Hell have different levels; the worst of people will be in the lowest depths of Hell, while the best of them will be in the highest parts of Heaven.

### Death and Life after Death

And they ask you concerning the spirit. Say: "The spirit, it is one of the things, the knowledge of which is only with my Lord, and of knowledge, you mankind have been given only a little. (17:85) . Although humanity has been permitted to know only a little about life after death right now, the Holy Quran still reveals some of the secrets surrounding the soul. The Quran says:

> It is Allah who takes away the souls at the time of their death, and those that die not during their sleep. He keeps

those souls for which He has ordained death and sends the rest for a term appointed. Verily, in this are signs for people who think deeply. (39:42)

The soul will be buried along with the body in the grave. It could get permission from Allah to depart from the grave, but it must go back to it again. Each individual, if faithful, faces two paradises after death, or if he is unfaithful and a sinner, two hells. One of them is for the souls before the Day of Judgement, and the second is the permanent abode.

Once Prophet Jesus (peace be upon him) sent two messengers to the city of Antioch to call for monotheism and the worshipping of Allah. One of the men of that town embraced the faith and followed them, so the king of the land ordered that righteous man to be killed. When he died, he said: "Verily I have believed in your Lord. So listen to me. It was said to him when the disbelievers killed him, 'Enter paradise.' He said, Would that my people knew what my Lord Allah has forgiven me for and made me one of the honoured ones.'" (36:25-27) The paradise that he had entered was of the kind, called barzakh, that the soul lives in before the Day of Judgement; on the Day of Judgement everyone will know the fate of everyone else, and there will be no need, as above, to tell others.

The descriptions of both types of hellfire are very vivid and painful: "Evil torment encompassed Pharaoh's people-the fire: they are exposed to it morning and afternoon, and on the day when the Hour will be established." (40:46)

Islam teaches that the parting of the soul is accompanied with severe pain. The moment of death has been described:

Nay! When the soul reaches the collarbone, and it will be said, "Who can cure him and save him from death?" and he, the dying person, will conclude that it is the time of departing, and he is shrouded; the drive on that day will be to your Lord. (75:26-30)

Remember that the two recording angels receive each human being after attaining the age of puberty, one sitting on the right and one on the left, to note his actions. Not a word does he utter but there is a watcher sitting by him to record it. And the stupor of death will come in truth; this is what you have been avoiding.

And the trumpet will be blown; that will be the day whereof warning had been given, and every person will come forth with an angel to drive him and an angel to bear witness. It will be said to the sinners: "Indeed, you were heedless of this. Now We have removed your covering, and sharp is your sight this day." (50:17-22)

But for the true believers, the departure of the soul will be peaceful:

It will be said to the pious: "O you in complete rest and satisfaction, come back to your Lord well-please yourself and well-pleasing unto Him. Enter then among my honoured servants, and enter my Paradise." (89:27-30)

## REPENTANCE AND FORGIVENESS

Repentance is the giving up of sin and is the best way of expressing regret for having committed one. It involves both sincerely regretting having committed the particular sin and then resolving never to do it again. Repentance is the source of and means to success: "Turn to Allah, O Believers, that you may be successful." (24:31) No matter how grievous a person's sin may be, the forgiveness of Allah is greater, and no one should be ashamed to turn towards Allah in repentance because Allah can erase the sins of whomever He pleases.

Say: "O My servants who have transgressed against themselves, despair not of the mercy of Allah; verily, Allah forgives all sins. Verily, He is the Forgiving, the Merciful. (39:53)

Tell My servants that I am the Forgiving, the Merciful. (15:49)

Will they not turn to Allah and ask His forgiveness? Allah is the Forgiving, the Merciful. (5:74)

Your Lord is full of forgiveness for mankind in spite of their wrongdoing. (13:6)

Despite His ability to destroy mankind if he so willed, the main characteristics of Allah are forgiveness and mercifulness, and for this reason Muslims begin nearly every action, speech, or endeavour with the words, "In the name of Allah, the most Merciful, the most Compassionate." Repentance is of benefit both now and during the Hereafter. Prophet Muhammad (peace be upon him and his family) has narrated that repenting brings an increase of wealth, protection from danger, and an easing of hardships and difficulties. Furthermore, it has been said that the fastest way to attain nearness to Allah is to humble the self before Allah and admit to wrongdoing. The benefits of repentance for the next life are obvious-entrance into Paradise and safety from the Hellfire.

Repentance will be accepted up until the moment of death. Prophet Muhammad (peace be upon him and his family) once said that if a person seeks repentance one year before dying, Allah will accept it. Even if a person seeks repentance one day before dying, Allah will accept it. Then he pointed to his throat and said that even if someone seeks repentance before his soul reaches here, Allah will accept it.

Nonetheless, repentance should be done as soon as possible and should not be delayed; this point has been emphasized again and again in the Islamic tradition. Imam 'Ali says: "How numerous are the procrastinators who postpone [repenting and doing good deeds] until death overtakes them!"

Repentance should be done in secrecy and privacy. People can establish a direct link to Allah while seeking repentance without the necessity of a third person interfering and in fact should not let others know about their sins. Prophet Muhammad (peace be upon him and his family) once told Imam 'Ali (peace be upon him): "O 'Ali, blessed is he whom Allah looks upon while he is weeping for the sin that none is aware of except Allah."

In addition to not revealing his own sins, every person must conceal the faults of his brother or sister in religion to preserve that person's honour and society. That person's faults may be dealt with personally and privately but must not be spread among society.

A person who sincerely repents is loved by Allah and is as if he or she had never committed any sins at all. Imam al-Baqir (peace be upon him) has said: "He who repents of his sins is as one who has not any burden of sin." But repentance must be sincere; Allah knows who sincerely regrets misdeeds and who is just saying words. A person came to Imam 'Ali (peace be upon him) and said, "Astaghfirullah, I seek Allah's forgiveness," and the Imam (peace be upon him) replied:

Do you know what asking Allah's forgiveness is? It is a word that stands on six supports. The first is to repent over the past. The second is to make a firm determination never to revert to it. The third is to discharge all the rights of people so that you may meet Allah quite clean with nothing to account for. The fourth is to fulfill every obligation which you ignored in the past so that you may now be just with it. The fifth is to aim at the flesh grown as a result of unlawful earning so that you may melt it by grief of repentance till the skin touches the bone and a new flesh grows between them. And the sixth is to make the body taste the pain of obedience as you previously made it taste the sweetness of disobedience. On such an occasion, you may say, "I seek Allah's forgiveness."

## RELIGIOUS TEXTS

### The Quran

The Quran is the last in a series of divine books revealed by Allah to mankind through the prophets. The Holy Quran was revealed to Prophet Muhammad (peace be upon him and his family) over a period of 23 years and consists of 114 chapters arranged from longest to shortest. Its length compares to that of the New Testament. The revelations were written down by a group of people appointed by the Prophet (peace be upon him and his family) and, after his death, first compiled by Imam 'Ali (peace be upon him).

The Quran sheds light on many different aspects of life-legal, moral, social, political, economic, philosophical, mystical, and scientific-and also contains stories of previous prophets. "We have sent down to you the Book as an exposition of everything-a guidance, a mercy, and glad tidings for those who have submitted themselves to Allah as Muslims." (16:89) Less rigid than poetry but more beautiful than prose, its peculiar music transcends all other forms of writing. It speaks only the truth, and its directives are universal for all places and times. In reality, it is the completion of the earlier revelations, such as the Old and New Testaments, and is the only divine revelation to exist in its original unchanged form: "Verily, it is We Who have sent down the Quran, and surely We will guard it from corruption." (15:9) From the time of the

Prophet (peace be upon him and his family) until today, not one word of the Quran has been edited, altered, added, omitted, lost, distorted, or otherwise changed.

The Quran plays an important role in Muslim life. It constantly reminds Muslims of their duties, rights, obligations, and destiny. Muslims are asked to study, memorize, ponder, and reflect on the Quran and then to implement its teachings. The chapters of the Quran contain the supreme divine wisdom which is meant for all seekers of truth-ordinary people, scholars, specialists, old, young, Muslims, and non-Muslims. It addresses all mankind; specific verses even clarify this fact by beginning with the words, "O mankind!" The Quran satisfies people with its symphony of words, its science, its narrations and intellectual discourse, and fascinates them with its richness and depth.

### Science and the Quran

Many scientific facts and realities are present in the Quran, which is the only religious book not to contradict science. Creation is described on the embryological and cosmological levels:

"And indeed We created man out of an extract of clay. Thereafter, We made him as mixed drops of the male and female fluids and lodged him in a safe lodging (womb of the mother). Then We made the mixed drops into a clot (a piece of thick coagulated blood). Then We made the clot into a little lump of flesh. Then We made out of that little lump of flesh bones. Then We clothed the bones with flesh. And then We brought it forth as another creation. So blessed be Allah, the best of creators." (23:12-14)

A careful comparison of this verse with the actual details of embryological development will reveal no contradictions. The creation of life, the earth, and the universe is also described in a way that parallels modern scientific theory:

"Do not those who disbelieve know that the heavens and the earth were joined together as one united piece, then We parted them? And We have made from water every living thing. Will they then not believe? And We have placed on the earth firm mountains, lest it should shake with them, and We placed therein broad highways for them to pass through that they may be guided, and We have made the heaven a roof, safe, and well-guarded. Yet they turn away from its signs. And He it is Who has created the night and the day, and the sun and the moon, each in an orbit floating" (21:30-33)

Human beings are asked to ponder the creation of the universe and consider their role therein: Verily, in the creation of the heavens and the earth, and in the alternation of night and day there are indeed signs for men of understanding-those who remember Allah always, standing, sitting, and lying down on their sides, and think deeply about the creation of the heavens and the earth, saying, "O Lord! You have not created all this without purpose! Glory be to You! Give us salvation from the torment of the fire." (3:190)

Are you more difficult to create or the heavens above? (79:27)

Many of the chapters are named after cosmological objects such as "The Star" and "The Sun", the latter of which begins:

By the sun and its brightness, and by the moon as it follows it, and by the day as it shows up in the sun's brightness, and by the night as it conceals it, and by the heavens and Him who built it, and by the earth and Him who spread it....

Although the people of the Prophet's time knew nothing about the lifetimes or mechanisms of the sun and stars, the Quran refers to the fact that stars exist for a fixed period of time: And the sun runs on its fixed course for a term appointed. That is the decree of the Almighty, the Omniscient. And the moon, We have measured for it mansions to traverse till it returns like the old dried curved date-stalk. It is not for the sun to overtake the moon, nor does the night outstrip the day. They all swim each in an orbit. (36:38)

Even the expansion of the universe is alluded to: "With power did We construct the heavens; verily, We are able to expand the vastness of space thereof." (51:47)

The end of this universe, too, is described: And remember the day when We will roll up the heavens like a scroll rolled up for books. As We began the first creation, We shall repeat it. It is a promise binding upon Us. Truly, We shall do it. (21:104)

When the sun has wound around and lost its light and has been overthrown, and when the stars shall fall, and when the mountains shall be made to pass away... And when the seas shall become a blazing far or shall overflow.... (81:1-3,6)

When the Heaven is cleft asunder, and when the stars have fallen and scattered, and when the seas have burst forth.(82:1-3)

When the Event befalls-and there can be no denying its befalling-it will bring low some, and others it will exalt. When the earth will be shaken with a terrible shaking, and the mountains will be powdered to dust so that they will become floating dust particles.... (56:1-6)

And they ask you concerning the mountains. Say, "My Lord will blast them and scatter them as particles of dust; then He shall leave it as a smooth, level plain. You will see therein nothing crooked or curved." (20:105-107)

The Quran does not contradict science because Allah Who revealed the Quran is the same Allah Who made this creation.

### The Qualities of the Quran

And know that this Quran is an adviser who never deceives, a leader who never misleads, and a narrator who never speaks a lie. No one will sit beside this Quran but that when he rises he will achieve one addition or one diminution-addition in his guidance and elimination in his (spiritual) blindness. You should also know that no one will need any thing after (guidance from) the Quran and no one will be free from want before (guidance from) the Quran. Therefore, seek cure from it for your ailments and seek its assistance in your distresses. It contains a cure for the biggest diseases, namely, unbelief, hypocrisy, revolt, and misguidance. Pray to Allah through it and turn to Allah with its love. Do not ask the people through it. There is nothing like it through which the people should turn to Allah, the Sublime.

### The Dua, or Supplications to God

Supplications and prayers (*dua*) focus on the idea that human beings are in constant need of God. Even those who reach the peak of wealth, knowledge, strength, and dignity still are in need of God. The word *dua* itself means to call out to God, and *dua* is of equal importance to those inflicted by calamities and hardships and to those living in comfort and abundance. Speaking with Allah through *dua* defends against adversity and tribulation and leads to salvation and relief. Islam encourages its followers to offer *dua* constantly, either using their own words, directly from the heart, or else repeating some of the beautiful words that have been left behind by the Prophet (peace be upon him and his family) and his successors (peace be upon them).

Allah has guaranteed His servants that He will answer their prayers:

When My servants ask you concerning Me, I am indeed close to them. I listen to the prayer of every suppliant when he calls upon Me. Let them also with a will listen to My call and believe in Me that they walk in the right way. (2:186)

And your Lord says, "Call on me, I will answer your prayer." (40:60)

### Dua Kumail

A man named Kumail ibn Ziyad once asked Imam 'Ali (peace be upon him) for a way to approach Allah. In response, Imam 'Ali (peace be upon him) gave him this prayer and told him to recite it every day, if he could, or else once a week, or even once a year-and if reciting it once a year was too difficult, then to recite it at least once in his lifetime. Muslims usually recite it once a week together on Thursday night:

In the name of Allah, the Beneficent, the Merciful

O Allah, I ask You by Your Mercy which embraces all things,

By Your Strength, through which You dominate all things, towards which all things are humble, and before which all things are lowly;

By Your Invincibility, through which You overwhelm all things;

By Your Might, which nothing can resist;

By Your Greatness, which has filled all things;

By Your Power, which towers over all things;

By Your Face, which subsists after annihilation of all things;

By Your Names, which have filled the foundations of all things;

By Your Knowledge, which encompasses all things; and

By the Light of Your Face, through which all things are illumined!

O Light! O All-Holy!

O First of the first and Last of the Last!

O Allah, forgive me the sins which tear apart safeguards!

O Allah, forgive me the sins which bring down adversities!

O Allah, forgive me the sins which alter blessings!

O Allah, forgive me the sins which hold back supplication!

O Allah, forgive me the sins which dash all hopes!

O Allah, forgive me the sins which bring about tribulation!

O Allah, forgive me ever sin I have committed and every mistake I have made!

O Allah, verily I seek nearness to You through remembrance of You, I seek intercession from You with Yourself, and I ask You through Your Munificence, to bring me nearer to Your Mercy, to bless me with gratitude to You and to inspire me with Your remembrance....

# 8

# OTHER ISLAMIC ISSUES

## LEADERSHIP OF THE MUSLIMS AFTER PROPHET MUHAMMAD (PEACE BE UPON HIM AND HIS FAMILY)

The Quran emphasizes the role and significance of leadership in Islam. Allah states: "And remember the day on which we will call together all human beings with their leaders (imams)." (17:71)

Therefore, Prophet Muhammad (peace be upon him and his family) was very keen on appointing a successor after himself by the command of his Lord. Allah commands the Prophet (peace be upon him and his family): "O Prophet! Proclaim what has been revealed to you from your Lord [the succession of Imam 'Ali], for if you do not, you will not have conveyed His message, and Allah will protect you from the people." (5:67)

This event has been remembered as the event of Ghadir Khum, which was the name of a place intersecting Mecca and Medina, and occurred when the Prophet (peace be upon him and his family)was concluding his Hajj rites and heading back with 110,000 companions. When he received the command of Allah, he immediately appointed Imam 'Ali (peace be upon him) as his successor after his death. In approval, the Quran says: "This day, I have perfected your religion for you, completed my favour on you, and have chosen for you Islam as your religion." (5:3)

All the companions of the Prophet (peace be upon him and his family) paid allegiance to Imam 'Ali (peace be upon him) and accepted him as the first caliph after the Holy Prophet (peace be upon him and his family). However, only 70 days after this monumental incident, the Prophet Muhammad (peace be upon him and his family) left this life, and the first setback to his teachings occurred when the Muslims did not honour their allegiance to Allah to accept Imam 'Ali (peace be upon him) as the first caliph. Confusion and disarray overtook the Muslims regarding who should succeed the Prophet (peace be upon him and his family) as leader of the Muslim community. In a hasty meeting at Saqifa Bani Saida in Medina, Abu Bakr assumed leadership (632-634), followed by 'Umar ibn al-Khattab (634-644), 'Uthman ibn 'Affan (644-656), and finally 'Ali ibn Abi Talib (656-661).

After the khilafa of 'Ali (peace be upon him), two dynasties followed--the Umayyids and the Abbasids--before massive political changes overtook the Islamic world.

### Social Life in Islam

Islam places tremendous emphasis on the social aspect of life. The Islamic practices have not only spiritual dimensions but also social ones. For example, Islam encourages people to perform their daily prayers in congregation; Prophet Muhammad (peace be upon him and his family) has said: "One prayer of a man in congregation is worthier than his forty years of prayers at home alone." Praying in congregation strengthens the ties between people by giving them the opportunity to interact with each other and discuss their issues in a holy place. Once a blind man came to the Prophet (peace be upon him and his family) and said that there was no one to take him to the mosque to attend the congregational prayer.

Prophet Muhammad (peace be upon him and his family) told him to stretch a thread from his house to the mosque and use it to go to the mosque to attend the congregational prayer. Similarly, fasting has many social aspects: it causes Muslims to feel the starvation and the agony of the poor and deprived in society and encourages them to extend their hands in help towards them. The Hajj undoubtedly is the largest religious and social convention bringing millions of people from around the globe into one arena to strengthen their ties, develop their skills, and exchange ideas and opinions as to how to improve their situations. Khums and zakaat (charity) also play an important social role in Islam by causing Muslims to think that they themselves are responsible for bridging the gap between the rich and the poor as well as for sharing their own wealth with the needy and disadvantaged in society. Enjoining the good and forbidding the evil is a social responsibility which falls on the shoulders of each and every individual in the Islamic society to promote goodness, kindness, peace and justice and to fight oppression, corruption, and evil. Therefore, Islam is truly a social religion.

## Marriage and Family Life

Another aspect of Islamic sociality is marriage and establishing families. Islam encourages its followers to get married and avoid celibacy; Prophet Muhammad (peace be upon him and his family) has said: "The person who marries gains half of his faith; then he must fear of Allah for the next remaining half." In another saying, the Holy Prophet has said: "He who wishes to be clean and purified when he meets Allah should marry and have a spouse."

The Quran describes the union between man and woman:

> "And among His signs is that he created for you spouses from among yourselves that you may dwell in tranquility with them, and He has put love and mercy between your hearts. Verily, in that are signs for those who reflect." (30:21)

This verse establishes the three pillars of a successful marriage. First, it should provide emotional and social shelter ("dwell in tranquility") whereby the husband and the wife find stability and financial, spiritual, emotional, and social security. The second pillar of a successful marriage is the love between the spouses. Marriage which is not based on love is apt to fail at any time. And the third pillar is the mercy between the spouses which leads to mutual understanding, appreciation, respect, and care for each other.

Although heavily discouraged, divorce is permissible in Islam. It exists as a safety valve for a failed marriage which has no possibility of progress or development. Allah does not want a couple to remain in misery and sustain emotional, physical, and financial damage. Thus, Allah explains the laws and rules of divorce in a chapter of the Quran called "Divorce." Islam encourages reconciliation between the spouses, and their families and friends have the responsibility to help them with this as much as possible, but if this process ultimately fails then the last resort is divorce. After divorce, there is a waiting period for women to consider their life and the fate of their children. Most people go back to their spouses sometime during this waiting period, but if it elapses and the two people show no interest in returning to each other, then the divorce will be finalized.

Part of Islamic social life is to have regard for kinship; he who wishes his sustenance to be increased and his death day to be delayed should pay attention to his kinsfolk. Kindness and respect for one's parents holds a high place in Islam:

The Lord has decreed that you worship none but Him, and that you be kind to your parents, whether one or both of them attains old age in your life. Say not to them a word of contempt nor repel them, but address them in terms of honour, and out of kindness lower to them the wing of humility and say, "My Lord, bestow on them Thy mercy, even as they cherished me in childhood." (23:24)

Respect and kindness towards parents is as important as worship. Imam al-Sadiq (peace be upon him) has said: "He who glares at his parents with wrathful eyes, although they have been unjust to him, Allah will not accept his prayers unless he repents." Respecting one's mother is particularly important; the Prophet (peace be upon him and his family) said: "Treat kindly your mother. Treat kindly your mother. Treat kindly your mother, and be kind to your father."

Imam al-Sadiq (peace be upon him) has narrated: He who wishes Allah, Almighty and Glorious, to lighten the agonies of death should have regard for his kinship and treat his parents with goodness. Then Allah will make the agonies of death easy for him, and he will not be stricken by poverty in his life at all.

In general, human beings should all serve one another whether they are related or not. Prophet Muhammad (peace be upon him and his family) has said: "He who decreases a grief out of the agonies for his Muslim brother, Allah will decrease for him a grief out of the agonies of the hereafter." He (peace be upon him and his family) also said: "People are the dependants of Allah for sustenance. So the most beloved person with Allah is the one who is helpful to the dependents of Allah and makes the family members of a house happy." As a social responsibility, Islam also encourages its followers to help the needy; Imam al-Sadiq (peace be upon him) has said:

Whoever satiates a hungry believer so that the one is satisfied fully, neither a human being among people nor a near-stationed angel nor a divine messenger knows how great his reward is in the Hereafter except Allah, the Lord of the Worlds.

And

Feeding a hungry Muslim is among the means of forgiveness.

Even those who are not indigent should still be helped in any way possible: "He who is referred to by his Muslim brother [to borrow] but does not give him a loan, Allah will forbid him from entering Paradise on the day when the righteous will be recompensed."

## Women in Islam

Islam equalizes men and women on the following issues: creation, religious obligations, honour and dignity. However, there are natural differences in the peculiarities of each gender. The female as a mother differs in her personality and peculiarities from the man as a father. For each one of them, there is a specified message in life.

The Holy Quran declares that men and women are born equal. It gives women such rights as owning property, engaging in businesses, choosing a husband, claiming inheritance, receiving education, and being treated with respect. An entire chapter of the Quran (chapter 4) discusses women's' rights in the society. It starts by addressing people: "O Mankind! Be dutiful to your Lord Who created you from a single soul, and He created its mate out of it, and from them both He created many men and women."

Some of the verses equalizing men and women are as follows:

There is a share for men and a share for women from what is left by parents and those nearest related, whether the property be small or large (5:7)

O You who believe, you are forbidden to inherit women against their will, and you should not treat them with harshness, and live with them honourably. If you dislike them, it may be that you dislike a thing and that Allah brings through it a great deal of good. (4:19)

For men there is reward for what they have earned, and for women there is reward for what they have earned. (4:32)

Whoever works righteousness, whether male or female, while he or she is a true believer, verily to him We will give a good life in this world, with respect, contentment, and lawful provision, and We shall certainly pay them a reward in proportion to the best of what they used to do. (16:97)

Islam grants women full political, financial, social, and educational rights in society. Women have the right to vote in Islam, and to participate in the democratic process. "O Prophet! When believing women come to you to give you political and religious allegiance... then accept their allegiance, and ask Allah to forgive them; verily, Allah is Oft-Forgiving, most Mericiful." (60:12) Women should also have the full right to choose their own husbands without pressure or intimidation. Arranged marriages in the sense of women being dragged into marriages that they are unaware of or dislike are unlawful in Islam.

Women have the right to participate in the educational and cultural activities as well as religious and spiritual endeavours. No field is closed to women unless it interferes with their dignity, respect, and chastity in society. Therefore, Islam does forbid women to display their attractions and physical appearance in society and calls for modesty and conservatism in their behaviour and dress, as well as loyalty to the family, ideals which Islam also enjoins upon men as well. Women are instructed to cover modestly which includes covering the hair as well as the rest of the body except the hands and the face.

Islam has laid down fundamental, universal rights for humanity which are to be observed and respected in all circumstances. These rights are those which were specified and granted by Allah and apply to all human beings, not just Muslims. An integral part of the Islamic faith is to accept, recognize, and enforce these human rights. The verdict in the Quran is unequivocal for those who fail to do so: "Those who do not judge by what God has sent down are the disbelievers." (5:44)

The rights guaranteed by Islam and the Quran include: the right to life, the right to safety, respect for women's honour and dignity, the right to a basic standard of life, the right to individual freedom, the right to justice, and the inherent equality of human beings.

## Mosques (Masjid)

Mosques are places of worship used by Muslims. Islam encourages people to perform their prayers in mosques and also encourages people to participate in building mosques. Prophet Muhammad (peace be upon him and his family) has said: "Whoever builds a mosque, Allah will build for him a house in Paradise." The mosque plays a vital role in Muslim life; in addition to the five daily congregational prayers and the recommended prayers, the mosque also accommodates Muslims during the Friday noon prayers and on the 'eid holidays. Therefore, the mosque is considered a sacred place, and it should not be sold or defiled, and men and women who are ritually impure may not enter.

The first mosque built by Prophet Muhammad (peace be upon him and his family) was called Kaaba and was located in the outskirts in the city of Medina, while the first house of worship built on earth was al-masjid al-haram, the sacred mosque in Mecca. This mosque is the holiest of the mosques, the second holiest being the Prophet's Mosque in Medina which was built after the Prophet's migration from Mecca to Medina.

Mosques have many distinctive features. There are the musallah, or prayer hall; the minbar, or pulpit, where the preacher or imam stands to deliver his sermon; the mihrab, the niche which faces the direction of the Kaaba in Makka (al-qiblah); and also there are minarets and domes from which the call to prayers is raised.

Before entering mosques, the shoes must be removed, and women should be dressed conservatively (this includes covering the head). Neither men nor women should carry on loud conversations inside. Mosques belong to Allah, not to specific individuals, families, communities, or tribes: "And the mosques are for Allah alone, so invoke not anyone along with Allah." (72:18) And Allah encourages people to construct and fill mosques:

"The mosques of Allah shall be maintained only by those who believe in Allah and the last day, perform prayers, and give zakaat and fear none but Allah. It is they who surely are on true guidance." (9:18) Hence, barring people from conducting their worshipping in the mosque is considered a grave sin in Islam: "And who is more unjust than those who forbid that Allah's name be glorified and mentioned much in Allah's mosques and strive for their ruin?" (2:114)

Allah exists everywhere and throughout all time, and the Quran states: "To Allah belong the East and the West, so wherever you turn your face there is the face of Allah." (2:115) Nevertheless, as a sign of unity Muslims are instructed to face the qiblah, the direction of the Kaaba in Mecca, during prayer.

### Islamic Law and Punishment

Before speaking of the law and punishment in Islam, many premises must be introduced regarding Islamic jurisprudence. Islamic ideology stipulates that Allah is the main source of Islamic law. These laws were revealed to all divine messengers in different eras and geographical places in accordance with the intellectual progress of the various societies, and reached their perfection through the Holy Quran which carries a universal message for mankind. Therefore, the Islamic law is not bound by time and place and is designed to cater to the different needs of the human race until eternity.

The Islamic law of punishment is based on prevention, not retribution-meaning that Islam cares to prevent criminal acts before they happen and disrupt the peace of society. These laws are dynamic, everlasting, and not bound by individualistic interests. They take into consideration the general interest of society. Allah speaks about the punishment of the criminals by saying: "O you who believe, the law of equality in punishment is prescribed for you in case of murder, but if the killer is forgiven by the relatives of the killed against blood money, then adhering to it with fairness and payment of the blood money to the heir should be made in fairness. This is an alleviation and a mercy from your Lord." (2:178) Although Islam tries to combat crime and terror with full seriousness, it leave room for mercy and forgiveness, emphasizing the human nature of people and that they should learn mercy and forgiveness from their Lord.

However, Islam has to be introduced as a whole to the people, and to incorporate Islam in all aspects of life, not only in the judicial system. Islam invites the rulers and the subjects alike to spread social justice, equality, and distribution of wealth in society. Once every individual in society has adequate food, shelter, clothing, and opportunities for work, education, and marriage and the gap between the haves and the have-nots has been bridged-then if an individual or group of people tries to jeopardize the safety and security of society and terrorize the people, then in this case Islam would stand firmly in their face and the law of punishment would be exercised.

## RELIGION

Religion refers to the beliefs and a series of practical and moral instructions that the prophets have related on behalf of Allah to guide and lead human beings.

Believing in these tenets and performing these instructions result in man's prosperity and happiness in this world and in the world Hereafter.

So if we abide by religion and follow the orders of Allah and the Prophet (SA), we will become prosperous not only in this short life, but also in the everlasting and endless world Hereafter.

We are aware that a happy and prosperous person is one who has a true objective in his life and who does not live in misdeed and aberration. He possesses a good and praiseworthy demeanour and performs good deeds and has a confident, strong, and peaceful heart in this turbulent world.

The religion of Allah directs us towards this happiness and prosperity. Without religion, there would be no prosperity and bliss. Religious tenets are like secret police in the heart of man and always accompany him. They keep man away from moral wickedness and force him to be virtuous.

Belief is the strongest and most solid refuge in which man never confronts fear and anguish in the ups and downs of life. The worshippers of Allah never lose their courage in any circumstances and never feel disdain and inferior, for they see themselves connected to the infinite might of the Creator of the world and under all circumstances, they remember Allah and seek refuge with Allah; they possess a confident, strong, and peaceful heart.

Religion commands us to have a praiseworthy behaviour and to perform good and decent deeds as far as we can.

Therefore, religion is divided into three parts:

(1) Beliefs;

(2) Ethics; and

(3) Commandments.

This brief account should be elaborated to be acceptable to the honourable readers.

## Beliefs

If we use our commonsense and conscience, we realize that this world of existence with its wonderful order could not be created by itself and this astonishing order of the world of creation could not be achieved without an organizer. Undoubtedly, there is a Creator Who has created this vast and magnificent world with His infinite capability and knowledge and who has established the world of creation with exact order by the invariable and unchangeable rules that He has set up throughout the world of existence. Nothing has been created uselessly and extravagantly. No creature falls outside the purview of the laws of Allah that govern the world.

Can it be believed that such a compassionate Allah with all the grace and blessings that He has toward His creatures would leave man, the masterpiece creation, on his own? And that He would leave human beings to man's wisdom which is mostly victim of carnal desires and is, as a result, faced with aberration and misery? The reply to this question is self-evident.

Consequently, Allah must send instructions to human beings by prophets-who are free from any kind of sin and error-to lead men to happiness and prosperity by following them.

We realize that in this world, the signs and valuable benefits of adherence to religious principles do not become completely evident. Neither the righteous are rewarded, nor the criminals and oppressors are punished for their deeds.

From this, we understand that another world must exist where people's deeds are closely investigated, so that if one has done a charitable act, he would be rewarded or if he has committed an indecent deed, he would be castigated. Religion encourages people with these tenets and other rightful beliefs, which will later be thoroughly discussed in this book, and warns them of paganism and ignorance.

### Ethics

Religion decrees that we adopt praiseworthy qualities in life, have a good nature, and accomplish ourselves with good and commendable attributes. We must be conscientious, benevolent, philanthropic, kind, faithful, good-natured, pleasing to meet, and just. We must defend our own rights. We must !lot transgress our own limits and rights and should not encroach upon the property, reputation, and lives of people. In search of knowledge and civility, we must not spare any effort for self-sacrifice and self-denial whatsoever. Finally, we must have equality and moderation in all affairs of life.

### Commandments

Religion decrees that we perform acts that are beneficial to ourselves and to our society during our life and refrain from acts that cause corruption and immorality. It also teaches us to engage in reciting salat (prayers), observing sawm (fasting), and performing similar other duties which are signs of servitude and obedience towards Allah. These are the laws and instructions the religion offers and invites us to perform. As it is evident, some of them are doctrinal, others ethical, and some others practical. As mentioned before, acceptance and performance of these principles is the only means of happiness and prosperity, for we are aware that man should be nothing but realistic and should live with good ethics and praiseworthy deeds.

## IS IT NECESSARY FOR MAN TO FOLLOW A RELIGION?

The foremost question that comes up here is "what is the relation of men's lives with religion and piety?" Is it not possible for a human society to continue its humanitarian existence without religion and faith in Allah? Is it not that a religious person is one who proves Allah's existence and performs specific acts for His satisfaction?

It is possible that in the society, according to the laws enacted by human beings, the duty of each member of the society determines the benefit and the loss. In this case, the laws of men replace religious laws and there will be no need for religion. But with little attention and deliberation on Islamic commandments and regulations, the opposite of this is proved, for Islam has not been concerned only with praying to and praising Allah, rather it has enacted comprehensive instructions and specific regulations for all individual and social positions of man.

Islam has considered the vast world of humanity in an astonishing manner and has enacted suitable regulations in accordance with man's individual and social actions and otherwise. Finally, Islam has provided and guaranteed the happiness and prosperity of the members of social community in every respect and to the maximum extent possible.

Every just person acknowledges that the laws sprang from man's limited thoughts and knowledge cannot equal those of religion. This power of the Almighty Allah has described the religion of Islam in the Holy Quran. As examples, we will cite few verses here:

> "Surely the (true) religion with Allah is Islam, and those to whom the Book had been given did not show opposition but after knowledge had come to them, out of envy among themselves: and whoever disbelieves in the communications of Allah then surely Allah is quick in reckoning (3:19)."

The religion towards which all prophets have invited people consists of theism and submission to Allah's orders. Though the religious scholars specified right through wrong, they did not accept what was rightful due to their prejudice and animosity. Each scholar adopted a specific course of action; as a result, different religions came into existence on earth. In fact, this category of people did not believe in the Divine verses. Allah will soon retribute their deeds.

"And whoever desires a religion other than Islam, it shall not be accepted from him and in the Hereafter he shall be one of the losers (3:85)."

"O you who believe! enter into submission one and all, and do not follow the footsteps of Shaytan (satan); surely he is your open enemy (2:208)."

"And fulfil the covenant of Allah when you have made a covenant, and do not break the oaths after making them fast, and you have indeed made Allah a surety for you; surely Allah knows what you do (16:91)."

The purpose of this verse is to indicate that any Muslim who makes a promise to Allah or to people must keep it and must not breach it.

"Call to the way of your Lord with wisdom and goodly exhortation, and have debates with them in the best manner; surely your Lord best knows those who go astray from His path, and He knows best those who follow the right way (16:125)."

This refers to the fact that to promote religion, a Muslim must converse with people according to their understanding and in a way that is beneficial to them. However, if he fails to guide a person through logic and advice then he must debate in the best manner, which is one of the means of proving something, to guide him towards truth.

"And when the Quran is recited, then listen to it and remain silent, that mercy may be shown to you (7:204)."

"O you who believe! Obey Allah and obey the Prophet and those in authority from among you; then if you quarrel about anything, refer it to Allah and the Prophet, if you believe in Allah and the Last Day; this is better and very good in the end (4:59)."

This verse means that in an Islamic society, disputes can only be settled by the Quran and the Hadith of the Prophet (SA). Every difference must be settled by these two factors. If a Muslim settles differences by the logic of reason, this is due to the fact that the Quran has accepted the rule of logic.

"Thus, it is due to mercy from Allah that you deal with them gently, and had you been rough, hard-hearted, they would certainly have dispersed from around you; pardon them therefore and ask pardon for them, and take counsel with them in the affair; so when you have decided, then place your trust in Allah; surely Allah loves those who trust (3:159)."

Good behaviour, benevolence, and taking counsel in the affairs result in fellowship and kindness. Members of the society must respect their leader to be influenced by him. Allah orders the honourable leader of the Muslims to be benevolent and to take counsel.

But since it is possible that people may make mistakes in their decisions, Allah orders the leader to be independent in his decision after taking counsel and to have trust in Allah, because no one can oppose Allah's will.

In like manner, the Almighty Allah introduces Judaism and Christianity with their Divine books of Tawrat (Old Testament) and the Injil (Bible) and their social precepts and provisions as:

"And how do they make you a judge and they have the Tawrat wherein is Allah's judgement... Surely We revealed Tawrat in which was guidance and light; with it the prophets who submitted themselves (to Allah) judged (matters) for those who were Jews, and the masters of divine knowledge and the doctors... And We sent after them in their footsteps 'Isa (Jesus), son of Maryam (Mary)... and We gave him the Injil in which was guidance and light, and verifying what was before it of Tawrat... And the followers of the Injil should have judged by what Allah revealed in it... And We have revealed to you the Book with the truth, verifying what is before it of the Book and a guardian over it, therefore judge between them by what Allah has revealed...(5:43-48)."

Tawrat and Injil which are now in the hands of the Jews and Christians emphasize this point, because the Tawrat contains many legal and judicial provisions and apparently the Injil confirms and certifies the religious laws of Tawrat.

### Conclusion

From the aforementioned statement, it becomes evident that religion as viewed by the Quran is the same as the method of living from which man cannot escape. The difference between religion and a social law is that religion is descended by the Almighty Allah, whereas social laws spring from people's minds. In other words, religion unites man's social life with his worship and obedience of the Almighty Allah, while no attempt at such unity is made by social laws.

## QURAN'S TEACHINGS ABOUT THE CREATOR OF THE WORLD

### The Existence of the Creator

"... Is there doubt about Allah, the Maker of the heavens and the earth... (14:10)?"

*Explanation:* In daylight, everything is visible. We can see ourselves, others, houses, city, desert, mountains, jungle, and sea. But when the darkness of night prevails, all these bright and evident things lose their brightness. Then we realize that this brightness did not belong to them, rather it was due to the sun which illuminated them by a kind of contact. The sun is bright and, with its reflection, makes the earth and all that is on it bright and visible. If these objects had a brightness of their own, they would never lose it.

Human beings and other living beings perceive objects by their eyes, ears, and senses. They em bark on activities by their hands, feet, and other internal and external organs. After a while, however, they lose their senses and motions and no longer show any movement or activity and apparently die.

By witnessing this scene, we come to the conclusion that the intellect, determination, and movement of these living beings are not due to their posture and figure, rather they spring from their soul and psyche. When their soul goes out they lose their livelihood and activity.

For example, if seeing and hearing were done only by the eyes and ears, these activities would continue so long as these two organs existed, but this is not the case at all. In like manner, if the undoubted existence and genesis of the vast world of existence, of which we are a part and can never doubt its existence, sprang from and belonged to itself, it would never lose them. In spite of this, we see that the components of the world lose their existence vitality one after another and are incessantly in the state of change and transformation. They replace one condition by another and assume another shape.

For this reason, one must decisively judge that the existence and genesis of all living things originate from something else which is their Creator and Generator. As soon as the Creator cuts off relation of creation with something, that object plunges into annihilation and obliteration and becomes invisible.

That Infinite Existence, which is the support of the world of creation and the Preserver of people, is Allah.

There is no annihilation and obliteration for Allah; otherwise, like all other living beings, His existence would not have been from itself and would have been dependent on others.

## Quran and Tawhid

If with a pure nature and peaceful heart, man glances at the world of existence, he will see proofs and signs for the pure existence of the Creator in its nooks and corners. He will find evidences from every place to back up this truth. In this world, everything that man faces is either a phenomenon created by Allah or possesses a characteristic endowed by Allah or is a system that runs and governs everything by Allah's command. Man is one such being and his entire body attests this fact. Neither does man's existence belong to himself nor are the traits that he manifests based on his will. Man has neither devised the plan of life that he takes up from the beginning of his life, nor can he consider this system based on chance and accident and, therefore, cut off. Man cannot attribute his existence and the system of his existence to the environment in which he came into being. This is because the existence of the above-mentioned environment and the system that governs it are not made by that environment and have not evolved by chance and accident.

Thus man has no choice but to prove an origin for the world of creation. This origin creates and fosters things. It gives life to every being and leads it in the path of survival to its specific perfection by a particular system. When man sees that the creation of objects is related and a unified system exists in the world, he is forced to accept that the source of creation and manager of its system is no one except Allah.

The Holy Quran states:

"If there had been in them any gods except Allah, they would both have certainly been in a state of disorder... (21:22)."

Explanation: If many gods governed the world and, as idolaters say, different gods ran various parts of the world, then the earth, heavens, seas, and jungles would each have a god for its own. As a result of the differences among such gods, various systems would be established in the world, so that inevitably the world would face corruption and annihilation. However, we see that all components of the world have complete relation and harmony with one another and comprise a system. Thus, it must be said that there is no partner for the Providence and Creator of the world.

Some might assume that since the supposed gods are wise and aware that their differences lead the world toward annihilation and corruption, they never differ with each other. But this is a depraved assumption because Allah, Who governs the world of existence or a part of it and Whose activity and motion are for the system of creation, performs no mental activity like us.

From the first day that our eyes open upon the world of creation and view the system at work in it, we acquire mental impressions from this system. These constitute our knowledge. Then as we work to provide our basic needs, we coordinate our action with our mental impressions to make it correspond to the prevalent system of creation. For example, we eat to satisfy our hunger. To quench our thirst, we drink water. To be relieved from cold and heat, we wear suitable clothes, because we realize that these exigencies are satisfied by such means in the world order.

Thus our action (in this view) in contingent upon and subsequent to our thoughts and our thoughts depend upon and are subsequent to the world order. Therefore, our actions are two stages subsequent to the world order. But for Allah Who governs the world or a part of it, the external world order is an action. It is not rational to believe that His actions occur due to premeditations on the system.

### The Almighty Allah Possesses All Attributes of Perfection

What is perfection? A house is perfect when it provides for all the needs of a family's living such as enough rooms to serve as a living room, a guesthouse, a kitchen for making food, a bathroom, and other rooms. If it lacks these utilities, it is proportionately deficient.

### Why Doesn't Man Accept this Truth at Times?

This fact is evident for man without the least speculation and there is no doubt in it, but that at times man becomes so entangled with the conflicts of life that he uses all the power of his wisdom for vital struggles. He spends all his time probing life, therefore, he has no time to spend on these kinds of thoughts. As a result, he becomes heedless of this fact or enchanted by nature's charming outward appearances and indulges in voluptuousness and pleasure. Since adherence to these facts precludes materialistic unrestrainedness, such a man naturally refuses to accept this fact and its like and is intolerant of it.

The Holy Quran has paid greater attention, in different ways, and has presented evidences for the creation of the creatures and the system prevalent and dominant among them. This is because most people, especially those who are infatuated by nature's charming appearances and who find prosperity in voluptuousness and worldly pleasures, are unable to think philosophically and to investigate subtle logical theories due to their fondness of material and perceptible things. In any case, man is a part of the world of creation and is not free from want of its other components and the general and particular systems that govern it. He can consider the world of creation and the system prevalent in it at any time to find out the existence of the Creator and Lord of the world. The Almighty Allah states:

> "Most surely in the heavens and the earth there are signs for the believers. And in your (own) creation and in what

He spreads abroad of animals there are signs for a people that are sure, and (in) the variation of the night and the day, and (in) what Allah sends down of sustenance from the cloud, then gives life thereby to the earth after its death, and (in) the changing of the winds, there are signs for a people who understand (45:3-5)."

*Explanation:* In the Holy Quran, many verses invite people to think about the creation of the heavens, the sun, the moon, the stars, the earth, mountains, seas, plants, animals, and human beings. The Quran also mentions the astonishing system that governs each of these kinds. Truly, the mechanism of creation and the system that leads different activities of the world towards the goals of creation and the causes for existence are very astonishing and wonderful. The seed of wheat or the kernel of almond, planted on the earth, respectively turn into a clustered shrub or a fruit-bearing tree.

From the moment they are planted deeply in the heart of the earth, they rip up, produce green tips, and strike their white roots into the heart of the earth. To attain their final goal, vast and enormous systems, whose magnitude and vastness astound the intellect, begin to operate. The stars in the skies, the bright sun, the luminous moon, and the earth all with their rotation, movement, and potential power along with the mysterious powers in the seed or kernel, the four seasons of the year, the atmospheric conditions, the clouds, rains, winds, and days and nights all contribute to the growing of a seed into a shrub of wheat. Like nurses, these factors foster this new phenomenon and turn it from one hand to another until it reaches the last stage of its growth and development.

Likewise, the coming into existence of a human infant is much more complex than the bud of a plant or other phenomena, because it is the product of millions or rather billions of years of complex and systematic activity of the mechanism of creation. Man's daily life, in addition to external connections with the world of creation, springs from an astonishing system within his being which has amused the perceptive minds of the scientists of the world engaged for many centuries in observation of its outward things. Each day another layer is removed from its secrets, but still their knowledge about the unknown is rather insignificant. If a human being possesses what is needful in the system of being of a normal man, he is perfect. But if he lacks one of them, for instance, if he does not have a hand, foot, or an eye, he is deficient in that respect.

From what has been said, the attribute of perfection is that which meets some of the needs of existence and obviates deficiency. For example, the epithet of knowledge obviates the darkness of ignorance and elucidates what is known to the scholar. Also power enables a powerful person to attain his ends and satisfy his demands and makes him competent to do so. Other epithets are life, comprehension, etc.

Our conscience judges that the Creator of the world (He, from whom the existence of the world and creatures originate and who meets any need that could be conceived and grants every blessing and perfection) possesses all attributes of perfection, because from a realistic point of view, it can never be assumed that anyone possessing an attribute can prevent others from having it. The Almighty Allah names all attributes of His perfection and declares Himself Immaculate and Pure from any fault and deficiency:

> "And your Lord is the Self-sufficient One, the Lord of Mercy... (6:133)."
>
> Allah states:
>
> "Allah-there is no god but He; His are the very best names (20:8)."
>
> (Allah is Living, Wise, Clear-sighted, Hearing, Mighty, Creator, and Free from want.) Thus the Almighty Allah possesses all epithets of perfection and His Holy Presence is Pure and Immaculate. Because if He had deficiency, He would be dependent in that respect and a superior god would have to provide His needs.
>
> "...Glory be to Him and exalted be He above what they associate (with Him) (30:40)."

### The Power and Knowledge of Allah

Observation of the interconnected components of this magnificent world, its astonishing usual revolution, its dazzling minute and interrelated systems which are at work here and there, as a result of which various phenomena move in an utmost orderly manner towards a specific goal and a particular destination, informs any wise man that the existence and survival of the world of existence and all that is associated with it originate from an Immortal One and Power. This Immortal One has created the world and all its inhabitants with His Boundless Might and Infinite Knowledge. Having placed His creatures in the cradle of nurturing, He leads them to an ideal perfection by His blessing. He has an immortal life and is Omnipotent and Omniscient. The Almighty Allah states:

> "His is the kingdom of the heavens and the earth; He gives life and causes death; and He has power over all things. He is the First and the Last and the Ascendant (over all) and the Knower of hidden things, and He is Cognizant of all things (57:2-3)."

Allah also states:

> "...And Allah's is the kingdom of the heavens and the earth and what is between them; He creates what He pleases; and Allah has power over all things (5:17)."

*Explanation:* When we say that such and such a person has the ability to purchase a car, we mean that he has whatever is needed (enough money) to do so. If we say that such and such a person is able to lift a weight of about 60 kilogrammes, we mean that he has the strength to lift a weight of 60 kilogrammes.

On the whole, possessing capability and power over some matter is contingent upon the availability of its requirements. Since the requirements of any phenomenon in the world of existence can be met through the Divine power of the Almighty Allah, it can be said that He is Mighty and Powerful over all things and His Holy Existence is the main source of existence. He also states:

> "Does He not know who He created...(67:14)?"

That is to say, since in his creation and existence, each creature relies upon the Infinite Entity of the Almighty Allah there can never be any barrier and isolation between that creature and Allah. Nor can that creature be concealed from Him because He is Knowledgeable and Aware of ins and outs of everything.

## Justice

The Almighty Allah is Just and Righteous, for justice is one of the attributes of perfection. Allah possesses all attributes of perfection. He, in His words, has repeatedly praised justice and has reproached injustice and cruelty. He commands people to do justice and prohibits them from injustice. How would it be possible for Allah to possess attributes that He considers indecent or to lack whatever He considers good and decent? The Almighty Allah states:

> "Surely Allah does not do injustice to the weight of a particle...(4:40)."

> He also states:

> "...And your Lord does not deal unjustly with any one (18:49)."

> Allah states:

> "...And Allah does not desire injustice for (His) servants (40:31)."

> He also states:

> "Whatever benefit comes to you (O man !), it is from Allah, and whatever misfortune befalls you, it is from yourself..(4:79)."

> Allah also states:

> "Who made good everything that He has created...(32:7)."

Thus, any phenomenon, in itself, has been created in an extremely proper manner. Any hideousness, injustice, deficiencies, or shortcomings that are seen in some creatures can only be experienced by way of comparison and in relationship with other beings. F or example, snakes and scorpions are evil and unjust in their relation to man. When compared with flowers, thorns are not so beautiful, but they are all, in their own right, wonderful and thoroughly beautiful creatures.

Indeed the Almighty Allah declares some of man's voluntary deeds religiously bad and evil and orders man to refrain from doing them. They include sins such as polytheism, disobedience of parents, killing the innocent, drinking alcoholic beverages, gambling, and any other acts which are against religious obligations. These kinds of actions, which are called sins, are evil acts and are not attributed to Allah because they bear the title of opposition to and rejection of obligation (title of negation). If these acts are willingly performed by religiously obligated people, then they will be attributed to these people, thus making them responsible and subject to punishment.

### Blessing

When we see an enfeebled needy, we try to meet his demands to the best of our ability. We help a desperately poverty-stricken man or take a blind man's hand in our own and lead him to his destination. We consider these acts as compassion and blessing and thus regard them as praiseworthy deeds.

Actions performed by the Capable and Independent Allah can be nothing but blessings. By granting His innumerable graces, He lets everyone enjoy them. Without being dependent upon anyone else, Allah provides part of the needs of the creatures. Allah states:

> "...And if you count Allah's favours, you will not be able to number them...(14:34)."

He also states:

> "...My mercy encompasses all things...(7:156)."

### Other Attributes of Perfection

> "And Your Lord is the Self-sufficient one, the Lord of mercy...(6:133)."

Explanation: Any goodness and beauty existing in the world and any attribute of perfection that can be conceived are favours that the Almighty Allah has bestowed upon His creatures, and through this means satisfied one of the needs of creation. Certainly, if He lacked that perfection, He would be unable to grant favours to others and would have a share in the needs of people. Thus, Allah possesses all attributes of perfection and is endowed with all attributes of perfection, such as, life, knowledge, might, etc., without having received a single aspect of perfection from others and without asking them for help. Attributes of imperfection and causes for need and indigence, such as weakness, ignorance, death, difficulty, etc., will not find a way to His Holy Presence.

## NUBUWWAH (PROPHETHOOD)

While independent in every respect, the Almighty Allah, with His immense power, has created the world of existence and its various creatures, allowing them to enjoy His countless blessings.

From the first day of creation till the last day of existence, man and other creatures are fostered by Allah. They are each led toward a known and determined goal with a particular order and system. They proceed towards their ends while being exposed to His noteworthy blessings.

If we study and deliberate upon our lifetime, namely the period of infancy, childhood, youth, and old age, our conscience will testify Allah's complete favours to us. When we become more aware of this matter, our wisdom will undoubtedly judge that the Creator of the world is more compassionate to His creatures than anyone else is.

Due to this compassion and favour, Allah always considers their interests and never consents to the corruption and defect of their affairs without wisdom and expediency. Mankind is one of the creatures of Allah. We know that man's interest and prosperity depend upon his being realistic and benevolent; that is to say, he must possess true beliefs, praiseworthy ethics, and good deeds.

One may say that with his Allah-granted wisdom, man can distinguish between good and bad and can recognize a well from a path.

It should be known, however, that wisdom alone cannot resolve this difficulty and lead man to realism and benevolence. All these indecent characteristics and unjust actions witnessed in the human society are committed by those who possess wisdom and discernment, however, as a result of selfishness, profit-seeking, and voluptuousness, their wisdom has been overcome by their sentiments and they have succumbed to their carnal desires, leading them astray.

Therefore, the Almighty Allah must lead and invite us to prosperity through some other ways and through means which can never be overcome by carnal desires and which never make blunders or mistakes in their guidance. This path is nothing but the path of Nubuwwah.

## The Logic in Nubuwwah

It becomes evident that since Allah creates everything, its fostering also depends upon Him. In other words, the Almighty Allah is the organizer and leader of the movement of any worldly creature or phenomenon that from the very beginning of existence endeavours for its survival, strives to remove its imperfections, eliminates its needs and shortcomings one after another, makes itself independent and self-sufficient as much as possible, and moves in an orderly manner in its path of survival and existence.

A definite conclusion can be drawn from this concept. That is to say, any one of the various kinds of phenomena of the world has a specific evolutionary process for its survival which is done by its special endeavours. In other words, in the path of their survival, worldly creatures of each particular group have a series of specific functions assigned to them by Allah. As the Holy Quran, with reference to this fact, states:

> "...Our Lord is He Who gave to everything its creation, then guided it (to its goal) (20:50)."

This order applies to all components of creation without any exception. It includes the stars, the earth, their components, compositions that generate primary phenomena, plants, and animals.

Man's condition is the same as others, in this universal guidance, but there is a difference between him and others.

## The Difference between Man and Other Creatures

The earth has supposedly been created millions of years ago. It employs all its hidden forces and endeavours in the environment of its existence to the extent permitted by opposing forces. It displays the signs of its entity in the field of its rotation and transitional movement, thus maintaining its survival. Unless faced with a stronger opposing force, it will continue this activity and will not fall short of carrying out any of its functions.

For example, from the time an almond tree takes root from a seed until it becomes a fully grown tree, it assumes duties, such as nourishing, developing, etc. (in other words, it performs these duties to pursue the course of its existence.) It will never refrain from carrying them out unless it is precluded by a stronger opposing force. This process also applies to any other phenomenon. But mankind performs his particular activities voluntarily and his actions originate from his thoughts and determination. Many a time, man refrains from a task which is entirely to his interests and which is not hindered by any opposing force and undertakes a task which is entirely disadvantageous to him knowingly and intentionally. Sometimes, he abstains from drinking antidote and sometimes he drinks a cup of poison and kills himself.

It is certainly clear that the divine universal guidance will not be compulsory for a creature born with free will. That is to say, the prophets conveyed the message of the Almighty Allah on good and bad and prosperity and wretchedness to the people and warned believers of Allah's chastisement, but the believers have always been free to adopt any one of them. It is true that, in general, man perceives his good and bad and advantage and disadvantage through his wisdom, but that very wisdom often loses its keenness, follows carnal desires, and makes error. Therefore, in addition to the medium of wisdom, divine guidance should positively be achieved through a different medium, which is entirely inviolable to sin and error. In other words, in addition to the medium of wisdom, the Almighty Allah confirms His orders by another medium.

This medium is the same medium of prophethood by which the Almighty Allah reveals His orders to one of His servants through wahy leading mankind to prosperity. Allah appoints him to communicate His orders to the people and to oblige them to follow the orders through hope, despair, encouragement, and threat.

The Almighty Allah states:

> "Surely We have revealed to you as We revealed to Nuh (Noah), and the prophets after him...(4:163)." "(We sent) messengers as the bearers of good news and as warners, so that people should not have a plea against Allah after the (coming of) messengers...(4:165)."

9

# ATTRIBUTES OF PROPHET

From what was discussed, it becomes clear that the Almighty Allah, with His divine teachings, must have provided some of His servants with intuitive knowledge and laws that guarantee man's prosperity and must have sent them to lead the people.

A person who possesses divine messages is called a "nabi (prophet)" and messenger of Allah and the entire set of messages from Allah which he has brought to the people are called "religion".

It has also become clear that a prophet:

(1) Must be free and immuned from error. In order to communicate what has been revealed to him to the people without error and mistake, he should be immuned from forgetfulness and other mental weaknesses; otherwise, divine guidance will not attain its goal and the general guidance rule will forfeit its applicability and lose its power to influence people.

(2) Must be inviolable to error and sin both in deeds and speech, because sinfulness has no effect in propagation. People do not esteem the speech of a person whose manner and speech are at odds. They even take his deeds for his mendacity and imposture by saying if he meant what he said, he would act accordingly.

By bringing these two aspects together in one phrase, we can say that a prophet must be inviolable to errors and sins to render preaching and propagation effective. In His words, the Almighty Allah, too, refers to this point and states: "The Knower of the unseen! so He does not reveal His secrets to any, except to him whom He chooses as a messenger for surely He makes a guard to march before him and after him, so that He may know that they have truly delivered the messages of their Lord...(72:26-28)."

(3) Must possess moral virtues such as chastity, courage, justice, etc., for these are considered as praiseworthy qualities. Anyone who is immune to any sins and follows religion in a perfect manner will never be blemished by moral vices.

## Prophets among People

History indicates that there were prophets among people who responded to the call of Allah; however, the details of their life is not so clear. Only the details of life of Prophet Muhammad (SA) is devoid of ambiguity. The Holy Quran, which is the divine book given to Prophet (SA), contains sublime religious aims, has clarified the call of the prophets in the past and has described their goals and objectives.

The Holy Quran stipulates that many prophets have been, assigned by Allah to lead the people, all of whom consistently invited the people to monotheism and the true religion. As Allah states:

> "And We did not send before you any messenger but We revealed to him that there is no god but Me, therefore worship Me (21:25)."

## Ululazm Anbiya' (Arch-Prophets) and All Other Prophets

There were five prophets who had divine books and independent teachings. They are referred to as Nuh (Noah) (AS), Ibrahim (Abraham) (AS), Musa (Moses) (AS), 'Isa (Jesus) (AS), and Muhammad (SA) in the following verse:

> "He has made plain to you of the religion what He enjoined upon Nuh and that which We have revealed to you, and that which We enjoined upon Ibrahim and Musa and 'Isa that keep to obedience and be not divided therein... (42:13)."

These five prophets, who have books and divine religious laws, are called the Ululazm Anbiya' (arch-prophets). The messengers of Allah, however, were not limited to these five prophets, rather each ummah (people) had a messenger. Many prophets were sent by Allah to lead the people, of whom only the names of less than twenty have been mentioned in the Holy Quran. The Almighty Allah states:

"... There are some of them that We have mentioned to you and there are others whom We have not mentioned to you...(40:78)."

He also states:

"And every ummah had a messenger...(10:47)."

Allah states:

"...And (there is) a guide for every people (13:7)."

Yes, prophets, who came after each of the Ululazm Anbiya' invited people to follow the divine religious laws of the same prophets. Thus, prophetic mission and the call continued until Allah appointed the Prophet Muhammad (SA) ibn Abdillah to bring the previous prophetic missions to perfection and to communicate the latest orders and the most complete divine religious laws. His divine book became the last book and consequently, the religion of Prophet Muhammad (SA) will remain valid until Qiyamah (Resurrection) and his religious laws will remain everlasting.

## Prophet Nuh (AS)

Nuh (AS) (prophet Noah) was the first prophet appointed to prophetic mission and sent towards mankind as bearer of divine religious laws and a divine book by Allah, the Merciful.

Nuh (AS) invited the people of those days to monotheism and belief in the Oneness of Allah and asked them to refrain from polytheism and idolatry. As evident from his stories in the Holy Quran, Nuh (AS) seriously struggled to settle class distinctions and to eradicate injustice and cruelty. He notified the people of his teachings by way of reasoning which was something new to the people of those days.

After a long period of suffering with ignorant, stubborn, and unruly people, Nuh (AS) guided only a small group of people. Thus, by means of Nuh's (AS) Deluge, the Almighty Allah annihilated unbelievers and cleansed the earth of their defiled entity. Nuh (AS) and a group of his followers who were saved laid the cornerstone of a religious society over again. This Holy Prophet (SA) is the founder of the religious laws of monotheism and the first divine representative who struggled against cruelty, injustice, and rebellion. Owing to his valuable services rendered to the divine religion, he is allotted a praise and greeting by Allah, a praise which will remain alive and perpetual as long as mankind exists.

"Peace and salutation to Nuh among the nations (37:79)."

### Prophet Ibrahim (AS)

A long time elapsed after Nuh. (AS). Although many prophets, such as Hud, Salih, and others also led the people towards Allah and righteousness, the polytheism and idolatry flourished day by day and finally became universal. By His sublime wisdom, the Almighty Allah appointed Ibrahim (AS) (prophet Abraham) as a prophet.

Ibrahim (AS) was a perfect example of a man with innate disposition who searched for truth with his pure and immaculate nature. He found out the oneness of Allah and struggled against polytheism and injustice all his life.

As revealed by the Holy Quran and confirmed by the Hadith of the Imams of Ahl al-Bayt (Members of the Household of the Prophet Muhammad [SA]), Ibrahim (AS) spent his childhood in a cave away from the clamours of people and the tumultuous urban life. He only saw his mother who carried food and water for him from time to time.

One day he came out of his cave and followed his mother to town and paid a visit to his uncle, Adhar, but everything seemed new and interesting to him. Amidst thousands of bewilderments and wonders and with utmost impatience and calmness, his immaculate nature focussed on the creation of things that he saw, trying to find out the secret of their existence and the cause of their creation. He saw idols which Adhar and others carved and worshipped. Ibrahim (AS) asked about their identity, but the explanation he got about their divinity was not convincing. He saw a group of people who worshipped venus, others who worshipped the moon, and yet another group who worshipped the sun. Their divinity was unbelievable to Ibrahim (AS) because each one of them set after a few hours. After these incidents, Ibrahim (AS), fearlessly, announced his worshipping of the Almighty Allah and his disgust of polytheism and idolatry. He thought of nothing but struggle against idolatry and polytheism. He struggled against idol-worshippers tirelessly and relentlessly and invited them towards monotheism.

Finally, he found a way to the idol-temple and broke the idols. Because of this deed, which people regarded as the greatest crime, Ibrahim (AS) was put to trial. After completion of the formalities, Ibrahim (AS) was thrown into the fire, but Allah saved him and he came out of the fire unharmed.

After a while, Ibrahim (AS) emigrated from his original birthplace, Babylon, to Syria and Palestine and continued his invitation of monotheism there.

In the last days of his life, he was blessed with two children: Ishaq (AS) (Prophet Isaac), the father of Israil (AS) and Isma'il (AS) (Prophet Ishmael), the father of 'Arab Mudar. By the order of Allah, Isma'il (AS), in infancy, and his mother were taken to Hijaz by Ibrahim (AS). They settled around Mount Tuhamah in an arid and barren land without inhabitants. In this manner, Ibrahim (AS) invited the nomadic Arabs to monotheism. Then he built Kaaba and described the rites of Hajj (pilgrimage to Mecca) which remained prevalent among the Arabs until the advent of Islam and the call of Prophet Muhammad (SA).

Ibrahim (AS) was endowed with the innate religion. According to the explicit wording of the Holy Quran, he had a divine book. He was the first person to call the divine religion as "Islam" and it's followers as "Muslims". Indeed, the religions of the world advocating monotheism, such as Judaism, Christianity, and Islam terminate at Ibrahim (AS), because Musa (AS), 'Isa (AS), and Prophet Muhammad (SA), the leaders of the aforementioned three religions, were all the descendants of Ibrahim (AS) and had followed his path of call and invitation to monotheism.

### Prophet Musa (AS)

Musa (AS) (Prophet Moses) ibn 'Imran is the third of the Ululazm Anbiya' and is bestowed with a book and shariah (divine religious laws). He was a descendant of Israil (AS) or Yaqub (AS)

(Prophet Jacob). Musa (AS) had a tumultuous life. He was born at a time when the Israelites were living in Egypt among Gipsies in a state of abjectness and servitude and when their sons were beheaded by the order of Firawn (Pharaoh*).

The mother of Musa (AS), according to the order given to her while asleep, placed Musa (AS), in a wooden box and left him in the Nile River.

The water carried the box directly to the castle of Firawn. By the order of Firawn, the box was picked up. When they opened it, they found a baby inside.

Because of the insistence of the queen, Firawn dispensed with killing the child. Since they did not have a son, they adopted him as their own son and put him under the care of a nurse (who was incidentally his own mother)

Up to the early stages of his youth, Musa (AS) lived in the palace of Firawn. Then, after an accidental murder, fearing Firawn, he ran away from Egypt. He went to Madyan and met Prophet Shuayb (Jethro) (AS). He married one of Shuayb's daughters and grazed his sheep for a few years. After a few years, he reminisced his birthplace, took his wife with him, and set out for Egypt, carrying his belongings along. On his way, when he reached Mount Sinai at night, he was assigned to prophetic mission by the Almighty Allah.

He was chosen by Allah to invite Firawn to the religion of Tawhid, to liberate the Israelites from the yoke of the Gipsies, and to designate his brother, Harun (Aaron), as his minister. But after he announced his mission and communicated the divine message, Firawn who was an idol-worshipper and who had also introduced himself to the people of Egypt as one of the gods, did not accept Musa's (AS) prophetic mission and refused to grant freedom to the Israelites.

Although for many years Musa (AS) invited people to tawhid and showed many miracles, Firawn and his people showed no reaction other than toughness and moroseness. Finally, by the order of Allah, Musa (AS) emigrated the Israelites and went from Egypt to Sinai desert at night. When they reached the Red sea, Firawn, too, came to know and chased them with his army.

Through a miracle, Musa (AS) split the water of the sea and crossed it along with his people, but Firawn and his army were drowned. After this event, Allah revealed the Tawrat to Musa (AS) and established the Shariah of Musa (AS) among the Israelites.

* In Egypt, kings were called "Pharaohs".

### Prophet 'Isa (AS)

Prophet 'Isa (AS) is the fourth of the Ululazm Anbiya' bestowed with a book and shariah. The circumstances of his birth were unusual. His mother, Maryam, a pious virgin, was worshipping Allah (in Jerusalem) when Ruhulqudus or Jibril (Gabriel) descended from heavens, gave her the good tidings of 'Isa's (AS) birth; and by Jibril's breathing on her sleeves, Maryam became pregnant with 'Isa (AS).

After his birth, 'Isa (AS) began to speak in the cradle in defence of his m other against unfair calumnies attributed to her. He also informed the people about his Nubuwwah and divine book (Injil). Later, in his youth, he proceeded to invite the people and revived the shariah of Musa (AS) with minor modifications. He sent missionaries from among his hawaris (disciples) to the surrounding places. After his call was spread among the people, the Jews (his ummah) embarked on killing him, but Allah saved him, and the Jews caught someone else in his place and crucified him.

It should be pointed out here that the Almighty Allah, in the Holy Quran, confirms a divine book called the "Injil" for 'Isa (AS), which was revealed to him. It is different from the Gospels written after 'Isa (AS) about his life and call. Among them, four Gospels compiled by Luke, Mark, Matthew, and John are formally recognized by Christians.

### Prophet Muhammad (SA) Ibn 'Abdillah

The biography of our Holy Prophet Muhammad (SA) ibn Abdillah is clearer than those of all prophets preceding him, because as a result of the lapse of time and historical changes, their books, shariahs, and even their personalities have been distorted and their biographies have become ambiguous.

In fact, there are no clear documents other than those imparted to us through the divine book of Islam, viz, Quran and the speeches and statements of Prophet Muhammad (SA) and the Ahl al-Bayt (AS). But there is a clear history on the life of Prophet Muhammad (SA) which describes the characteristics of his life adequately.

The Holy Prophet (SA) of Islam is the last prophet appointed by the Almighty Allah to lead the people of the world.

Fourteen centuries ago, mankind lived in such a condition that nothing was left of Tawhid except nominally and when people had completely deviated from Tawhid and theism. Human manners and justice had died away in their society. Holy Kaaba had turned into an idol-temple and the religion of Ibrahim (AS) had converted into idolatry.

Arabs led a tribal life and even a few of their cities in Hijaz and Yemen and elsewhere were governed in the same tribal manner. The Arabs lived in the meanest and most backward conditions. Instead of culture and civilization, they indulged in unchastity, sensuality, alcoholism, and gambling. They buried their daughters alive. Most people subsisted by Way of theft, banditry, murder, and plundering each other's belongings, livestock, and cattle. Cruelty and bloodshed were regarded as the greatest honours.

In such an environment, the compassionate Allah appointed Prophet Muhammad (SA) to reform and lead the people of the world. Allah revealed the Holy Quran to him, consisting of divine education, theism, the ways of implementation of justice, and beneficial advice. Allah commissioned him to invite people toward humanity and adherence to the truth using that divine authentic Book, Quran.

Prophet Muhammad (SA) was born in the city of Mecca in 570 AD (53 years before Hijrah) in the noblest and most honourable Arab family.

Muhammad's (SA) father died before he was born. He lost h is mother when he was six years old. After two years, his grandfather (Abdul Muttalib), who was his guardian, died. Then the Prophet (SA) was put under the guardianship of his kind uncle, Abu Talib (the father of the Leader of the Faithful, 'Ali [AS]). Abu Talib held him den just like one of his own children. Until a few months before Hijrah, he always did his best for the protection and support of Muhammad (SA) and he was never negligent.

The Arabs of Mecca, like other Arabs, indulged in breeding sheep and camels. They sometimes used to trade with neighbouring countries, especially with Syria. They were illiterate people who made no effort to educate their children.

Like all his people, the Prophet (SA), too, had not learnt to read and write, but from the beginning of his life, he was privileged by having a series of praiseworthy attributes. He never worshipped idols, lied, and committed theft and treachery. He guarded against evil, disrespectful, and indecent actions and was wise and efficient. Therefore, he gained considerable popularity among the people within a short period and became known as "Muhammad al-Amin" meaning "Muhammad the trustworthy". The Arabs often entrusted him with their belongings and talked about his honesty and efficiency. When he was about twenty years old, a wealthy lady of Mecca, Khadijah al-Kubra, designated him as her representative in commercial trade. As a result of his truthfulness, honesty, wisdom, and efficiency, she earned a great deal of profit. She was naturally attracted by the personality and magnanimity of the Holy Prophet (SA) more than ever and finally proposed to him for marriage. Afterwards also for years, she continued commercial works with her husband.

Being considered as one of the people, the Holy Prophet (SA) had an ordinary association with people until the age of forty. Of course, he differed from them in that he had a praiseworthy and decent behaviour and guarded against indecent deeds and conducts which had spoiled others. He did not possess cruelty, hard-heartedness, and status consciousness, thus had earned the respect and confidence of people. It was such that when the Arabs were reconstructing the House of Kaaba, a quarrel and dispute arose among the tribes on the erection of Al-Hajar al-Aswad (the Black Stone). The people unanimously chose the Holy Prophet (SA) as an arbitrator. He then ordered the people to spread a cloak to place Al-Hajar al-Aswad within. The nobles of the tribes lifted the sides of the cloak and the Holy Prophet (SA) installed the Al-Hajar al-Aswad in its place, thus bringing the conflict of the people to an end without any massacre and bloodshed.

Before his Al-Bithat al-Nabawiyyah (appointment for prophethood), although the Holy Prophet (SA) worshipped Allah and refrained from idol-worshipping, the people did not bother about him because he did not explicitly struggle against the superstitious beliefs of idolatry. The same applied to those belonging to other religions such as Jews and christians, who lived respectfully among the Arabs without being bothered by them.

## THE INCIDENT OF MONK BUHAYRA

While the Holy Prophet (SA) lived with his uncle, Abu Talib, and while he had not yet reached adolescence, Abu Talib set out for Damascus on business and also took the Holy Prophet (SA) along. It was a massive caravan and a great number of people travelled along with a huge quantity of merchandise until they arrived in Syria and entered the city of Busra. In the vicinity of a monastery, they pitched a tent and took rest. A monk, whose title was "Buhayra", came out of the monastery and invited them to a feast. Everybody accepted Buhayra's invitation and entered the monastery. Leaving his nephew, Muhammad (SA) with his belongings, Abu Talib also attended the feast along with others.

Buhayra asked: "Is everybody present?" Abu Talib replied, "Everybody is here except a youth who is the youngest of all." Buhayra said: "Bring him along as well!" Abu Talib called on the Holy Prophet (SA) who was standing under an olive tree and came to the monk.

Buhayra cast a deep glance at the Holy Prophet (SA) and said: "come a little bit closer, I have something to tell you." Then, he took the Holy Prophet (SA) aside. Abu Talib also went near them.

Buhayra told the Holy Prophet: "I am going to ask you a question and, by swearing on Lat and 'Uzza, would you answer me" (Lat and 'uzza were the names of two idols worshipped by the people of Mecca).

The Holy Prophet (SA) stated: "These two idols are the most hated ones to me".

Buhayra said: "By swearing on Allah, would you tell the truth". The Holy Prophet said: "I always speak the truth and I have never told a lie; you ask your question".

Buhayra asked: "What do you like the most"?

The Holy Prophet (SA) answered: "Loneliness".

Buhayra asked: "What do you look the most at and what do you like to look at"?

The Holy Prophet said: "The sky and the stars within it".

Buhayra asked: "What do you think of"?

The Holy Prophet (SA) remained silent, but Buhayra carefully glanced at his forehead.

Buhayra asked: "When do you sleep and with what thoughts"?

The Holy Prophet stated: "When I fix my eyes upon the sky, I see the stars and I find them in my lap and myself above them".

Buhayra asked: "Do you see dream also"?

He stated: "Whatever I see in dream, the same I see while I am awake."

Buhayra asked: "What do you dream of, as an example"?

The Holy Prophet (SA) kept quiet, Buhayra also kept quiet.

After a while, Buhayra asked: "May I take a look at the centre of your shoulders"?

The Holy Prophet (SA), while standing still, stated: "Come and see."

Buhayra stood up, came closer, and pulled the dress of the Holy Prophet (SA) off his shoulders. A mole appeared. Buhayra took a look and said in a murmuring voice: "He is the very person".

Abu Talib asked: "Which one? What do you mean"?

Buhayra said: "Tell me, what is your relationship with this youth"?

Since Abu Talib loved the Holy Prophet (SA) as one of his own children, he said: "He is my son".

Buhayra said: "No, the father of this youth must have died".

"How do you know"? said Abu Talib; "That is true, this youth is my nephew".

Buhayra told Abu Talib "Listen, this youth will have a very bright and astonishing future. If others see what I have seen and recognize him, they will kill him. Hide and protect him from the enemies".

Abu Talib said: "Tell me, who is he"?

Buhayra replied: "His eyes bear the signs of the eyes of a prominent prophet and a clear mark of prophethood is on his back".

### The Story of Monk Nestorius

After a few years, the Holy Prophet, acting as a representative, set out for Damascus once again along with the merchandise belonging to Khadijah al-Kubra. Khadijah sent her servant, Masirah, along with the Holy Prophet (SA) and advised him to fully obey his orders. In this trip, too, when they arrived in Syria, they landed under a tree in the vicinity of the city of Busra. There was a monastery belonging to a monk called "Nestorius" who was acquainted with Masirah.

Nestorius asked Masirah: "Who is the man resting underneath that tree"?

Masirah replied: "He is a person from the family of Quraysh".

The monk said: "under this tree, no one but a prophet from among the prophets of Allah has lodged or can lodge".

He added: "Is there redness in his eyes".

Masirah said: "Yes, his eyes are always like this".

The monk said: "That's it. He is the last prophet of the prophets of Allah. I wish I could find out the day when he will invite the people."

### Good Tidings Given by the Jews of Madinah

Many Jewish tribes, having read about the attributes and location of the Holy Prophet (SA) in their books, had left their homeland for Hijaz and taken abode in Madinah and its suburbs, waiting for the advent of the Holy Prophet (SA), the Ummi (unschooled). As they were a group of wealthy and rich people, the Arabs used to disturb them from time to time and robbed them of their belongings. Complaining against the injustice of the Arabs, the Jews told them that they would tolerate their cruelty and robbery until the migration of the Ummi prophet from Mecca to Madinah. They said that on that day, they would have their faith in him and would take vengeance on them. One of the main factors that led to the rapid belief of the people of Madinah in the Holy Prophet (SA) was the memory they had about these news. Finally, they acknowledged their faith, but the Jews refrained from believing in him due to their strong communalism and prejudice.

### Quran's Reference to Prophetic Tidings

In His words the Almighty Allah refers to these good tidings in many instances. Regarding the faith of a group of people endowed with a book, the Quran states:

> "Those who follow the Apostle-Prophet, the Ummi, whom they find written down with them in the Tawrat and the Injl, (who) enjoins them good and forbids them evil, and makes lawful to them the good things and makes unlawful to them impure things, and removes from them their burden and the shackles which were upon them...(7:157)."

Again, He states:

> "And when there came to them a Book from Allah verifying that which they already had, and aforetime they were seeking victory against those who disbelieved-yet when there came to them that (Book) which they had recognized, they disbelieved in it...(2:89)."

### From Al-bithat Al-nabawiyyah to the Hijrah

In the gloomy atmosphere of the Arabian Peninsula that can literally be called "the swamp of misery" and the centre of corruption and in a world full of cruelty and injustice, the Almighty Allah appointed His Prophet (SA) as a blessing for the people of the world and ordered him to invite the people to Tawhid and worshipping the One Allah.

He also ordered him to call people to justice, righteousness, and strengthening their social relations. Allah also ordered him to rise in observance of truth and follow the path of the followers of righteousness and to lay the foundation of man's prosperity on the basis of faith, piety, cooperation, and self-sacrifice.

Initially, the Holy Prophet (SA) was charged with the responsibility of inviting the people. Since the environment was full of obstinacy, ruthlessness, and injustice, the Prophet (SA) talked his mission over only with people who were more or less susceptible to conversion. Thus a limited number of people believed in him and (according to narrations) the first man was 'Ali ibn Abi Talib (AS), the son of his uncle and educated by the Prophet (SA) himself, and the first woman was his wife Khadijah al-Kubra (AS).

Then, Muhammad (SA) was commissioned to invite his close relatives and companions (who were about forty people) to his house and described his divine mission. Then, by the order of Allah, the Holy Prophet (SA) proceeded to an overt and public invitation, thus bringing forward the luminous torch of divine guidance from within the house to the arena of the world.

The reaction of the Arabs, especially the people of Mecca, was very severe against this invitation specifically after it was publicized. Unbelievers and polytheists responded negatively, savagely, and in a cruel way to this immaculate and pure invitation without using any proper logic whatsoever.

Sometimes, they called the Holy Prophet (SA) a soothsayer and magician, while at times they called him lunatic and poet and used to make fun of him. Whenever he wanted to invite the people to the newly-grown religion of Islam or wanted to worship Allah, the people used to make noise and disrupt his actions. They threw garbage and thorns on his head and used to beat and abuse him. Sometimes, they stoned him, while at times, they tried to allure him by giving enticing and sweet promises such as of wealth and leadership, so that through these means they could shake up his resolution and determination. But the Holy Prophet (SA) displayed no weakness and withdrawal. Sometimes, he regretted and became sad because of the ignorance and stubbornness of his people. In this regard, Quranic verses were frequently revealed by which the Almighty Allah expressed His consolation to him and ordered him to be patient and forbearing. Sometimes, verses were revealed to prohibit the Holy Prophet (SA) from showing the least willingness to the remarks of the people or from displaying any weakness and leniency.

Those who believed in the Holy Prophet (SA) were severely tortured and punished by the kafirin. In many instances, they died under torture. Sometimes, the matter became so serious that they were tortured to the extreme and then they sought the permission of the Holy Prophet (SA) to start a bloody movement and finalize their destinies. The Holy Prophet (SA) said: "I do not have an order from the Almighty Allah in this respect. You must wait". A group of people took their belongings with them and left their homeland due to the heavy pressure on them.

After a while, things became much harder on the Muslims due to the extreme torture. The Holy Prophet (SA) allowed his disciples to migrate to Ethiopia to be relieved of the torture and harassment of their people for a while. This group of people, led by Jafar ibn Abi Talib, the brother of 'Ali (AS) (Jafar was one of the most trusted friends of the Holy Prophet [SA]), migrated to Ethiopia along with their families.

After being informed of the Hijrah of the Muslims, the Kafirin of Mecca sent two of their experienced men, along with a large number of gifts and souvenirs, to the king of Ethiopia, requesting the extradition of the immigrants of Mecca. But with a speech delivered in the presence of the king of Ethiopia, Jafar ibn Abi Talib explained the entirely illuminating personality of the Holy Prophet (SA) and the sublime principles of Islam for the king, the Christian priests, and top authorities present at the time. He also cited several Quranic verses of Surah (Chapter) Maryam.

The immaculate statements of Jafar ibn Abi Talib were so attractive that the king and the audience started shedding tears. Thus the king rejected the request of the people of Mecca and declined all gifts and souvenirs sent to him. The king issued instructions to provide all means of convenience, peace, and comfort for the immigrant Muslims in every respect.

After this event, the Kafirin of Mecca decided to break their relations with Banu Hashim (family of Hashim) who were the relatives of the Holy Prophet (SA) and his followers. They also decided to totally stop all relations, discourse, and transactions with them. In this respect, they wrote a special agreement, got it signed by everyone, and left it in Kaaba. Banu Hashim, accompanied by the Holy Prophet (SA), had to inevitably leave

Mecca and take refuge in a valley known as "Shib Abi Talib" and lived there almost in utmost hardship and hunger. In this period, no one dared to come out of the Shib. During the days, they had to endure the burning heat and in the nights, they were faced with the wailing of women and children.

After three years, as a result of the obliteration of the agreement and because of the denouncement by the tribes settled around, the unbelievers dispensed with their agreement and Banu Hashim came out of their refuge.

But at that time, Abu Talib, who was the lone supporter of the Holy Prophet (SA), and also Khadijah al-Kubra, the kind wife of the Holy Prophet (SA), died. As a result, things became much harder for the Holy Prophet (SA) and he was unable to appear in public or reveal his identity to anyone, or stay in a specific place. Altogether, he had no life-security.

### A Trip to Taif

The year in which the Holy Prophet (SA) and Banu Hashim came out of the Shib Abi Talib, was 13th year after al-Bithat al-Nabawiyyah. The Holy Prophet (SA) made a short trip to Ta'if (a city about 100 kilometres from Mecca) at that time and invited the people of Taif to embrace Islam. But the ignorant people of Ta'if attacked him from every place, abused and stoned him, and at last drove him out of the city.

The Holy Prophet (SA) returned to Mecca from Ta'if and remained there for a while. But since he had no security of his life, he did not appear among the people. Since the circumstances were favourable to exterminate the Holy Prophet (SA), the elders of Mecca assembled in Darun-Nadwah, which was like a consultative assembly and hatched up the final plot in a secret session to exterminate him once and for all. The plot was designed to select one man from each Arab tribe. The selected men were then to rush into the house of the Holy Prophet (SA) collectively and kill him. The purpose of selecting one representative from each tribe was to prevent the relatives of the Holy Prophet (SA) from rising in revenge and from fighting with all those tribes who would direct the murder. Also the participation of one person from Banu Hashim would also keep the mouths of Banu Hashim shut regarding this matter. This decision was finalized. About forty people from various tribes were nominated to kill the Holy Prophet (SA). They surrounded his house at night, so as to enter it at dawn in order to carry out their plot, but the divine will was above the determination of these people and thwarted their plans. The Almighty Allah sent His revelation to the Holy Prophet (SA), informed him of their intention, and ordered him to come out of Mecca at night itself and set out for Madinah.

The Holy Prophet (SA) informed 'Ali (AS) of the current situation, ordered him to sleep in his place, and gave him his last wills. He left the house at night and seeing Abu Bakr along the way, he took him also along and set out for Madinah.

Some of the dignitaries of Madinah had already met the Holy Prophet (SA) in Mecca and had expressed their faith prior to his Hijrah. They had also made an agreement to support and vindicate the Holy Prophet (SA), if he came to Madinah, just as they would defend their own life and honour.

### The Hijrah of the Holy Prophet (SA) to Madinah

The Holy Prophet (SA) reached a cave in Mount Thawr near Mecca and hid there for three days. After three days, he left the cave and continued his journey until he reached Madinah where he was welcomed by the people of Madinah.

On the other side, the infidels of Mecca who had surrounded the house of the Holy Prophet (SA) at night, dashed inside at dawn, and went to his bed with their swords pulled out. They unexpectedly found 'Ali (AS) sleeping in the bed of the Holy Prophet (SA). As soon as they found out that the Holy Prophet (SA) had left Mecca, they began searching for him around Mecca, but after a thorough search they returned with a great disappointment.

The Holy Prophet (SA) stayed in Madinah where the people most willingly converted to Islam and wholeheartedly supported him. The city of Madinah turned into an Islamic city. Until then, this city was called "Yathrib", but after this occurrence, it assumed the name of "Madinat al-Rasul" (the City of Prophet) and became the first Islamic city. Of course, although munafiqin (hypocrites), the Arab minorities of Madinah who formed about one-third of the city's population, being scared of the majority, pretended to be Muslims.

The sun of Islam began shining in the clear sky of Madinah and began shedding its light. In the first place, the state of conflict which had existed for many years between the two main tribes of Aws and Khazraj turned into peace and compromise. The believers of Madinah encircled like butterflies around the candle of prophetic mission.

Gradually, the tribes in the territory of Madinah embraced Islam and the divine precepts descended one after the other and were implemented. Everyday one of the roots of corruption and indecent behaviour was eradicated and replaced by piety and justice. Gradually, the followers of Islam, who had remained in Mecca after the Holy Prophet's (SA) Hijrah and were under the harassment and severe torture by the unbelievers, left their homes and fled to Madinah where they were received with warm hospitality by their religious brethren.

Muslims who had remained in Mecca gradually migrated and gathered in Madinah. These people were called muhajirin (immigrants) and the believers in the city of Madinah were called "Ansar"(helpers).

There were many tribes of Jews in Madinah, its suburbs, Khaybar, and Fadak whose information and scholars constantly notified the Arabs of Madinah of the good tidings of the Holy Prophet's (SA) mission. But when these tribes were invited to Islam after the Hijrah, they did not accept this invitation and turned away from Islam. Finally, a non-aggression treaty was signed between the Jews and Muslims with specific terms.

The rapid advancement of Islam seriously annoyed the unbelievers of Mecca and increased their wrath and animosity towards the Holy Prophet (SA) and the followers of Islam. They were after a pretext to disrupt the unity of the followers of Islam. On the other hand, the followers of Islam, too, especially the Muhajirin of Mecca who were quite unhappy with the unbelievers, expected a divine permission to punish the cruel unbelievers for their evil deeds and to liberate their women, innocent children, and helpless old people living under persecution and torture in Mecca.

## The Battle of Badr

The first battle between the Muslims and the unbelievers of Mecca took place at Badr (a valley between Mecca and Madinah) in the second year of the Hijrah. In this battle, the number of fully equipped unbelievers was about one thousand. The Muslims were about one-third of them and lacked all necessary war equipment, but divine dispensation afforded the Muslims a bright victory and defeated the unbelievers in the worst possible way.

Suffering heavy casualties and many captives and losing their entire stock of equipment in this battle, the mushrikin (polytheists) ran away to Mecca. It is said that in this battle, seventy unbelievers were killed, out of which almost half of them were killed by the sword of 'Ali (AS). Also seventy people from the unbelievers were taken as captives.

## The Battle of Uhud

In the third year of Hijrah, the unbelievers of Mecca, led by Abu Sufyan again rushed towards Madinah with three thousand men (and according to one narration with five thousand men). They confronted the Muslims at Uhud outside Madinah. In this battle, the Holy Prophet (SA). arrayed seven hundred Muslims to face the enemy. In the beginning of the battle, the Muslims had the upper hand again, but after a few hours due to the mistake of some Muslims, the army of Islam was defeated. At this time, the unbelievers attacked from all sides and the Muslims suddenly found themselves surrounded on all sides by the swords of unbelievers.

In this battle, the Muslims sustained heavy losses. Hamzah, the uncle of the Holy Prophet (SA), along with seventy other disciples of the Holy Prophet (SA) who were mostly Ansar were martyred. The forehead of the Holy Prophet (SA) was wounded and one of his front teeth broke. One of the unbelievers who inflicted a blow on the Holy Prophet's (SA) shoulder shouted: "I killed Muhammad". Hearing this, the army of Islam dispersed. Only 'Ali (AS), along with a few men, remained steadfastly near the Holy Prophet (SA). All these were killed but 'Ali (AS) resisted the enemy until the end of the battle and defended the Holy Prophet (SA).

On the last day, those who had fled away from the army of Islam gathered around the Holy Prophet (SA) once more and prepared for battle. But the army of Abu Sufyan, however, considered only that much success as enough, stopped fighting, and set out for Madinah.

After travelling a few kilometres, the army of the unbelievers seriously regretted why they had not pursued the battle to final victory and why they had not taken Muslims' women and children as captives, and plundered their properties. They even got busy with consultation to attack Madinah once again, but received the information that the information that the army of Islam was following them to continue the battle. Having received this information, the unbelievers became intimidated, gave up the idea of returning to Madinah, and hastily set out for Mecca.

Surely what they had heard was true, because the Holy Prophet (SA), by the order of Allah, had mobilized an army from the injured who were led by 'Ali (AS) to follow the enemy.

Although the Muslims sustained heavy casualties in this battle, in fact, it finished to the advantage of Islam and Muslims. The Muslims drew a more important conclusion out of this battle and experienced the inauspicious consequence of violating the order of the Holy Prophet (SA). Having given up the battle, both the confronting sides promised to fight another battle in Badr next year at the same time. The Holy Prophet (SA), with a group of his disciples, went to Badr on time, but the unbelievers refrained from coming.

After this battle, the Muslims became very well prepared and made advancement on all sides in the peninsula except in the region of Mecca and Ta'if.

### The Battle of Khandaq

This was the third battle declared by the Arab unbelievers against the Holy Prophet (SA). It was also the last battle under the leadership of the people of Mecca. It was a very severe battle in which the unbelievershad fully equipped themselves with their forces and powers. In the history, this battle is known as the "Battle of Ahzab" and "Khandaq". After the battle of Uhud, the leaders of Mecca, led by Abu Sufyan, decided to inflict the final blow upon the Holy Prophet (SA) to put off the light of Islam for good. To this end, they instigated the Arab tribes and asked for their cooperation and assistance. In spite of the non-aggression treaty signed by the Jews and Muslims, the Jewish people also had secretly involved themselves with the plot and violated the treaty and signed a cooperation agreement with the unbelievers.

Thus, in the fifth year of Hijrah, a fully mobilized army comprising of Quraysh, various Arab tribes, and Jewish people rushed to Madinah totally equipped.

Having come to know of the intention of the enemy beforehand, the Holy Prophet (SA) consulted his disciples over the matter. After a long discussion, they dug a trench all around the city of Madinah according to the proposal of Salman al-Farisi who was an intimate Companion of the Holy Prophet (SA). They then got fortified within the city. After reaching Madinah, the army of the enemy found no way to enter the city. They inevitably besieged the city and started the battle in that position. The siege and battle continued for sometime.

It was in this battle only that ' Amr ibn 'Abdwudd, a most renowned equestrian and a most famous brave man of Arabia, was killed by the powerful hands of 'Ali (AS). Finally, as a result of wind, cold, the fatigue of the Arab idolaters from the extended duration of the siege, and the difference and separation between the Jews and Arabs, the siege got broken without any result; thus the army of the unbelievers dispersed from around Madinah.

### Battle with the Jews-The Battle of Khaybar

After the Battle of Khandaq, originally provoked by the Jews who cooperated with the Arab unbelievers and who had openly breached their treaty with Muslims, the Holy Prophet (SA) proceeded to punish the Jewish tribes in Madinah by the order of Allah. He fought several battles, all of which ended in the victory and triumph of Muslims. The most important of these battles was the Battle of Khaybar. The Jews of Khaybar had several fortifications in hand and a considerable number of belligerents with adequate equipment at their disposal.

In this battle, 'Ali (AS) killed Marhab of Khaybar, the well-known hero of the Jews, and dispersed the Jewish army.

Afterwards, he rushed to the Fort of Khaybar, unhinged its door, and entered the fort along with the army of Islam.

He then hoisted the banner of victory on its top. With these very battles which ended in the fifth year of Hijrah, the problem of the Jews of Hijaz came to an end.

## Inviting the Rulers and Kings to Islam

The Holy Prophet (SA) settled in Madinah. Gradually, a great number of the Muslims of Mecca, who were under the torture by the unbelievers, relinquished their homes and belongings and migrated to Madinah. Ansar also kept their promise and received them wholeheartedly.

The Holy Prophet (SA) constructed Masjid al-Nabi at Madinah. Other mosques were also built. Missionaries of Islam were sent to the outskirts and treaties were signed with Jewish tribes of Madinah and its suburbs and also with some Arab tribes. Thus Islam began to flourish with its enormous luminosity.

In the 6th year of the Hijrah, the Holy Prophet (SA) sent letters to the rulers and kings such as the King of Iran, Qaysar (Caesar) of Rome, Khedive of Egypt, and Al-Najashi (Negus) of Ethiopia and invited them to embrace Islam.

After some time, the unbelievers of Mecca breached the treaty and, as a result of this, the Holy Prophet (SA) decided to conquer Mecca. In the 8th year of the Hijrah, the Holy Prophet (SA) rushed to Mecca with ten thousand soldiers and conquered Mecca without any fighting and bloodshed. He also toppled and broke many idols placed in Kaaba. People of Mecca accepted Islam.

The Holy Prophet (SA) summoned all the leaders of Mecca, who had in the last 20 years shown their animosity and behaved inhumanely with him and his followers, and pardoned them all with utmost magnanimity and without showing the slightest harshness and moroseness.

## The Battle of Hunayn

After the conquest of Mecca, the Holy Prophet (SA) proceeded to clear out the suburbs of the city and fought numerous battles with the Arab idol-worshippers, one of which was the Battle of Hunayn. The Battle of Hunayn was one of the most important battles of the Holy Prophet (SA). It took place in the valley of Hunayn against the tribe of Hawazin. The army of Islam, with twelve thousand soldiers, arrayed in front of the army of Hawazin which was equipped with a few thousand men. A heavy battle took place between them.

In the beginning of the battle, Hawazin severely defeated the Muslims, so much so that everybody ran away, except Ali (AS) who was carrying the banner of Islam and a few others, who fought in front of the Holy Prophet (SA). But after a few hours, initially the Ansar and then other Muslims returned to their bases and defeated the enemy after a very heavy fighting. In this battle, five thousand enemies were taken as captives by the Muslims, but all of them were released by the Muslims at the request of the Holy Prophet (SA). The Holy Prophet (SA) bought the share of the dissatisfied Muslims by paying them money and released their captives.

### The Battle of Tabuk

In the 9th year of Hijrah, the Holy Prophet (SA) despatched an army to Tabuk (located at the borders of Hijaz and Damascus) to fight a battle with Rome, because the rumours had spread that the Qaysar of Rome was preparing an army comprised of Romans and Arabs in that area. The Battle of Mutah was previously fought there with Rome, leading to the martyrdom of the commanders of the army of Islam such as Jafar ibn Abi Talib, Zayd ibn Harithah, and 'Abdullah ibn Rawahah. The Holy Prophet (SA), with an army of thirty thousand soldiers, proceeded towards Tabuk, but the people gathering there had dispersed before the arrival of the army of Islam. The Holy Prophet (SA) stayed in Tabuk for three days, cleared out that territory, and then returned to Madinah.

### Other Battles

Within ten years of his stay in Madinah, the Holy Prophet (SA) fought almost eighty major and minor battles other than those previously mentioned. The Holy Prophet (SA) personally participated in almost one-fourth of the number of these battles.

In the battles in which he participated, unlike other commanders who remained in shelters and only issued the orders for attacks and killing, the Holy Prophet (SA) himself took part in the battlefield along with other soldiers, but no occasion arose for him to embark upon killing anyone.

## GHADIR KHUMM AND THE ISSUE OF SUCCESSION

Mecca was the last city whose conquest led to the absolute domination of Islam over the Arabian Peninsula. It has the Haram (Sacred premises) of Allah and the site of Kaaba. This city fell in the hands of the army of Islam in the 8th year of Hijrah. Shortly afterwards, the city of Ta'if was also conquered.

In the 10th year of Hijrah, the Holy Prophet (SA) set out for Mecca to perform the Hijjatul Wada' (last Hajj). After performing the Hajj manasik (rituals) and giving necessary instructions to the people, the Holy Prophet (SA) headed for Madinah. In the course of his journey, he ordered to stop the caravan at a place called "Ghadir (Pond) Khumm." Among one hundred and twenty thousand Hujjaj (pilgrims) who had gathered for Hajj from all parts of the Arabian Peninsula, the Holy Prophet (SA) took 'Ali's hand in his own, lifted him up, and announced his Imamah (succession of Prophet Muhammad [SA]).

By this action, the matter of succession, which controls the affairs of the Muslims, guards the Book and Hadith, and protects the divine instructions and laws, was resolved. Thus the order given by Allah in the following Ayah was executed:

> "O Messenger! deliver what has been revealed to you from your Lord; and if you do it not, then you have not delivered His message;...(5:67)"

Shortly, after returning to Madinah, the Holy Prophet (SA) passed away.

## THE SETTLEMENT OF THE HOLY PROPHET (SA) IN MADINAH AND THE ADVANCEMENT OF ISLAM

The invitation of the Holy Prophet (SA) to Islam was widely extended in Madinah and it had embraced every home, association, district, and quarter. The people embraced Islam in groups and multitudes in such a way that the people in Mecca, Madinah, and all the tribes in the surrounding areas submitted to Islam. During the ten years of the Holy Prophet's (SA) stay in Madinah, absolute domination of Islam established in the entire Arabian Peninsula. In these ten years, the Holy Prophet (SA) was preoccupied with carrying out his mission and never took rest.

He received wahy and taught the people the sublime teachings of Islam concerning education, ethics, and laws revealed to him by the Almighty Allah. The Holy Prophet (SA) gave people the necessary advice, answered their questions, discussed and debated with the opponents and scholars of various nations especially those of the Jews, and managed the affairs of the country, thus enabling the people to administer lives.

In spite of all these preoccupations, the Holy Prophet (SA) devoted a considerable part of his time for worshipping Allah. He observed Sawm on many days of the year, that is to say, he observed Sawm almost continuously during the three consecutive months of Rajab, Shaban, and Ramadan and also observed Sawm for about a month on different occasions during the year. Sometimes, the Holy Prophet (SA) observed the Sawmul Wisal (continuous fasting) which was one of his special characteristics, i.e., he did not take anything for several consecutive days and nights. He used to spend some of his time in the management of household affairs and necessities of life. Also, at times, he spent his time to earn his subsistence. The Almighty Allah has briefly mentioned the events of these ten years in His words:

> "They desire to put out the light of Allah with their mouths, but Allah will perfect His light, though the unbelievers may be averse (61:8)"

Allah is the One who has sent His messenger with divine guidance and true religion to the people to make His religion dominant over all other religions and faiths, even if this is unpleasant for the polytheists.

As it is evident, this divine promise had been well realized during the lifetime of the Holy Prophet (SA) and after his passing away to the present day when more than one billion Muslims live all over the world.

He also states:

> "You are the best of the ummahs (peoples) raised up for (the benefit of) men; you enjoin what is right and forbid the wrong and believe in Allah... (3:100)"

## A Glance at the Intellectual and Spiritual Personality of The Holy Prophet (SA)

According to authentic historical documents, the Holy Prophet (SA) was brought up in an atmosphere which was the meanest environment for living and was the centre of ignorance, corruption, and moral vices. In such an environment and without academic education, the Holy Prophet (SA) spent the period of his infancy and youth. Although the Holy Prophet (SA) never worshipped an idol and was never involved with inhumane demeanours; nevertheless, he was among such people, and his ordinary life did not indicate such an eventful future; indeed it was unbelievable on the part of a poor, unschooled, and inexperienced orphan.

The Holy Prophet (SA) spent some time in this way until during one night, while worshipping Allah with usual peace of mind and freedom from worldly affairs, he suddenly gained a different personality.

His quiet inner personality converted into a divine one. The Holy Prophet (SA) regarded the thoughts and beliefs of thousands of years of human societies as superstitious. With his realistic views, he considered the customs and rites of the inhabitants of the world as cruel and unjust. He linked the past and the future of the world and fully recognized the path of man's prosperity. His observations and vision changed totally. He did not see or hear anything except the truth and reality. He began to speak of divine and heavenly words, wisdom, and guidance. His natural state of mind which was occupied with reforming daily routines in a poor atmosphere of trade and transaction grew stronger and, so he embarked on reforming the world and its inhabitants and subverting the thousands of years old organization of human aberration and cruelty. He rose to revive the truth and reality all by himself and challenged the terrifying and intense opposing forces of the world as if they were nothing. He talked about divine teachings and derived all the realities of existence from the Oneness of the Creator of the world.

The Holy Prophet (SA) described the sublime human ethics in the best possible manner and comprehended and clarified their relationships. He first believed what he said to anyone else. Also, he first carried out whatever he asked the people to do.

The religious laws and precepts brought forth by him consist of a series of worships and services which beautifully express the servitude of man towards the grandeur and power of the Almighty Allah. He brought other laws such as legal and penal laws which are completely interrelated and which are established on the basis of monotheism and respect for the sublime human ethics.

The set of laws brought by the Holy Prophet (SA) on worships and transactions is so comprehensive that it deals with every aspect of individual and social life that can be conceived of in the world of humanity, as well as various needs and requirements resulting from the lapse of time and issues instructions to fulfil them.

The Holy Prophet (SA) considered the laws of his religion as universal and everlasting, i.e. he believed that his religion is capable of eliminating the worldly and heavenly needs of all human societies for ever. He thought that the people must adopt the same stance in order to secure their prosperity. He frequently stated:

> "The religion that I have brought guarantees your worldly and heavenly prosperity and happiness."

Surely, the Holy Prophet's (SA) statement was not in vain and groundless, rather he arrived at this conclusion after studying the creation and foreseeing the future of the human world. In other words, firstly, after he recognized the complete harmony and coordination between his laws and the physical and mental creation of man and secondly, after he generally considered the changes that would take place in the future and the harms that would be done to the Muslim society, he passed a judgement on the durability and perpetuity of his religious precepts. The prophecies of the Holy Prophet (SA), that have reached us through authentic documents, have described the general circumstances and conditions after his passing away up to the remote future.

The Prophet (SA) performed all these tasks in a period of twenty three years, out of which, he spent thirteen years under severe torture and harassment of the unbelievers of Mecca. He spent the remaining ten years in battles, campaigns, and external struggles against overt enemies; in domestic campaign against the munafiqin and trouble-makers; and the management of the affairs of the Muslims, the reformation of their beliefs, ethics, and deeds, and thousands of other involvements. The Holy Prophet (SA) achieved so much due to his firm resolution in pursuit of truth and its revival. His realistic views were only directed to truth. He did not follow what was contrary to truth even if it was in his own interest or in the interest of the public. He accepted wholeheartedly what was true and never refused it. On the other hand, he refused whatever was false and never accepted it.

## The Spiritual Personality of The Holy Prophet (SA) was Extraordinary

If we impartially consider the subject already covered we will have no doubt that the appearance of such a personality in those conditions and circumstances was nothing but an extraordinary occurrence and miracle and had no reason other than the special support by Allah. Therefore, the Almighty Allah repeatedly mentions in Quran about the earlier unschooledness, orphanage, and poverty of the Holy Prophet (SA). The Almighty Allah states:

> "Did He not find you an orphan and give you shelter? And find you unable to see and show the way? And find you in want and make you to be free from want? (93:6-8)."

Allah also states:

> "And you did not recite before it any book, nor did you transcribe one with your right hand...(29:48)."

Again the Almighty Allah states:

> "And if you are in doubt as to that which We have revealed to Our servant, then produce a chapter like it...(2:23)."

## The Character of The Holy Prophet (SA)

The only basis and principle upon which the Holy Prophet (SA) laid the foundation of his religion is the principle of Tawhid which he recognized as the source of the prosperity for the people of the world. According to the principle of Tawhid only Allah is the Creator of the world and worthy of being worshipped. We must not bow down and pay homage to anyone except the Almighty Allah. Thus the principle that must be practised in human societies is for all to act like brothers and be equal with one another and not to regard anyone as their unconditional sovereign except Allah.

As the Almighty Allah states:

"Say: O followers of the Book! come to an equitable proposition between us and you that we shall not serve any but Allah and (that) we shall not associate aught with Him, and (that) some of us shall not take others for lords besides Allah... (3:64)."

The Holy Prophet (SA) pursued no objective other than the propagation of the religion of Tawhid. He invited the people to Tawhid by the best morality, the most cheerful disposition, and the most convincing reasoning and proof. He also advised his friends to follow the same principle accordingly. As the Almighty Allah issued His order upon him:

"Say: 'This is my way I call to Allah, 1 and those who follow me being certain...(12:108)."

On the basis of his character, the Holy Prophet (SA) regarded all people as brothers and equal to one another. He never showed prejudice in carrying out the divine precepts and penance. He did not discriminate between his acquaintance and the stranger, the weak and the strong, the rich and the poor, the man and the woman, the black and the white. He provided the people with their rights on the basis of the precepts and laws of religion and states: "Even if my daughter Fatimah, who is the most beloved of all people for me, commits a theft, I will cut off her hand." No one had the right of domineering, commanding, and oppressing others. The people enjoyed the utmost freedom outside the domain of the law (certainly freedom against law bears no meaning not only in Islam but also in any other social order).

This freedom and social justice is stated by the Almighty Allah in introducing His Holy Prophet (SA).

"Those who follow the Messenger Prophet, the Ummi, whom they find written down with them in the Tawrat and the Injl, (who) enjoins them good and forbids them evil, and makes lawful to them the good things and makes unlawful to them impure things, and removes from them their burden and the shackles which were upon them; so (as for) those who believe in him and honour him and help him, and follow the light which has been sent down with him, these it is that are successful. Say: 'O people! Surely I am the Messenger of Allah to you all'..(7:157-158)."

This is why the Holy Prophet (SA) desired no privileges for himself in his life. One could never tell that the Holy Prophet (SA) differentiated from other people someone having a former acquaintance with him. The Holy Prophet (SA) managed the chores of the house, welcomed everyone in person, and listened to those who turned to him out of need. He did not sit in the position and seat of honour. He did not have any means of riding and official protocol for moving from one place to another. If he earned some money, he would give to the needy over and above his necessary expenses. At times, he gave even his least available money to the needy and lived with hunger. He always lived like the needy and associated with them. He did not display the slightest procrastination in granting the rights of the people, but he used the maximum connivance and condonation for his personal rights. When the dignitaries of Quraysh were brought before him after the conquest of Mecca, he did not display the slightest harshness and pardoned them all, although they had treated him most cruelly before the Hijrah and had even provocated sedition after the Hijrah.

In his humane ethics and virtues, the Holy Prophet (SA) was conspicuously recognized among friends and foes. He was matchless in sociability, cheerfulness, forbearance, modesty, soberness, and dignity. As the Holy Quran has praised his munificent conduct by a statement: "And most surely you conform (yourself) to sublime morality (68:4)."

He took the lead in greeting those whom he met, even women, children, and subordinates. One of his friends asked his permission to bow down, i.e., to prostrate in front of him. The Holy Prophet (SA) stated: "What do you mean? These are the customs of Caesar and Caṣra. And I am for prophecy and servitude".

Ever since he was appointed to a mission by Allah to propagate the religion and to guide and lead the people, the Holy Prophet (SA) did not neglect his duty for a moment and did not refrain from his untiring efforts. Thirteen years before the Hijrah, when he was in Mecca although he faced unbearable difficulties caused by the Arab polytheists, the Holy Prophet (SA) was constantly engaged in the worship of Allah and the propagation of the religion of Allah. During the ten years after Hijrah, the Holy Prophet (SA) conveyed the teachings of religion and the laws of Islam with its amazing enormity to the people, despite the ever-increasing troubles made by the enemies of religion and the hindrances caused by the Jews and munafiqin pretending to be Muslims. The Holy Prophet (SA) also fought more than eighty battles with the enemies of Islam.

In addition to handling the affairs of the Islamic society which at that time included the whole Arabian Peninsula, the Holy Prophet (SA) personally looked into the complaints and minor requirements of people without a doorkeeper and chamberlain attending on him. With regard to the bravery and courage of the Holy Prophet (SA), it suffices to say that with his rightful invitation, he rose all alone against the world of that time which ruled the people with nothing other than coercion and injustice. All the tortures and sufferings inflicted on him by the oppressors never produced weakness and disappointment in him. He never retreated in any battle.

The Holy Prophet (SA) kept himself very clean and neat. He considered cleanliness and neatness as a sign of faith. "Cleanliness is a part of the belief."

In addition to the cleanliness and neatness of his clothes and body, the Holy Prophet (SA) was well-dressed and well-behaved also. Whenever he wanted to leave the house, he would set out in the best outward appearance. He particularly liked to use perfumes. He never changed his disposition in the course of his life. His life came to an end with the same modesty and humbleness. Although he had such a valuable position, he never gave preference to himself to demonstrate his social value.

During his lifetime, the Holy Prophet (SA) never insulted anyone and never used empty remarks. He never laughed boisterously and never performed disrespectful and worthless deeds. He was highly interested in thinking and reflection. He listened to the remarks of every afflicted person and the complaints of every protestor and then replied. He never interrupted the speech of others and never marred the freedom of thought; however, he clarified their mistakes and eased their discomfort.

The Holy Prophet (SA) was very kind and tenderhearted and was always saddened by sufferings; nevertheless, he did not waver in punishing the criminals and the wicked and did not discriminate between the individuals in carrying out the divine laws.

Once a Jew and a Muslim were accused of a theft in the house of one of the Ansar. In this connection, a great crowd of Ansar went to the Holy Prophet (SA) and insisted that the Jew be punished for the sake of the prestige of the Muslims, specifically the Ansar and keeping in view the overt enmity of the Jews. Since the Holy Prophet (SA) discovered the truth contrary to what they had demanded, he openly supported the Jew and punished that Muslim man. Amidst the throes of the Battle of Badr, when the Holy Prophet (SA) was personally organizing the arrays of the division, he saw a fighter standing a little bit ahead of the others. The Holy Prophet (SA) pressed his stick at the belly of the man to move him back a little and get him in line with others. The fighter said, "O, Messenger of Allah! I swear by Allah that my stomach is hurt and I should go for qisas (Islamic reprisal)". Giving the stick to the man, the Holy Prophet (SA) pushed his dress aside from his stomach and said, "Go for qisas". The man ran towards the Holy Prophet (SA), kissed his stomach, and said, "I know that 1 will be killed today and I wanted to touch your holy body". Then he attacked the enemy and stroke with his sword until he was martyred.

The Holy Prophet (SA) always patronized the weak and the oppressed and urged his friends to inform him of the exigency of the needy and of the complaints of the weak and not to procrastinate in this regard.

It is related that the Holy Prophet's (SA) last words were a recommendation to the people regarding the slaves and women, after which he ceased speaking and passed away.

Peace be upon him and his holy family.

# BIBLIOGRAPHY


Abdul, Hamid Siddiqui : *The Life of Muhammad (PBUH)*, Islamic Pub., New Delhi,1997.

Amery, Reeves : *The Anatomy of Peace*, Oxford, New York, 2001.

Arnold, Sir Thomas : *The Caliphate*, MacMillan, London, 1965.

Arnold, T. W. : *Preaching of Islam*, Luzac & Co., London, 1913.

Aurobindo, Sri : *The Foundations of Islamic Culture*, New York, 1973.

Bawer, Raymond : *The New Man in Soviet Social Psychology*, Oxford, New York, 1990.

Calverley, Edwin Elliot : *Worship in Islam*, University of Madras, Madras, 1925.

Edward, Mortimer : *Faith and Power, the Politics of Islam*, Oxford, New York, 2002.

Ernst, Carl W. : *Teaching of Sufism*, Deep & Deep, New Delhi, 2000.

Fatima, T. : *Islamic Law and Judiciary*, Deep & Deep Publications, New Delhi, 2001.

Gins Berg, M. : *Evolution and Progress*, William Heinemann Ltd., London, 1982.

Halepota, A.J. : *Philosophy of Shah Waliullah*, Feroz Pub., Lahore, 1986.

Harun, Yahya : *Islam : the Religion of Ease*, Goodword Books Pvt. Ltd., New Delhi, 1993.

Husain, Wahed : *Administration of Justice during the Muslim Rule in India*, Kitab Ghar, New Delhi, 1977.

Imamuddin, S. M. : *Arab Muslim Administration*, Kitab Bhavan, New Delhi, 1984.

Jalbani, G. N. : *Teachings of Hazrat Shah Waliyullah*, Kitab Bhavan, New Delhi, 1997.

Jamila, Khatun : *The Face of God,* Adam Pub., New Delhi, 1996.

Kalerji : *From War to Peace,* Oxford, New York, 1991.

Landau, R. : *The Philosophy of the Ibn Arabi,* Century Pub., London, 1959.

MacDonald, D.B. : *Development of Muslim Theology,* New Century Pub., London, 1903.

Muir, Sir William : *The Caliphate, its Rise, Decline and Fall,* Oxford, Edinburgh, 1915.

Muir, William : *Early Caliphate,* Oxford, New York, 1970.

Narayan : *Pan Islamism,* MacMillan, New York, 1953.

Oudha, Abdul Qadir : *Criminal Law of Islam,* Kitab Bhavan, New Delhi, 1999.

Poole, Lane, S. : *The Mohammedan Dynasties,* MacMillan & Co., London, 1895.

Qureshi, A. Iqbal : *Islam and the Theory of Interest,* Kitab Bhavan, New Delhi, 1994.

Rizvi, Hasan Askari : *Islami Reassertion : a Socio Political Study,* Progressive Publishers, Lahore, 1981.

Rodinson, Maxime : *Islam and Capitalism,* Penguin, London,1974.

Schacht, J. : *The Origins of Muhammadan Jurisprudence,* Clarendon Press, Oxford, 1953.

Stern, S.M. : *Fatimid Decrees,* Faber and Faber, London, 1964.

Syed, M. H. : *Islam and Science,* Anmol Publications, New Delhi, 2003.

Titus, M. : *Indian Islam,* Milford, New Delhi, 1979.

Ullah, M. : *Administration of Justice in Islam,* Kitab Bhavan, New Delhi, 1990.

Valliuddin, Mir : *The Quranic Sufism,* Motilal Banarsi Das Publishers, New Delhi, 1989.

Watt, W.M. : *Islamic Surveys,* Edinburgh University Press, Edinburgh, 1999.

Wolfson, H.A. : *The Philosophy of the Kalam,* Oxford, London, 1976.

Yousuf, Abbas Hashmi : *Rasul (PBUH),* Adam Pub., New Delhi, 2001.

Zahid, Malik : *Subjects of Quran,* Kitab Bhavan, New Delhi, 1998.

# INDEX

♦♦♦